Let the
cooking
Be - GIN!

ginspired

THE ULTIMATE GIN COOKBOOK

Heather E. Wilson
and Kate Dingwall

Paperback Edition ISBN: 978-0-2288-6847-7
Hardcover Edition ISBN: 978-0-2288-6848-4
Ebook Edition ISBN: 978-0-2288-6849-1

First published 2021

For more information, please contact:
Heather E. Wilson
The Gin Shop, Stratford, PEI
support@theginshop.ca | theginshop.ca

Food and Cocktail Photography:
Heather Ogg Photography, North Wiltshire, PEI

Food Stylist:
Jennifer Bryant, Canada's Smartest Kitchen, Charlottetown, PEI

Design and Layout:
Roberta MacLean and Blair Sweeney, TechnoMedia Inc., Charlottetown, PEI

Edited by:
Shannon Courtney, Shanco Studio, Charlottetown, PEI

Please drink and eat responsibly.

This book is dedicated to our families, who put up
with us as we wrote and developed the cookbook,
who tried every recipe more than once, and
who supported this project from day one.
You are the gin to our tonic.
Thank you so much!

Best Ever Burger with Gin Mayo. find recipe on page 79.

Table of Contents

Kazuki Negroni
Brownies.
find recipe on
page 161.

gintroduction

We believe in
love at first gin.

Heather E. Wilson

It all began in Temple Bar in Dublin, Ireland. Larry and I were sitting at the bar contemplating life, sampling various gin brands and somehow the conversation turned to food. I wondered why there wasn't a cookbook for gin lovers. There are cookbooks for cooking with wine, beer, whiskey and many other spirits. Why wasn't one of the more flavourful spirits - gin - featured as a star culinary ingredient? It was a mystery.

Once I got back home, I started looking for a cookbook, ANY cookbook, that would take me on a GINtastic food adventure. I found a few recipes but no complete guide to cooking with gin. And an idea was born - I could do it!!!

I LOVE to cook and I LOVE gin. Why not combine the two and open others up to the wonderful flavours and versatility of cooking with gin? I began to experiment and experiment and test and test. Some recipes were hands-down winners and others not so much. But it proved to me that cooking with gin was not only doable but something I had been missing in my life up until that point.

I had others test the recipes. Many others. My family began to ask me at every meal if there was gin in the dish and the answer was pretty much always "yes". That's what happens when you are testing a cookbook.

The recipes in this cookbook ALL use gin in some way. I have discovered a world of gin that I never knew existed. I've tried gins from all over the world. I am not a gin expert (I'll leave that to Kate and others), but I can tell you that each gin has its own unique botanical flavour profile that augments a recipe in a beautiful and tasty way.

This is NOT your grandmother's gin that I'm talking about. Modern gins offer a variety of flavours never before truly appreciated in relation to food.

This book is truly a passion project for me. It's my mission to tell the world that "Yes! You can cook with gin. And you are going to love it!"

Let the cooking BeGIN!!

Heather E. Wilson

Kate Dingwall

I can credit my love of gin to my grandmother. She's one of the most glamorous women alive, and some of my earliest memories are of her, perfectly quaffed in her evening wear, with big pearls hanging off her ears and an ice-cold gin Martini in her hand. Every day at five she would dutifully add her vermouth and gin into a vintage silver cocktail shaker, gracefully give it a rattle, and pour it into an antique crystal coupe.

My grandmother, who is 85, and I still go for Martinis every single Friday.

At 4:30, we sit on a couple of barstools at AloBar (the staff now reserve them for us) and have exactly one Martini each. We gossip, and graciously let the bar manager, Lee, test out his new recipes on us. I've been trying to replicate his dill-infused vermouth for a year now.

I'm now a fervent gin lover, and have taken my admiration around the world. I've sipped gin and tonics on a camping trip in Northern India (it helps with malaria, locals promised me) and I ooed and awed at the Martini cart at the Ritz-Carlton in Macau. I spent a month's going-out budget on one Martini at the Connaught in London, though I swear the best Martinis in the world are to be found at Bar Goto - a tiny little East Village, New York City, Japanese spot that tops their Martini with a sakura blossom flower.

That said, I'm excited to dive even deeper into gin across these pages, sharing the history of what makes the category so fascinating and whipping up liquid partners for Heather's dishes.

I'll cheers to that!

Kate Dingwall

How to Use this Book

You hold in your hands a cookbook. But it's so much more than that. It's a new cooking adventure. It's a taste bud explosion. It's information and fun facts that you may not have previously known. It's a challenge to step out of your comfort zone and try something new.

The book is divided into a few sections. The first section is all about the history and process of making gin. It's pretty fascinating, so we suggest you read it first. Next, we move into GINportant facts that will help you make the most of your cooking with gin journey.

Then, of course, we have the recipes which make up the bulk of the book. Each recipe includes GINspirations to help you adapt the recipe to your preference. We've also suggested a gin brand and a cocktail to round out your meal.

We urge you to try different gins. Don't just stick to your go-to, everyday gin. There is a WORLD of gins out there to try and some of the more specialty craft gins are simply scrumptious in a recipe. Give them a try, you won't be disappointed.

Be sure to read the recipe in full a few times before attempting to make it.

Some recipes involve creating a GINfusion the day before or require marinating. You may need extra time, so preparation is key. Ensure you have all the ingredients before starting. Again, read the recipe in FULL before attempting.

There are a variety of quick-to-prepare dishes along with the more fancy or special occasion dishes. Don't be afraid to try something new!

At the back of the book is a list of gin distilleries. We also have a section dedicated to our sponsors, test cooks and tasters. There is a resource guide if you are looking to find something we reference along the way.

You do not need to read this book from start to finish. You can jump around in whatever fashion pleases you. We've added fun facts, gin quotes and sayings, as well as direct quotes from our test cooks all throughout the book. We do recommend that you read the entire book as there are some fun surprises along the way.

in the beGINning

*Good friends
offer advice.
Real friends
bring gin!*

a Brief History

You may think gin is a distinctly British drink, but the roots of this storied sip actually date back through the Netherlands to ancient Egypt. The word 'gin' comes from the Dutch 'genever.' This is born from the French word 'genevre', which in turn stems from the Latin word for juniper, 'juniperus'.

Clearly, gin's history crosses the world. Way back in 1550 BCE, the ancient Egyptians used juniper water as a cure for jaundice.

By 1055, Benedictine monks in Italy were making tonic-wine infused with juniper berries in a medicinal elixir.

In the 1220s, a Belgian medical author noted that juniper berries cooked in wine would cure a host of different illnesses and ailments.

But it wasn't until a few years later that gin as we know it was born. Next time you sip a Martini, you can thank Arnaud de Villanova for it.

In the thirteenth century AD, Villanova developed the European practice of distillation. The physician and alchemist started distilling wine through, you guessed it, juniper berries. Why juniper? The berry was thought to have healthful properties – during the black plague, doctors would fill masks with juniper berries to protect them from the disease.

Historically, juniper berries were used to help treat kidney infections and juniper teas were used as a disinfectant for surgeon's tools. Canadian First Nations peoples would use juniper for tuberculosis and ulcers and apply a juniper salve on wounds.

Villanova's experiments with this early take on gin ended there. It's the Dutch who grew the gin category to what we know today.

The Dutch spent a lot of time sailing the high seas through the fifteenth, sixteen, and seventeenth centuries. Their swashbuckling sailors travelled the world, trading with major global powers and bringing their treasures of foreign spices back home to the Netherlands. When the Dutch ships docked at Rotterdam, they unloaded their worldly treasures at a local warehouse in the shipping port of Schiedam. But the fruits, spices, and other raw goods didn't last long in the warehouses, especially after weeks on the high seas.

Dutch distiller Lucas Bols caught on to this and became a shareholder of the Dutch East India Company. The Dutch started to use a fleet of four hundred pot stills in the warehouses to turn these spices, herbs, and the grains that were also stored at Schiedam into something with a longer shelf life – genever.

As a result of this Dutch ingenuity, brandy was born (or as they knew it, brandewijn, or burned wine). They started distilling it with grain beer, which made early forms of gins.

Early genever was a rich, whisky-like, malt-based alcohol. Juniper was the main part of the brew, but it also included global spices that came off the ships and into the stills. Bols took the concept of a local grain brandy (korenbrandwijn) and added these exotic global spices to the grain-based spirit to make the low-class swill more enticing to the Dutch upper crust.

The idea took off, and genever became the drink of the who's who in Amsterdam. Given the frequent outbreaks of war with France, brandy was hard to come by. The Dutch started trading the spirit through their shipping routes, and the spirit spread across Europe, landing in England.

Gin found popularity in England in the late 1600s, when William III of England, originally a Dutchman, became the king of England, Ireland, and Scotland. In an effort to curb trading from other countries and promote the local economy, he blocked off trading of French wine and Cognac and promoted English-made gin.

With the Dutch and British monarchs bickering, the English Crown convinced British subjects to start distilling Dutch Courage (gin) to get Brits drinking local spirits.

In the 1700s, gin swept the country in what was dubbed the 'gin craze' - a period of vice and debauchery. A widespread wave of public drunkenness hit England. Every store in the country started brewing its own concoctions. No licenses were required to make gin, so folks were brewing with anything they could get their hands on.

People caught on that you could replicate the taste of real gin by adding juniper oil and glycerin to moonshine. These semi-poisonous homemade spirits started taking their toll on the population. Gin was blamed for the death of thousands through overconsumption, murder, insanity, and negligence.

After much moral outrage, the British government stepped in and regulated gin distillation with the *Gin Act* of 1751. It was meant to curb the amount of public drunkenness and illnesses caused by underground distillers that had popped up around the country. The parliament opened ornate, government-run gin distilleries to encourage more civilized ways to sip gin. It quickly became the country's national tipple. British dandies and ladies sipped gin punches at tennis matches, horse races, and cricket matches.

So, gin became the country's national spirit, spreading through the British empire to North America, India, and beyond.

In the later 1700s, a slate of poor harvests made gin expensive, so wealthy members of the upper crust began distilling as a hobby. A few of them still boast brands in their name to this day, including Gordon's and Booth's.

When phylloxera wiped out French grapes in the nineteenth century, gin - a product that can be made without grapes - surpassed French brandy's market share.

In the 1830s, a French-born Irishman named Aeneas Coffee invented a new still that made a cleaner, purer spirit in a shorter amount of time.

England is responsible for making gin into a soldier's spirit. The addition of angostura bitters, an herb-based, high-proof spirit often used to cure stomach ailments, was added to make a medicinal (and delicious) pink gin. Quinine was added to gin to prevent malaria. In India, gin and quinine water became the drink of choice of British expats. Lime cordial was added to make a Gimlet – the citrus prevented scurvy.

English colonizers brought the spirit to far-flung regions around the world. Gin landed in the British colonies in the nineteenth century, but even after the United States gained independence, gin remained a popular spirit.

Americans particularly loved Old Tom, a slightly sweet version of gin. What really put gin on the map in the USA was cocktails. The craft cocktail movement solidified gin as one of the most popular spirits in the world.

There are Martinis, Gin Fizzes, Gimlets, and more. All were served in cocktail bars in the late 1880s in San Francisco, New York, and beyond.

Enter the Prohibition era.

With drinkers desperate to imbibe during the decade-long drought, bathtub gin became all the rage. It didn't require barrel ageing or tough-to-source ingredients like fresh juniper berries - just moonshine and juniper extract bought from mail-order catalogues.

English bootleggers kept sending gin to bootleggers in Canada and the Bahamas, which was then distributed to the US mob. After Prohibition, gin thrived in the United States.

Gin was so beloved by the navy that when Plymouth was bombed by the Germans in World War II, one sailor declared, "Hitler has lost the war now!"

Gin's popularity was overshadowed in 1967 when vodka crashed into the market. In the 80s and 90s, vodka was crowned the penultimate party drink and gin began disappearing from bar carts and back bars.

Over the past two decades, however, new gins started hitting the market, reviving interest in the botanical spirit. New brands started popping up around the world, highlighting juniper gins, but also distilling gin with local ingredients. Canada's **Raging Crow Spruce Tip Gin** is an excellent example of this — made from spruce tips foraged from spruce trees within 30 minutes of the distillery.

Bartenders are unearthing pre-Prohibition cocktail books and discovering the gins that appeared in them.

Part of this new guard of gins is actually the old guard. There has been a wave of reissues of historic formulas that died off decades ago — Hayman's Old Tom gin in 2007 and Plymouth in 2004. In 2008, Bols launched a modern version of genever. The category had come full circle.

Legal Definitions

At its essence, gin is a triple-distilled spirit made with neutral grain alcohol, infused with botanicals, and cut with distilled water. The neutral grain alcohol is distilled through a double or triple-column distill, then distilled one last time in a big pot still with a mixture of botanicals.

Gin can legally be made anywhere that distillation occurs, so there is a world of gin to be sipped. There are roughly four categories of gin: London Dry, Genever (or Holland), Plymouth, and international-style gins. Let's look at each type.

London Dry Gin

London Dry gin can be made anywhere, but it must be made to the strict rules of the category.

Dry gins don't need to come from London, but this category is incredibly popular in the city. Traditional London Dry gins boast strong juniper and citrus flavours and have a round, dry mouthfeel.

This style of gin was invented by Englishman Charles Tanqueray in the 1830s, and today Tanqueray is still one of the more popular styles of London Dry gin (Bombay Sapphire, Beefeater, and Sipsmith are other great styles). Grains were expensive and London Dry was far cheaper to make than the malty Dutch gin.

So what's the difference between London Dry gin and regular gin? London Dry is an EU-recognized style of gin that can be made with any high-strength neutral base spirit (wheat, grape, or corn).

Dry gins are made by redistilling high-strength, neutral grain alcohol together with botanicals in a pot still. The mixture is distilled until it reaches a minimum strength of 70% ABV (alcohol by volume), or 140 proof.

Only a neutral spirit of the same type may be added to strengthen the spirit after distillation. No colouring or sweetener is permitted. Juniper must reign the botanical mix.

Traditional London Dry gins are a whopping 47% ABV, but modern producers have tweaked theirs — some are as low as 37.5% while others are a hair-raising 55%. Regardless, to earn the title of a London Dry, the spirit must be distilled to a minimum of 70%, then redistilled in a pot still with juniper as the key botanical.

Genever

Often known as Holland's gin, genever is local to the Netherlands and Belgium, though there are distillers in France and Germany. In colour, genever ranges from pale yellow to a rusty gold depending on the producer.

Genevers are made from pot-stilled barley or rye distillate (known as malt wine) with a neutral grain spirit blended in. Some use rye, wheat, corn, or malted barley, all of which can make a huge difference to the flavour and characteristics of the end spirit.

Genevers must, by law, include juniper, but it doesn't need to be the main flavour. Some genevers push the malty flavour profile forward while others play about by adding different botanicals.

Rather than build the spirits in the still, it's common for genever makers to craft everything — the neutral spirit, malt wine, and botanical distillate — separately, then blend it all together at the end. Genevers range in ABV from 35% to 50%.

Think of it as gin's country cousin — it's malty and cereally, rather than spicy and herbal like the gin you probably know.

Genever fell from American shelves after the world wars. Brands like Bols, the biggest brand in North America and the oldest genever company in the Netherlands, and Old Duff, a newer genever made by American bartender Philip Duff, have since revived the category.

Plymouth Gin

Plymouth gin must be made in the town of Plymouth, England.

Plymouth is home to a lone gin distillery, Black Friars, which makes its own distinct style of gin, fittingly named Plymouth Gin. It's lower in alcohol and earthy on the palate. With the rise of vodka in the 1970s, gin struggled and styles like Plymouth gin disappeared from shelves.

International Gin

Anything that doesn't fit in those three categories is dubbed an 'international gin.'

If distillers want to get creative with flavours, colours, and sweeteners, the product has to be dubbed a 'distilled gin' or 'international gin'. You will, for example, never find a flavoured London Dry gin.

These run the gamut of funky pink gins from England to lemon gins from Sicily.

The Gin Process

One of the most common misconceptions about gin is that the spirit is simply flavoured vodka. But the production process is far more complex than sprinkling the essence of juniper in a vodka.

There are two steps to making a decent gin. The first is to take a neutral spirit (this can be akin to vodka). Once the spirit is created, the liquid is re-distilled, where it's flavoured with any number of seeds, berries, roots, fruits, herbs, and spices. These flavourings are referred to as botanicals.

Turkey & Green
Apple Salad with
Ginty Dressing.
find recipe on
page 129.

To make the base spirit, distillers take their raw material of choice (grains are popular, though it's not uncommon to see spirits made from potatoes) and distill them through a pot still. Grain (traditionally wheat though often barley) is commonly used for this base spirit, but traditional genevers use heavier grains. Nowadays, producers are getting more creative. Potatoes are normal, as are grapes, sugar cane, and even whey and milk.

This is distilled again and again either through a pot still, or continuously through a pot still, or continuously through a column still to strengthen (or rectify) the spirit. The more the liquid is distilled, the purer the spirit.

That base spirit is then redistilled through a pot still with a custom blend of botanicals. Every distiller has their own secret recipe - some use a juniper base, while others will lean on ingredients like dulse, spruce tips, rosemary, or other local ingredients that add a custom edge to the spirit.

From here, the distillation method varies from distiller to distiller. Some work with botanicals to extract the oil and flavour the gin as it re-distills. Other distillers add the botanicals to a small shelf in the top of the still. As the steam of the gin rises, it passes through the botanical shelf and flavours the gin. The botanicals only ever encounter the gin as a vapour. When the vapour cools, the gin turns back into a spirit. This spirit is super high-proof (it'll put hair on your chest!), so distillers add purified water to reduce it to the usual 40% ABV.

Other distillers use the 'steep and boil' method. Here, the botanicals are steeped (just like tea) in that neutral spirit created in step one. Distillers will let the botanicals sit for up to 48 hours. As soon as it's ready, the mixture is redistilled through a pot still.

During distillation, there are three different parts of a spirit that are produced: the head, the heart, and the tail.

The head is the first part of the vapour that comes up through the still. This is the first part of the gin that evaporates: usually comprised of methanol and other harmful alcohol. Distillers don't want that, so the heads are put aside.

The second part of the liquid that turns to vapour and comes up through the still is the heart. This is the good stuff, the purest part of the spirit with the best flavours. Eventually, the hearts are what gets bottled and sent off to be poured in your glass.

The last part of the spirit that evaporates is the tail: sludgy discards that stick to the bottom of the still. The heads and tails can be redistilled to make pure spirits.

What makes a bad gin? Sub-par distillers will skip steps and miss cutting out the heads and the tails, letting sub-par liquid into the bottle. Or, they'll opt for non-copper stills. While pricey, copper stills are essential in creating super smooth spirits. The copper removes unwanted sulphur that can form in spirits (you know, the stuff that makes the smell of rotten egg — not ideal for a G&T).

This is the nitty-gritty, but there are a number of factors that can impact the quality of the gin.

The first is the botanicals. A distiller can decide on their blend of botanicals, but botanicals are based on natural plants. Some growing seasons may produce a bounty of botanicals, but if it's rainy one year, distillers may face a shortage of their botanicals. Even the world's juniper is mainly found in nature — not juniper farms — so a bad crop can cripple the gin world.

Every ingredient, including the water, can affect the final product. Regular tap water won't work, the water used for distillation needs to be purified or filtered. Some distillers like to flex unique water sources like underground springs, mountain snow, or even iceberg ice.

After deciding on botanicals, water, and their distillation method, it's up to the distiller to either bottle the gin or play around with aging and flavourings.

Unlike whiskey and brandy, few gins are aged these days. But the ones that are aged are wonderfully unique, with rich flavours and a warm, brown colour.

The oriGINs

ginophobia –
the fear of running
out of gin!

The Origins

Belgium/The Netherlands

Looking at the history of gin, it's largely thanks to the Dutch that we have gin as we know it today. Gin has been produced in Belgium and The Netherlands (Holland) for over 500 years, and the countries' gin makers have had the opportunity to craft incredibly unique gins from the grains that have passed through ports and bloomed from fields surrounding Schiedam in South Holland.

From a British perspective, genever as a spirit only really became truly fashionable when it gained wider popular appeal with the arrival of the Dutch King, William of Orange in 1689. But that all came to an end in the mid-17th century, when a distilling ban in Belgium sent distillers to the Netherlands, France, and Germany.

Today, genever (a category of gin) can only be made in Holland, Belgium, two areas of France (Nord and Pas-de-Calais), and western Germany (Nordrhein-Westphalia and Niedersachsen), and it must be made from rye, corn, and wheat. Visitors to both Belgium and Luxembourg are likely to encounter two predominant styles of genever: *oude* and *jonge*, or old and young.

Oude genever is a more traditional recipe, which tends to be stronger in character; it's often served in small, tulip-shaped glasses and drunk neat. **Jonge** genever, on the other hand, is lighter in body and often used in cocktails. Other subtle variations — like the extra-malty *corenwijn* and cream- and fruit-laced versions — can also be found.

Interested in learning more? You can stop into Belgium's **Jenever Museum** to learn about the historic spirit.

fun fact:

To give you a sense of this region's gin abilities in the 1800s, Schiedam had a population of 77,000. At the time, it boasted 392 distilleries – an impressive number for a city of that size.

While Belgium has a long history of making serious genevers, the next generation of drinkers is making Dutch gin decidedly au courant.

Belgium's vibrant bar scene has helped gin find its stride across these two regions over the last few years. Gin and genevers play a huge role in cocktails, so it makes sense that the city's bars quickly adopted the spirits. Many brands are leaning back on the Dutch history of jenever.

Bols 1820 genever launched in 2009, when bar master Philip Duff decided it was time to further shed a light on the category. The brand he helms, Old Duff, is bottled at the Herman Jansen 'De Tweelingh' Distillery near

Rotterdam, which has been operating since 1777. The bottle is specifically designed for cocktails, be it craft cocktails, classic cocktails, or boiler makers.

Duff's iteration is milled, mashed, fermented, distilled, and bottled in Holland, making it a uniquely Netherland's spirit. If you're looking for more traditional expressions of genever, consider Smeets, Hertekamp, and Peterman.

Outside of the jenever realm, Belgian gin is starting to gain steam. There are brands like Martini Whisperer, which pulls together Piedmont hazelnuts, cacao beans, vanilla, and chilies to produce a chocolate-inflicted gin. Filliers makes a tangerine gin perfect for Negronis.

England 💙

You could say gin's history is quintessentially British – its heritage is interwoven with tales of war, adventure, aristocracy, innovation, and, of course, cocktails.

Many assume the name gin is British – it's commonly thought the British anglicized the Dutch genever to the monosyllable 'gen' to better roll off the tongue (we assume Martinis were involved in this decision!).

fun fact:
One of the world's most famous vodka brands, Ketel One, started as a genever distillery. Its genevers are available in Europe, but unfortunately, not in Canada or the United States. You can, however, get their gin, Nolet's Silver Dry, in North America.

In the 1600s, William III of England took the throne of England, Ireland, and Scotland. He raised taxes on French distillates and wines and loosened restrictions on spirits production in England to boost the local economy. This lit a fire for home distillers and fueled a period dubbed 'the gin craze.'

Distillers, large and small, good and bad, popped up across the country. Gin became de rigueur among the upper crust, while the poor drank gin by the gallon. A pint of gin quickly became cheaper than a pint of beer.

But not all gins were created equally. While a host of excellent distilleries had opened up in the country, home distillers were making juice in their bathtubs, adding things like sawdust and turpentine to the process.

That said, the gin craze also sparked the opening of excellent distilleries, many still operating today.

Submitted photo

For example, **Whitley Neill** is an established English brand with eight generations of distilling expertise dating back to 1762. Their range of gins are distilled at the multi-award-winning City of London Distillery based within the Square Mile. Established in 2012, it was the first gin distillery to operate in the City of London in over 200 years and remains the only distillery in the City of London.

Rather than rely on unnatural flavourings, **Whitley Neill** uses 29 botanicals sourced locally and globally. They add botanicals like cape gooseberry and baobab fruit to round out the rich juniper notes, resulting in a smoother, softer dry gin.

This exquisite London Dry gin was the start of a love affair with exciting flavours and pushing boundaries in gin distillation. The range is unparalleled when it comes to innovation. With a delicious and hugely exciting range of flavoured gins inspired by tastes from around the world and the Neill family's holidays abroad, every bottle has a unique story to tell.

Outside of standard gin flavours, they work with a rainbow of innovative ingredients, like the beloved Rhubarb and Ginger Gin. Inspired by English country gardens and the citrus groves of coastal Spain, it's bright and versatile - sip it in a sunny spritz!

In the 1830s, Charles Tanqueray opened his namesake distillery, intending to craft the finest London Dry gin available. He worked like a chemist, tinkering and toying with botanicals and spices from around the world to craft his perfect gin. After extensive trials, he discovered a perfectly balanced recipe that combined a rich, full flavour with a bold, invigorating taste and **Tanqueray** gin was born. He began bottling it, and it took off like wildfire, gaining popularity in England and abroad - even becoming the favourite gin of spice traders in Jamaica.

Today, the **Tanqueray** brand continues to showcase Charles' eponymous London Dry gin, alongside a range of boundary-pushing flavours, from Rangpur lime to Sevilla orange, plus cocktails in a can for all your alfresco drinking needs!

Scotland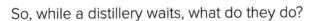

Think England is the gin king of the UK? In 2020, Scotland accounted for 70% of the UK's overall gin production.

But Scotland's signature spirit is Scotch (duh). So why all the gin?

Consider how long it takes to make Scotch. You have to let the whisky age in barrels for years before it's ready to drink. Only after ageing for five, ten, twenty-plus years will Scotch develop those elegant flavours and nuances whisky nerds fawn over.

So, while a distillery waits, what do they do?

One of the most popular solutions is to make gin! Distilling gin gives savvy distillers an activity, a way to make money, and a way to flex their creativity beyond the confines of the Scotch category while they wait for it to age.

So, it makes sense that some of the world's best Scotch distilleries are also responsible for some excellent gin.

Bruichladdich makes The Botanist, an elegant sipping gin with well-balanced botanicals (all foraged from Islay). Caorunn Gin is made by Speyside's Balmenach distillery, primarily using mystic Celtic botanicals — bog myrtle and Coul blush apple.

The Scottish swear by water from their respective regions. In the highlands, the water is mineral-rich (or hard) while down in Speyside, the water from the River Spey is low in minerals with a basic pH. Out in the islands, ocean water is soft and acidic, and high in salt. These factors are key in crafting the specific flavour profiles that each region births.

Submitted photo

fun fact:

Many distilleries name their stills. Bruichladdich calls theirs 'Ugly Betty' while Edinburgh gin has 'Flora' and 'Caledonia'.

It gets even more specific than regions. Ardbeg refuses to use any water but the water from a nearby loch. Laphroaig pulls all its water from the Kilbride stream. They once went to court after a rival distiller started using it.

Outside of Scotch makers, the country is full of fascinating gin distilleries. There's Teasmith out of Aberdeenshire that makes a gin made with hand-picked black tea. Arbikie gin looks to Scottish botanicals, like kelp, blaeber-ries (yes, they are real berries), and carline thistle, that grow wild in the hills surrounding the distillery. On the Isle of Jura, Lussa Gin employs women on the remote Hebridean island - the women head out on row boats to collect sea lettuce and climb trees to collect pine needles.

Ireland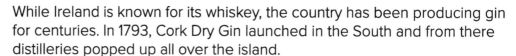

While Ireland is known for its whiskey, the country has been producing gin for centuries. In 1793, Cork Dry Gin launched in the South and from there distilleries popped up all over the island.

While distilleries across the country were producing gin, many just looked to the spirit as a stopgap while whiskey sat maturing.

Over the last few decades, that's changed. Dedicated distillers are betting on gin, making distinct gins with fascinating flavours. Now, gin is one of the fastest-growing spirits among Irish consumers - you can even take a curated gin trail in County Mayo. There are over 50 different brands across the country, all making a case to skip the Irish whiskey and pour yourself a dram of gin.

Galway distills gin with dillisk, a type of seaweed harvested by the coastal city. Drumshanbo Gunpowder Gin uses gunpowder green tea and vapour distills it through the gin (the tea earns its name from the bullet-shaped leaves). Dingle makes gin using water from an underground well and distills it with rowan berry from the mountain ash trees, fuchsia, bog myrtle, hawthorn, and heather. The botanicals in Glendalough Wild Botanical Gin are foraged from the Wicklow mountains outside of Dublin.

United States of America

America is currently undergoing what local producers dub a 'ginaissance.' Seemingly daily, new innovative distillers and unique bottlings are popping up across the country - so much so that in 2021, a gin association was formed to promote more American gins across the land.

What is American Gin? It can be a lot of things. While all will have gin's characteristic juniper, the growing ranks of 'New American' gins look to everything from local citrus and fruit to far-flung spices to define their botanical mixes. It's a creative category, allowing distillers to step beyond the confines of London Dry and experiment with a globe of botanicals.

In the US, mixology is a major factor for gin. Take **Aviation Gin**, for example. The brand was founded by bartenders Christian Krogstad and Ryan Magarian in 2006. Magarian came up with the term "New Western Dry Gin" to describe what the distillery was doing: gins where the first taste was botanical, not juniper. Named after the Aviation cocktail, it blends cardamom, coriander, French lavender, anise seed, sarsaparilla, juniper, and two kinds of orange peel. The botanicals are suspended in a pure, neutral grain spirit for 18 hours in macerating tanks before being distilled. It's bigger, rounder, and smoother than the juniper-forward London options. In part due to the brand's famous face (Ryan Reynolds), **Aviation** has solidified its role as one of the go-to gins for American drinkers.

Submitted photo

While American gin is wildly different from London Dry gins, the category has a range of smaller subcategories. West Coast gin, for example, leans away from the sharp, menthol nature of juniper and rounds out with the coniferous botanicals available locally. St. George Spirits use ingredients like coastal sage, Douglas fir, and California bay laurel to make a gin that sips with a very clear sense of place. Elk Rider out of Washington also leans on that West Coast flavour profile, balancing out the juniper.

While British distillers are tied to gin's deep-rooted British heritage, American distillers have no history to uphold, meaning they can do really whatever they please with their bottles. In the Midwest, Minnesota's Far North Spirits makes a mushroom-y, rye grain-based gin. Out of Oregon, Ransom makes an Old Tom gin - they partnered with spirits historian David Wondrich to replicate the historic method of distilling malted barley, giving the gin a rich, almost whiskey-like flavour. In the South, Waterloo makes a Texas-style gin that's acidic and floral with notes of pecans.

Canada 🍁

While gin has roots across the globe, Canadian producers are running with the category, crafting incredible products with a spotlight on local ingredients. And, for some homegrown pride, (both authors are Canadian), local bottles are starting to clean up on the global stage, winning accolades from major spirits competitions.

What's particularly interesting about Canadian gins is they run a gamut of flavour profiles. There are traditional iterations, with big bouquets of juniper, just as there are more curious boundary-pushing iterations that place interesting botanicals such as frankincense, Labrador flower, and myrrh at the forefront.

As a case in point, the award-winning distillery Black Fox Farm & Distillery in Saskatoon is making creative gins from scratch with grains grown in their fields. Their oaked gin is a prime example of this. (The fact that it earned World's Best Gin at the World Gin Awards is a bit of a hint.) They follow the vapour method of distillation to infuse botanicals, then age it for six to eight months in virgin American White Oak barrels. Black Fox is one of the few farm distilleries in the country, a distillery that grows everything that they craft into their bottles - no outsourcing. Using ingredients such as mustard seed, calendula flowers, rhubarb, haskap berry juice, local tea leaves, and gentian roots, the distillery is pushing the envelope on creativity.

Why don't these ingredients sound familiar to Canadians?

Ingredients like haskap and Saskatoon berries are found across the country, but you won't spot them on grocery shelves. Black Fox and other distilleries using these ingredients marks a paradigm shift that happened in the Canadian industry decades ago.

Canada is a vast country with a spectrum of climates and microclimates, where ingredients grow that aren't found anywhere else in the world such as the red hairy skunk currant, a delicious berry with tiny spikes and crunchy seeds; and the pawpaw, a mango relative that grows in cold climates.

The 'support local' movement of the last decade is pushing forward local Canadian ingredients. Chefs and distillers are waving the banner for Canadian wild foods. Through creative gins, we're seeing a Canadian gin renaissance, as distillers work with Canadian ingredients to put the country on the world gin map.

Another reason Canada's gin scene is thriving is that the country is blessed with an abundance of pure water sources. While botanicals and distillation methods are crucial to crafting excellent spirits, water is truly the secret ingredient.

The country has glaciers, access to thousands of lakes of freshwater, mountainous streams, and oceans galore. Canada's landscape hints at how diverse the gin scene can be. On the West Coast, there are glacial rivers and towering mountains. In the centre, millions of miles of flat land; ideal grain-growing territory. On the very eastern shores of the country, the crisp sea air gives the area a climate similar to Scandinavia or Scotland.

This terroir is perfect for spirits production. Canadian distilleries are now sourcing water from glaciers and arctic streams, making spirits from incredible Canadian water sources with creative Canadian ingredients, from spruce tips to foraged kelp to mustard seed.

Empress 1908 Gin is one of the most successful brands to do so. This remarkable spirit could have only been created in the city of Victoria, on beautiful Vancouver Island in British Columbia, where rugged mountains meet the Pacific coast. It's a place where tradition is honoured, nature is revered, and artistic expression drives innovation.

Empress 1908 is a collaboration between the legendary Fairmont Empress Hotel and the not-quite-yet legendary Victoria Distillers, one of Canada's oldest artisan distilleries. It is a partnership that combines tradition, nature, creativity, and a touch of audacity.

Submitted photo

Built in 1908, the Empress Hotel is known for its stately Victorian architecture, picturesque setting, and regal afternoon tea service. They started their collaboration by exploring 20 different teas from the Empress Hotel for their recipe. They eventually selected the signature Empress Blend Tea to provide hints of floral and fruity flavours for the gin.

In addition to the classic gin botanicals of juniper, coriander seed, and rose petal, they also added unique twists to the recipe. Instead of traditional lemon, they use grapefruit peel for its aromatic and lively bright notes. Ginger root imparts a unique peppery/citrus note, and cinnamon bark offers an unusually warm, spicy note.

Their eighth and final botanical is perhaps the most unusual of all - exotic butterfly pea blossom that was found in another bespoke tea blend at the Empress Hotel. When molecular biologist-turned-master distiller Peter Hunt discovered the earthy flavours of the herb, he knew he needed to use it in a gin. But he didn't realize that the unique green came with an alluring shade of violet. It was only after distilling that he realized the gin had turned a bright shade of purple. This blossom balances the traditional citrus notes of gin with a warm herbal earthiness and imparts a deep indigo colour that changes to bright lavender, soft pink, or fuchsia depending on the mixer.

Mixologists have found that the extraordinary flavour, remarkable mixability, and dramatic visual properties of **Empress 1908** offer bold new ways to create exquisite cocktails and the wow factor that the social media generation craves.

Ungava is another brand flying the flag for Canadian gin across the globe. The almost unsettling shade of yellow is easily identifiable on store shelves and holds an identity strongly rooted in Northern Canada. The base spirit is made with local Quebecois corn, while the flavour profile is built out with six botanicals sourced from Labrador: rosehips (a relatively common fruit that blooms on the wild rose), bakeapple (a small berry known as cloudberry similar to a blackberry, but bright amber in colour), Labrador tea (a flowering bog plant used in teas), and crowberries (evergreen, low-lying berries). It's a crisp, cold-weather gin that pairs beautifully with warm cocktails.

Raging Crow Distillery and **Still Fired Distilleries** are both East Coast distillers creating gins that have a serious sense of Canadiana. They use land and ocean botanicals hand-harvested in Nova Scotia. The gins are uniquely maritime, with a variety of botanicals such as spruce tips, citrus salt, haskap, honey, dulse, and, of course, local juniper.

Submitted photo

Back on the West Coast, **Sheringham Distillery** is also flexing a uniquely Canadian accent to their spirits. They rolled out a grain-forward single malt made with whole-grain red fife wheat in late summer. (Red fife was the industry standard of wheat in 19th century Canada, and the oldest strain of grain in the country, brought over from Scotland in 1842. It almost disappeared a few years back, but the country's bakers and whiskey makers can be credited with bringing it back.) Their gin has a similar air, made with organic white wheat and local winged kelp hand-harvested by Amanda Swinimer, known locally as the Mermaid of the Pacific.

Australia

Despite strong ties to England, arguably the gin capital of the world, Australia's gin scene was slow to launch, but is gaining traction quickly. In 2013, there were just ten gins crafted in Australia. In 2020, over 700 different gins could be found in the country.

And we're thankful for it. Australia has a fascinating wealth of ingredients seldom seen elsewhere in the world, including bush tomato, wattle seed, Davidson plum, Aniseed myrtle, finger limes, pepperberry, and sea parsley.

Today's distillers are getting creative with the bounty Australia offers. West Winds Distillery uses bush tomato to make a salty gin dubbed The Broadside. Archie Rose Distilling Co. uses blood lime, Dorrigo pepper leaf, lemon myrtle and liver mint to balance out the juniper in a uniquely Australian way (try it in a Gimlet!). Garden Grown Gin picks ingredients like mandarin leaf, horehound (a green herb typically used for indigestion), curry leaf, and murraya (a flowering plant in the citrus family) from the Royal Botanic Garden in Sydney to make their Australian gin. Over in Tasmania, Forty Spotted uses Tasmanian pepper berry to add a spicy kick to the gin.

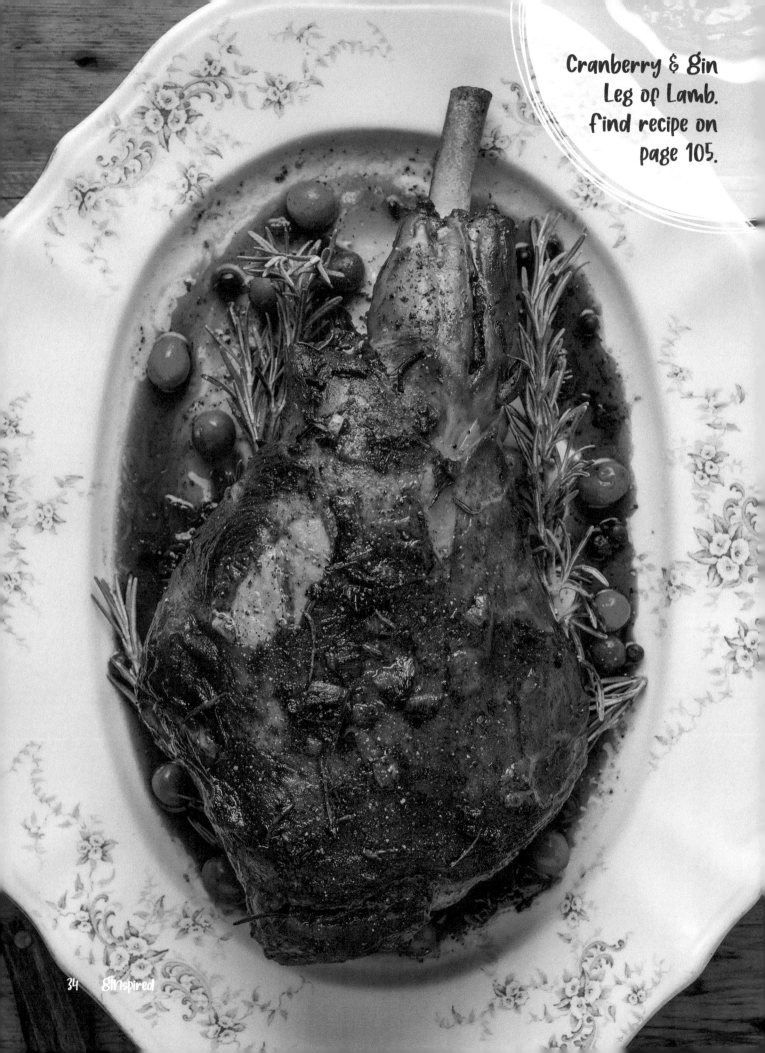

Cranberry & Gin
Leg of Lamb.
find recipe on
page 105.

gINportant facts

Step aside coffee. This is a job for gin!

Choosing the Perfect Gin

With hundreds, if not thousands, of gins on the market today, how do you choose the perfect gin for what you're whipping up? The choice can be overwhelming!

We say stop reaching for that same old bottle of gin and listen to us. Pairing a gin to a recipe or a cocktail doesn't have to be complicated. Once you know the basic gin flavour profiles, you can experiment and try different gins in different recipes. Swap out the flavour profile and you have a whole new recipe!

Primary Gin Flavour Profiles

Juniper-forward (or juniper-led or juniper-driven) - Juniper is present in every gin, but these gins let the pine-y, peppery botanical shine. Most London Dry gins are juniper-forward.

Citrus - Bursting with hints of lemon, lime, grapefruit, yuzu, or other citrus fruits

Fruity - Defined by berries, cherries, apples, haskap, rhubarb, or other non-citrus fruit

Floral - Lavender, rose, or other floral notes are the dominant flavours

Herbaceous - Expect cilantro, basil, rosemary, thyme, sage, or other herbs

Spicy - Peppercorn, coriander seed, or clove

Malty - Malt or cereal-driven and heavy- bodied; only found in genever or aged gins

Gin Flavour Wheel

To help guide you to your next favourite gin, we laid out a flavour wheel covering all the different styles of gin, our must-have bottles, and how they sip. There are so many bottles out there we can't cover them all, but follow this wheel for a dose of GINspiration.

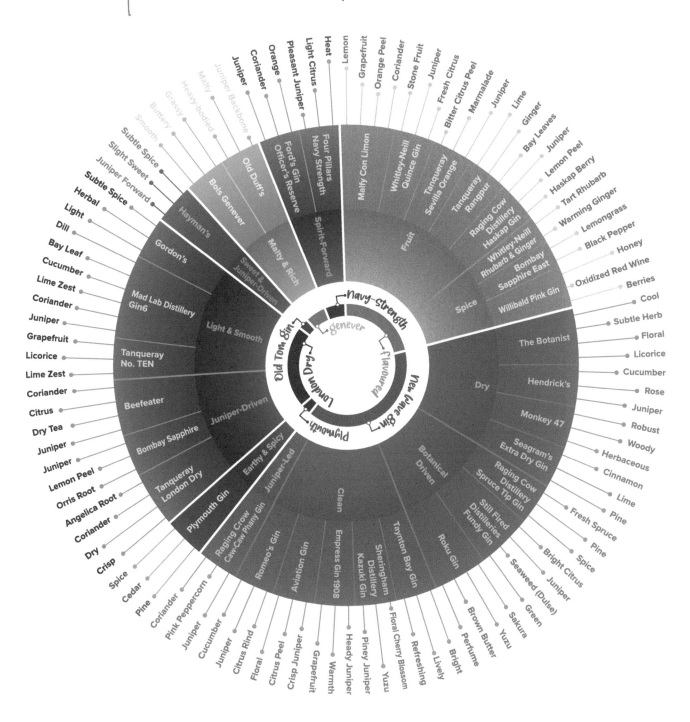

Mixers

What is gin without a great tonic? Tonic water is carbonated water infused with quinine, an extract pulled from the bark of the South American cinchona tree. It's been used by the indigenous of South America for years.

In the British colonies in the 1800s, English scientists began using cinchona as an antimalarial remedy. But the bark is bracingly bitter, so to make it more palatable, it was incorporated into tonic waters and fortified wines. The Brits started spiking it with gin.

Canada Dry launched a bottled take on a tonic at the 1939 World's Fair, and the drink took off across the globe.

Over the last few decades, tonic has gone from a standard cocktail ingredient to a decidedly exciting one, largely thanks to the work of two men. In 2003, Charles Rolls and Tim Warrilow (of what is now **Fever-Tree**) set out on a quest to rethink the G&T. They had one simple goal in mind: if three-quarters of your G&T is the tonic, wouldn't you want it to be the best?

Submitted photo

Fuelled by consumers' increasing awareness of the provenance of what they ate and drank, they looked to the history books for inspiration on where to find the best ingredients. They then travelled to some of the world's most remote, beautiful, and dangerous places to source the highest quality ingredients to create their range of premium tonics, ginger beers, and ginger ales.

Over 18 months, they combed through the archives of the British Library to track down the best flavours from the best locales. Quinine from the Democratic Republic of Congo, ginger from the Ivory Coast, India and Nigeria, and lemons from trees that grow along the seaside Sicily coast. They traveled to Colima and Michoacán to source the ideal Key limes and Tahitian limes, and Veracruz to find the best tangerines.

Fever-Tree continues to distinguish itself from mass-produced fizz and artificial flavours, offering thoughtfully-made mixers that stand up to your gin (or vodka, or whisky—you get our drift) of choice. If you're sipping a $100 bottle of gin, why the heck are you mixing it with a convenience store can of soda? Since its launch, **Fever-Tree** has collected many awards, including the Best Selling & Top Trending Tonic Water for seven consecutive years by Drinks International's World's Best Bars surveys.

For pink gin fans, the brand's aromatic tonic offers an easy alternative, relying on South American angostura bark, cardamom, pimento berry and ginger, for a gentle bitterness. **Fever-Tree** also has a cucumber tonic, elderflower tonic, and floral tonics spiked with Mediterranean herbs.

The brand has also rolled out a range of other ginger ales, ginger beers and sodas to make a strong case for a spritz or a highball. A sparkling Sicilian lemonade is an instant classic, so is an effervescent pink grapefruit. In the ginger realm, smoky or spiced ginger ales are made with whisky fans in mind.

The **Fever-Tree** story is about going to the ends of the earth in pursuit of the best, and the most exciting thing is they've only just scratched the surface.

GINfusions

You don't need a still and distillery to create delicious gin infusions. It's fun to make and the flavour potentials are limitless. Many of the recipes in this cookbook use GINfusions. We suggest creating some of the more common infusions on a regular basis so you always have some on hand for your favourite recipes.

The process is basically the same for any GINfusion - add something yummy to gin and let it sit.

Here is a more detailed explanation.

What You'll Need

- Gin
- Herbs, spices, fruits, or your flavour of choice
- A clean, airtight jar, at least 500 mL (2 cups) in size
- A fine strainer (a coffee filter or cheesecloth will do just fine!)

GINstructions

1. Prepare your ingredients. If appropriate, wash any herbs or fruit first to remove dirt or dust. Keep in mind to only add the flavours you want - remove the stems or tops of fruit. For harder fruit (apples, cherries, cucumber), cut it into smaller slices or carefully add slits in the skin. For citrus, slice into wedges, or peel or zest (for the latter, remove the white pith - it will add bitter flavours).
2. Add the ingredients to a clean jar.
3. If you're using herbs, lightly muddle to release flavours.
4. Pour the gin over.
5. If you're looking to make a sweeter infusion, you can add a teaspoon or two of honey or sugar here.
6. Seal the jar, give it a shake, and place it in a cool, dark place (a pantry or cupboard will do!) for two weeks.
7. Feel free to give it a shake or a taste every few days - it's your infusion, so remember it's ready when you like how it tastes.
8. When it's ready, strain through a fine strainer to remove any sediment.
9. You're ready to drink and cook with your GINfusion!

Toffee Gin

Toffee gin is used in many dessert recipes and yummy cocktails.

1. Make a toffee gin by adding one bag of hard toffee candies (such as Werther's Originals) to a food processor and blitz into a powder.

2. Add the toffee powder to the gin and infuse.

3. Give it a good shake every day. Since it's a powder, this should be ready in a few days.

Cinnamon Gin

Cinnamon gin or what we like to call cinnaGIN, is a quick cinnamon-infused gin that is amazing in baking or anywhere you would use cinnamon.

1. Make a cinnaGIN by adding 3 - 4 cinnamon sticks to gin (approximately 1 cup but you can do more or less to your taste)

2. Give it a good shake every day and a taste. It can take anywhere from a few hours to a few days to get to where you like it.

3. When it's ready, remove the cinnamon sticks and enjoy!

Cooking with gin

"I had never previously cooked much with anything beyond wine or sherry and the gin did add nice flavours. I was surprised how much adding juniper berries added great flavour to meat dishes. I now cook mushrooms with rosemary and juniper berries and gin all the time." - Jenny Wilson, test cook

Getting Started

Whether you are cooking with gin or preparing any recipe, there are a few things to remember.

1. Always read through the ENTIRE recipe before beginning. This way you'll know exactly what ingredients you'll need and how much time the recipe will take. It will also tell you if you need to set out some ingredients to come to room temperature.

2. Review any of the techniques mentioned. If something is unfamiliar, read it extra carefully or Google it just to be sure.

3. Use fresh ingredients. The quality of your ingredients will determine the taste of your dish. Make sure your baking powder is fresh.

4. Always use the highest quality gin. This really makes a difference in the long run.

5. Set out and measure your ingredients in advance (especially those ingredients that need to be at room temperature such as eggs and butter). It's a good idea to set out your equipment too.

6. Clean as you go! It can be very confusing cooking and baking in chaos, so put ingredients away after you use them and wipe up any spills as they happen.

7. Try to keep distractions to a minimum so you don't accidentally miss an ingredient or key step.

8. Always use quality cookware, it makes a huge difference in how your recipes turn out. We suggest Canadian-made **Meyer** cookware (it's all we use). The design, materials, and craftsmanship in **Meyer** cookware make it perfect for busy kitchens, with heavy-duty 18/10 stainless steel, durable handles that never loosen or fall off, and a special heat conducting base that is safe for all cooktops, as well as oven and dishwasher friendly.

9. Use an instant-read meat thermometer to test your meat for doneness. It'll save you a lot of headaches.

10. Have fun! Cooking and baking with gin is a pleasure, so pour yourself a beverage and enjoy the process.

Things to Have on Hand

It's a good idea to have some staples on hand at all times so that when the urge to cook with gin comes upon you, you'll be ready and avoid a trip to the store.

- Gin - a variety of flavour profiles and brands is best (the highest quality you can find)
- Juniper berries
- Fresh citrus fruits (e.g. lemons, limes, oranges, etc.)
- Pantry staples (e.g. flour, sugar, baking soda, etc.)
- Salt (preferably Kosher) and fresh ground pepper
- Fresh herbs
- Variety of spices
- The usual cooking and baking accoutrements (e.g. bowls, frying pans, wooden spoons, electric mixer, etc.)
- A quality instant-read meat thermometer

Temperature Considerations

"I did not know gin could give such a nice, unique kick without any bitterness. I also did not know how to cook down a recipe using a lot of gin (or any alcohol), but have learned to do so by cooking the Lime in the Coconut Chicken. It gets mellower and mellower as it bubbles along."
- Susan Sirovyak, test cook

While you most likely keep your gin in the freezer in anticipation of your favourite cocktail, the gin you use for many recipes in this book needs to be at room temperature. We won't go into the chemistry here, but the temperature of your gin DOES MATTER especially when you are baking with gin. You don't want to add ice-cold gin to a hot dish, believe us. So when in doubt, have your gin (and tonic, if applicable) at room temperature.

There are a few exceptions to this rule, including scones and pie pastry dough. Those recipes will tell you the correct temperature to have your gin.

In many hot dishes, the alcohol in the gin is cooked off so minors can consume the food you are making. However, be sure to check whether or not the gin is added during the cooking process or afterwards. If it's afterwards, there will still be alcohol present so that recipe is not suitable to serve to minors.

If you want your dish to have a stronger gin flavour or would rather dial it back a bit, you can play with the gin amounts in a recipe a tiny bit. However, rather than messing with the measurements, we suggest changing the gin you use to one with a lesser or higher alcohol content.

Freezing

Just in case you have leftovers (though that may be a challenge), many recipes in this cookbook can be frozen. Each recipe explains its own freezing considerations so be sure to watch out for that information in the GINspirations section.

Please do not try to freeze a recipe that is not recommended to be frozen - that is just a disaster waiting to happen and we'd hate for you to be disappointed.

Be sure to cool a recipe completely before putting it in the freezer. Wrap any breads, cakes, cookies or other baked goods tightly. Store soups and main dishes in airtight containers. Using moisture-proof wraps or containers will make all the difference and keep your food fresher longer. Ensure that you leave room for expansion when filling containers.

Thaw frozen dishes in the fridge overnight for best results.

Spirited Roast
Chicken.
find recipe on
page 117.

begin here

according to chemists, gin is a solution.

BOOZY TOMATO SOUP

GINTER VEGETABLE SOUP

MIXED GREENS WITH GINAIGRETTE

GINGER NOODLE SOUP

GINFUSED SUN-DRIED TOMATO & BACON PINWHEELS

CREAMY DIRTY MARTINI DIP

WATERMELON & GIN CUCUMBER SALAD

GIN & HERBED OLIVE TAPENADE CROSTINI

BOOZY GUACAMOLE

GIN MAPLE MUSTARD DIP

GIN & LIME SCONES

DIRTY MARTINI BREAD

SEASIDE TOMATO JAM

RASPBERRY GIN JAM

WILD BLUEBERRY & GIN PANCAKES

GRILLED CARROTS WITH GIN GLAZE

SOUSED MASHED POTATOES

DIRTY MARTINI SALSA

"The gin takes a regular tomato soup and gives it a delicious botanical kick without overpowering it, so even those who don't like gin will love the flavour. I still haven't admitted to my husband that I added gin to it, and he never guessed what the delicious secret ingredient was!"

Marnie Armstrong, test cook

Boozy Tomato Soup

Serves: 6 to 8
Total Time: 2 hours +

GINSPIRATIONS

🍸 We dare say this is the best tomato soup you'll ever make. Try dunking some of our **Dirty Martini Bread** (p. 64) and you'll be in heaven.

🍸 An optional garnish is cooked bacon bits. Believe us, you'll thank us for this suggestion. You could also use croutons or if you aren't eating carbs, those little dried cheese crisps. If you prefer a thicker soup, stir in some crème fresh, sour cream, or cream.

🍸 For a real flavour kick, drizzle a bit of gin on top of your soup AFTER pureeing (but only if you aren't serving it to minors).

🍸 You can use any brand of gin for this soup. We tend to prefer either a gin with more of a peppery taste such as Monkey 47 or you could also go with a more traditional gin if you wish to keep your soup mild. Remember, the alcohol cooks off in this soup (making it safe for those not imbibing), so you want to use a more flavourful gin where possible. This soup pairs nicely with a **Gin Basil Smash** (p. 235).

GINGREDIENTS

2 tablespoons of butter

1 large onion, diced

1 cup of celery, diced

1 tablespoon of all-purpose flour

1 cup of gin

8 cups of fresh or frozen tomatoes, diced
 (or 3 - 28 oz cans of diced tomatoes)

6 cups of chicken stock
 (only use 5 cups if using canned tomatoes)

½ teaspoon of fresh ground pepper

Salt to taste

¼ teaspoon of cayenne pepper OR smoked paprika *(optional)*

Optional garnishes: parsley, cooked bacon bits, drizzle of gin

GINSTRUCTIONS

- In a large stock pot, melt 2 tablespoons of butter on medium heat.

- Add diced onion and celery. Stir and cook until the onion starts to brown and caramelize and there are brown bits on the bottom of your pot. This could take 10 minutes or more.

- Once cooked and your onions and celery have some browning, sprinkle 1 tablespoon of flour over the mixture and stir to combine. Cook for 30 seconds.

- Add 1 cup of gin and stir to deglaze the bottom of the pot (meaning the liquid pulls the flavour bits off the bottom of the pot). All the nice brown bits should come up.

- Add the chicken stock and remaining GINgredients and season as you like with salt and pepper and cayenne or smoked paprika if you are using it.

- Simmer on the stovetop for at least 1 hour on low or place in a slow cooker and cook on low for 6 - 8 hours.

- Just before you are ready to serve, use an immersion blender (or transfer to a blender in batches) to blend the soup so that it purees, and the chunks are gone. Blend until your soup is a smooth and silky pot of awesomeness or leave it chunky if you prefer. Garnish as you like with parsley, bacon bits, and a drizzle of gin.

- This soup stores in the fridge for 3 days or you can freeze it (ungarnished) very nicely in an airtight container for a few months.

gInter Vegetable Soup

GINSPIRATIONS

This is a winter go-to soup but is also great any time of year. It is easy to find ingredients and you can spice it up as you like. If you like spice, try adding a can of diced chilies or a diced jalapeno for a spicier kick. It goes wonderfully with a nice crusty bread for dunking. This soup is especially yummy the next day.

For gin, we used Canada's Alpine Gin which has more of an herby aromatic, or you could also go with a more traditional gin. Remember, the alcohol cooks off in this soup (making it safe for those not imbibing) so use a more flavourful gin. This soup pairs nicely with an **It's About Thyme Gin & Tonic** (p. 230).

"The gin and tonic has saved more Englishmen's lives than all the doctors in the Empire."

Winston Churchill

GINGREDIENTS

2 tablespoons of butter

1 large onion, diced

1 cup of celery, diced

1 tablespoon of all-purpose flour

1 cup of gin

1 cup of dried red or green lentils
   (or one 19 oz can of cooked lentils)

2 cups of cabbage, shredded (or one bag of coleslaw mix)

1 - 28 oz can of diced tomatoes, including juice

1 - 28 oz can of crushed tomatoes

4 cups of chicken or veggie broth (you might need more once the soup is cooking to thin it a bit more)

3 carrots, diced

1 clove of garlic, crushed

1 teaspoon of salt

½ teaspoon of black pepper

¼ teaspoon of white sugar

½ teaspoon of dried basil

½ teaspoon of dried thyme

½ teaspoon of dried parsley

¼ teaspoon of curry powder *(optional)*

GINSTRUCTIONS

- In a large stock pot, melt 2 tablespoons of butter. Add onion and celery. Stir and cook until browned and there are brown bits on the bottom of your pot (could take 10 minutes or more).

- Once cooked and your onions and celery have some browning, sprinkle 1 tablespoon of flour over the mixture and stir to combine. Cook for 30 seconds.

- Add 1 cup of gin and stir to deglaze the bottom of the pot. All the nice brown bits should come up.

- Place celery/onion/gin mixture into the slow cooker. Add all remaining ingredients to the slow cooker.

- Cook on low for 6 hours or more until all veggies are tender. Remove from heat.

- Use an immersion blender (or transfer to a blender in batches) to blend the soup so that it purees, and the chunks are gone. Blend until your soup is smooth and silky or leave it chunky if you prefer. Garnish as you like.

- This soup stores in the fridge for 3 days or you can freeze it in an airtight container for a few months very nicely.

Mixed Greens with GINaigrette

Makes: 1 cup of dressing

Total Time: 15 minutes

GINSPIRATIONS

This is a very versatile dressing. You can use it on any greens and even add other veggies to your salad if you like. It's best to use a variety of greens for more depth of flavour. The dressing has a Mexican flair, so this salad goes great with pretty much any Mexican food. It DOES have alcohol so beware of serving it to minors.

The dressing works best with a lime or citrus flavoured gin such as **Aviation** but, of course, any gin will do in a pinch. We recommend you pair this salad with a **Serrano Cilantro G&T** (p. 232).

GINGREDIENTS

Mixed salad greens of your choice

Dressing

½ cup of fresh cilantro, chopped

½ cup of olive oil (or other salad oil of your choice)

1 tablespoon of freshly squeezed lime juice

2 tablespoons of gin

1 tablespoon of apple cider vinegar

2 teaspoons of honey

1 teaspoon of garlic salt

½ teaspoon of oregano

Fresh ground pepper to taste

GINSTRUCTIONS

- Wash and dry your salad greens and put aside.

- Add the dressing GINgredients into a mini-food processor or blender. Pulse until well-blended and emulsified. Taste and adjust the seasonings, adding more lime juice, gin, salt, and/or pepper if necessary.

- Alternatively, measure all the GINgredients into a jar with a tight-fitting lid and shake like crazy, OR whisk the GINgredients together in a bowl — just make sure your cilantro is chopped finely if you do.

- If you make the dressing ahead, store it in a sealed container in the fridge. Remember to allow it to come to room temperature and shake well before using.

- Right before eating, toss your greens with the dressing and enjoy!

"Light, refreshing, and tasty dressing for salad. Highlights our summer grown lettuce, fresh herbs and lime-infused gin."

Jenny Wilson, test cook

ginger noodle Soup

Serves: 2 to 4

Total Time: 25 minutes

GINSPIRATIONS

🍸 While this soup is meatless as written, you can easily add cooked chicken, shrimp, or thinly sliced beef. When in a hurry (or lazy), we like to strip the meat off of a grocery store rotisserie chicken and add that to the pot. It's quick and easy and dinner can be on the table in less than 30 minutes.

🍸 A ginger craft gin, such as Russell Henry Craft Gin is really awesome in this recipe. If you can't find one, you can always infuse your own favourite traditional gin with ginger, star anise, and garlic to make your own Asian-inspired GINfusion. Feel free to add a splash of gin before serving if you want that little extra something-something. Sooooo good!

🍸 This soup pairs wonderfully with a **Gin Old Fashioned** (p. 233) - try garnishing it with a slice of ginger!

GINGREDIENTS

1 tablespoon of olive oil

3 shallots, diced

1 bunch of green onions, chopped, green and white divided

4 cloves of garlic, minced

2 tablespoons of fresh ginger, minced

5 ½ cups of chicken broth

¼ cup of gin

2 whole star anise

2 tablespoons of soy sauce

10 oz of mushrooms, sliced

6 oz of rice noodles, uncooked

1 ½ heads of bok choy, roughly chopped

Optional garnishes: sesame seeds and red pepper flakes

GINSTRUCTIONS

- Heat the olive oil in a medium-sized stockpot over medium heat. Add the diced shallots and mix well. Cook for 4 - 5 minutes, or until the shallots turn translucent and start to soften. Stir often.

- Add the white part of the green onions, minced garlic, and ginger to the shallots and stir. Cook, stirring occasionally, for 1 - 2 minutes or until garlic and ginger are fragrant.

- Carefully add the chicken stock and gin to the pot and bring to a simmer. Add the star anise and soy sauce. Cover and continue to simmer for 10 minutes.

- Remove the lid from the pot and carefully discard each star anise from the soup (you don't want to eat these).

- Add the sliced mushrooms, uncooked noodles, and bok choy to the pot and simmer for 5 - 8 minutes, or until noodles and bok choy are tender. Season to taste.

- Divide soup between bowls and garnish with sesame seeds, the green parts of green onions and red pepper flakes (if desired).

"This is a great weeknight meal. The star anise is a wonderful addition."

Maggie Richards, test cook

gINfused Sun-dried Tomato & Bacon Pinwheels

Serves: 4 to 6

Total Time: 1 hour, plus overnight to infuse the gin

GINSPIRATIONS

This onion, bacon, sundried tomato mixture will be your new go-to appetizer. You'll have your guests moaning in delight with one bite. If you don't want to go to the trouble of rolling out puff pastry, try slathering Boursin on a cracker or a slice of toasted baguette and topping it with the yummy mixture. That way the gin isn't cooked off. The pinwheels, however, really are amazing so give that a try too.

We used Muskoka Butterfly Effect Pink Peppercorn Gin because of its light, peppery taste, but you can also use a gin with oregano or other Italian spices. These pinwheels pair nicely with a **Chef's Little Helper** (p. 227).

"It was a total hit! It was the one pandemic garden meal we shared at a distance with friends in the most sanitary way possible and everyone loved them. I had forgotten how much I like sundried tomatoes... put them with my other loves, bacon, puff pastry, and gin and good grief."

Susan Sirovyak, test cook

GINGREDIENTS

4 sun-dried tomatoes
4 strips of bacon
2 large Vidalia onions, thinly sliced
1 clove of garlic, minced
1 tablespoon of balsamic vinegar
¼ cup of gin, divided
Fresh ground black pepper
1 - 5.2 oz package of Boursin cheese
1 package of puff pastry
Egg wash: 1 egg beaten with 1 tablespoon of water

GINSTRUCTIONS

- The day before you plan to make the recipe, place the sundried tomatoes and 2 tablespoons of gin in a tightly sealed container. Chill in the refrigerator overnight (if you don't have a lot of time, you can chill for 4 - 5 hours but overnight is best).
- When ready to begin, first prepare a baking sheet with parchment paper.
- In a large frying pan, cook the bacon until it's crispy. Remove the bacon from the pan and set it aside, leaving the bacon grease in the pan.
- Add the sliced onion to the bacon grease and sauté on medium-low heat until the onions are caramelized and soft. This can take 25 - 30 minutes, so be patient. Add the garlic and sauté until fragrant, about 1 minute more.
- Remove the sundried tomatoes from the gin and finely chop. Crumble the bacon.
- Add the balsamic vinegar, chopped sundried tomatoes, and crumbled bacon to the onions. Season the mixture generously with pepper. Remove from heat. Add 2 tablespoons of gin and the sundried tomato infused gin. Stir to combine.
- Preheat the oven to 350°F.
  - Roll out your puff pastry into a 12-inch x 12-inch square.
    - Spread the Boursin over the pastry, covering the entire square. Spread the warm onion, tomato, bacon mixture over the cheese.
      - Starting at one end, tightly roll up the puff pastry into a log. Using a sharp knife, cut the roll into ¼-inch slices. Place each pinwheel onto the parchment lined baking sheet. Brush each pinwheel with the egg wash.
      - Bake in the preheated oven until golden brown, approximately 15 - 20 minutes depending on your oven. Serve warm.

Creamy Dirty Martini Dip

Makes: 2 cups of dip

Time: 10 minutes, plus 2 hours to chill

GINSPIRATIONS

This dip will be your new obsession. It can be easily changed up to suit your tastes. Change the gin, change the taste. Use just sour cream or just mayo (though the combination really works well). Use fresh chives if you don't have green onions. Add chilies or jalapenos. Use pickled beans instead of olives. Make it your own!

We like to use **Aviation** gin but have had great success with many other gins as well. Or leave the gin out (the HORROR!!) if you are serving it to minors.

Serve your dip in a Martini glass and garnish it with olives and paprika to complete the look. We suggest pairing this scrumptious appetizer with a classic Gibson Martini.

GINGREDIENTS

1 - 8 oz package of cream cheese, softened

1 tablespoon of mayonnaise

1 tablespoon of sour cream

4 green onions, chopped

¼ cup of sliced green olives with pimentos, drained and chopped

2 or 3 tablespoons of gin

2 tablespoons of olive juice

¼ teaspoon of garlic salt

¼ teaspoon of fresh ground pepper

1 small can of chopped chilies or jalapeños *(optional)*

Optional garnish: paprika and additional olives

GINSTRUCTIONS

- In a large bowl, beat the cream cheese, mayonnaise, and sour cream until well blended and no lumps remain.
- Stir in the green onions, olives, gin, olive juice, garlic salt, and pepper. Taste and adjust as you like.
- Stir in chilies if you are using them. Taste and adjust again if required.
- Refrigerate your dip for at least 2 hours.
- Garnish with paprika and olives. Serve with raw veggies, pretzels, or crackers.

Watermelon & gin Cucumber Salad

Serves: 4
Total Time: 15 minutes

GINGREDIENTS

3 tablespoons of honey

2 tablespoons of white balsamic vinegar

2 tablespoons of cucumber gin

½ teaspoon of Chinese five spice blend

1 English cucumber, cubed (seeded if desired)

3 cups of seedless watermelon, cubed

1 tablespoon of fresh mint, chopped

⅓ cup of feta or goat cheese, crumbled

Fresh ground sea salt

GINSTRUCTIONS

- Add the honey, white balsamic vinegar, gin, and Chinese five spice blend into a jar with a tight-fitting lid and shake like crazy OR whisk it all together in a small bowl.

- Place cubed cucumber, watermelon, and mint in a large salad bowl.

- When ready to serve, add the dressing and gently toss. Sprinkle feta cheese and ground sea salt over the salad and serve.

GINSPIRATIONS

You'll impress your guests at your next BBQ if you serve this salad. It's light, refreshing, and SO quick and easy to make. If you can't find a Chinese five spice blend, you can make your own out of star anise, fennel, cinnamon, peppercorns, and cloves. It's more work but definitely doable.

Be sure not to add the dressing to this salad until just before you want to serve it, otherwise it can get soggy. You'll also want to eat it all up immediately as it doesn't store well (but it'll all be devoured quickly, so leftovers aren't ever an issue).

We highly recommend using a cucumber gin for this salad such as Burwood Distillery's Cool Cucumber Gin. It also pairs well with a cool glass of **Watermelon Gin Punch** (p. 236).

fun fact:

Theodor Seuss Geisel was banned from writing for his university's paper after he was caught drinking gin. So, he started writing under a pseudonym, Dr. Seuss.

Made this GINspired recipe? Post your photo on Instagram and tag @the.gin.shop.ca

Gin & Herbed Olive Tapenade Crostini

**Serves: 10 to 12
(2 crostini each)

Total Time: 30 minutes**

GINSPIRATIONS

🍸 If you want an easy and impressive appetizer to serve, this is it. It's simply a matter of mixing up the tapenade, slathering the cheese mixture on little toasts and voilà - an appetizer or snack to die for. You may not want to share it.

🍸 You can totally change things up as well by changing the olives, leaving out the sundried tomatoes, and/or changing the gin.

🍸 We used Compass Distillers Autumn GiNS because of its hints of rosemary and thyme, but you can use whatever gin you like. Remember, the gin is NOT cooked off, so your tapenade will have a bit of a punch. We suggest pairing this recipe with a classic Dirty Martini.

GINGREDIENTS

1 cup of Kalamata olives, pitted and chopped

1 cup of Manzanilla olives, chopped

4 sundried tomatoes, chopped

3 large cloves of garlic, finely minced

3 tablespoons of fresh oregano, chopped

3 large basil leaves, chopped

Salt and fresh ground pepper to taste

3 tablespoons of extra virgin olive oil

2 tablespoons of red wine vinegar

2 tablespoons of gin

Fresh squeezed juice of 1 lemon

4 oz of cream cheese, softened

4 oz of goat cheese

1 fresh baguette, sliced

Olive oil for brushing

Optional garnish: chopped fresh parsley

GINSTRUCTIONS

- Preheat the oven to 350°F.

- Place olives, sundried tomatoes, garlic, herbs, and salt and pepper in a bowl.

- In a separate small bowl, whisk together olive oil, red wine vinegar, gin, and lemon juice.

- Add the oil mixture to the olive mixture and stir to combine. Put aside to rest.

- In a medium-sized bowl, beat cream cheese and goat cheese until smooth and fluffy.

- Lay baguette slices out on a baking sheet. Brush each slice with olive oil. Place the baking sheet in the oven and bake the bread slices just until golden brown, approximately 10 minutes. Keep a close eye out so that they don't overcook.

- Once the baguette slices are done, remove them from the oven. Spread a dollop of the cream and goat cheese mixture on each slice and top with the olive tapenade. Garnish with freshly chopped parsley and serve.

"Of all the gin joints in all the world, she walks into mine."

Casablanca

Boozy Guacamole

Makes: 2 cups

Total Time: 15 minutes

GINSPIRATIONS

Who doesn't love a good guac? And with a splash of gin, it's THAT much better. Seriously. As with any good guacamole, you need to season it to your own taste. Feel free to adjust the lime juice, garlic, salt, and gin as you like (or any of the GINgredients). Don't skimp on the salt. It needs it and does make all the difference.

We used a lime gin, Seagram's Lime, for our guac but have also used a spicier gin with good results. We suggest you indulge in a Gin Margarita when you snack on your boozy guac and tortilla chips.

GINGREDIENTS

4 ripe avocados

¼ cup of lime juice

1 Roma tomato, diced

¼ cup of red onion, finely diced

½ cup of fresh cilantro, chopped

1 jalapeño, chopped (*optional*)

2 large cloves of garlic, minced

1 - 3 tablespoons of gin

Kosher salt, to taste

Fresh ground black pepper, to taste

Optional garnish: cilantro leaves

GINSTRUCTIONS

- Add the lime juice and the meat from the avocados into a medium-sized bowl and mash, leaving it a little chunky.

- Add diced tomato, onion, cilantro, jalapeño, and garlic. Stir to combine.

- Add gin, salt, and fresh ground pepper.

- Taste and adjust as needed. Taste and adjust again until you have it tasting just the way you like.

- Place the guacamole in a serving bowl and garnish with fresh cilantro leaves. Grab some tortilla chips and serve.

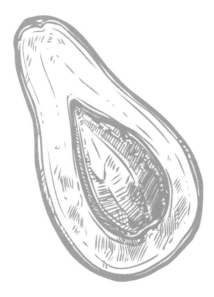

"Love this version of guacamole!!"

Susan Epstein, test cook

Made this GINspired recipe? Post your photo on Instagram and tag @the.gin.shop.ca

ginspired

gin maple mustard Dip

Makes: ¼ cup of dip

Total Time: 5 minutes

GINREDIENTS

2 tablespoons of grainy Dijon mustard

2 tablespoons of yellow mustard

1 teaspoon of maple syrup (or honey)

2 - 3 teaspoons of gin

GINSTRUCTIONS

- Place everything in a bowl and stir to combine. Taste and adjust as you like.
- Serve with fried pepperoni, sausages, or pretzels (warm or cold).

GINSPIRATIONS

If you've ever wanted a better mustard dip for your warm pretzel bites or sausages, this is IT! With only 4 GINgredients, this dip is crazy easy to make in moments and adds so much flavour to your favourite pub snacks. You can easily double or triple the recipe for more dip and any leftovers store well in the fridge in a sealed container.

For our dip, we used Black Fox Gin #10, a mustard gin that goes wonderfully in this recipe. Pair your dip with some warm pretzel bites and a classic G&T for a delightful snack any time of day.

"So so so good! Is amazing with warm pretzels and sausages!"

Larry Colbran, test cook

Made this GINspired recipe? Post your photo on Instagram and tag @the.gin.shop.ca

ginspired 61

Gin & Lime Scones

Serves: 8
Total Time:
45 minutes

GINGREDIENTS

2 cups of all-purpose flour

⅓ cup of granulated white sugar

1 tablespoon of baking powder

½ teaspoon of salt

4 tablespoons of COLD unsalted butter (the colder the better)

1 teaspoon of lime zest

1 ¼ cup of COLD heavy whipping cream, plus more for brushing the tops

1 large egg, COLD

1 tablespoon of COLD gin

OPTIONAL GLAZE
(do not serve to minors)

1 cup icing sugar

1 ¼ teaspoon of lime zest

1 - 2 tablespoons of gin

1 - 2 tablespoons of milk

GINSTRUCTIONS

- Preheat the oven to 450° F. Line a large baking sheet with parchment paper or a silicone baking mat and set aside.

- In a large mixing bowl, stir together the flour, granulated white sugar, baking powder, and salt.

- Grate the butter into the mixture using the large holes on a box grater, and blend it in using your fingers or a pastry blender until it resembles oatmeal. It's even better if some of the butter is not totally mixed in and there are still little pebbles of butter.

- Add lime zest.

- In a small bowl, whisk together cream, egg, and gin.

- Make a well in the centre of the dry mixture. Add the wet ingredients to the dry ingredients. With as little action as possible, stir just until the dough comes together. You may need to add an extra touch of cream or gin to gather up the bits of flour left at the bottom. The dough should be slightly sticky.

- Turn the dough out onto a floured surface and knead it gently a few times to make sure everything is combined. DO NOT over knead or you will have tough scones. Flatten your dough into a 7-inch circle then use a sharp knife to cut it into 8 equal-sized wedges (or use a round cutter to make round scones if you prefer).

- Place the scones on the prepared baking sheet, making sure to leave a little room between each one. Place the baking sheet in the freezer for 5 - 10 minutes or until the scones are chilled.

- Brush the tops of each scone with a little heavy whipping cream. If you're not adding the glaze, you can top them with coarse sugar if you desire.

- Place the tray of scones in the preheated oven and bake for 12 - 15 minutes or until they are nicely golden brown and sound hollow when tapped.

- Once cooked, remove the scones from the oven and wrap them with a clean tea towel to keep them warm and retain the moisture, or cool them completely on a rack.

- To make your glaze, place icing sugar and zest into a bowl. Add the gin and milk. Mix until fully combined. You may find it quite thick to start. You want it to be just runny enough to drip off a spoon slowly. Keep adding in a drop of gin at a time until you reach your desired consistency. If you accidentally add too much gin, add a tiny bit more icing sugar.

- Once your glaze is the right consistency, dip in a spoon and drizzle it over your scones. Sprinkle with more lime zest to garnish. Serve warm or cold.

GINSPIRATIONS

🍸 Scones remind us of teatime. And by teatime, we mean happy hour.

🍸 Here are a few tips to make your mouth-watering scones.

🍸 Start with everything cold. We even pop the butter in the freezer a bit to make it extra cold and easy to grate. Grating the butter gives it an even consistency. You can also chop it and then use a pastry blender or a fork to blend. Make sure your egg, gin, and cream are also cold. The mix of cream and gin means you will have fluffy scones – do not replace ALL the cream with gin (we know you are tempted). You can use milk or buttermilk if you don't have cream.

🍸 Resist adding more flour as the dough is meant to be slightly sticky. Do NOT over-knead – a few quick times is all that is required. Pop your scones in the freezer a few minutes before baking. This chills your butter even more.

🍸 Your oven must be HOT. Make sure it's 450°F before putting in your scones. As soon as the scones come out of the oven, wrap them with a clean tea towel to retain the moisture. Add your drizzle right before serving. We like to garnish the scones with a tiny bit more zest but that is totally optional.

🍸 You can use either lemon or lime zest in this recipe or both! The gin you use also makes a difference. Try changing it up. We like to use **Tanqueray Rangpur Gin** but have also used many others with great success.

🍸 Put on your best fancy hat, place one of these scones on your plate with some clotted cream and grab an **Earl Grey Mar-TEA-Ni** (p. 227) for a lovely teatime (aka happy hour) treat.

Made this GINspired recipe? Post your photo on Instagram and tag @the.gin.shop.ca

ginspired 63

Dirty Martini Bread

Makes: one loaf of bread

Total Time: 5 minutes to mix, 24 hours to rise, 40 minutes to cook

GINSPIRATIONS

🍸 This is the easiest bread you will ever make. You don't have to knead it; you just need patience. It's definitely worth the wait. Simply mix it up the afternoon or evening before you want it - let it rest 24 hours. Then put it in your pan and let it rest another 2 hours and then bake. Easy breezy.

🍸 The cast-iron skillet or Dutch oven DOES make a difference. You can use a cake pan in a pinch but there is something about cast-iron and how the bread bakes - it just gives the crust that extra something special.

🍸 Store any leftover bread in a large sealable bag or container at room temperature.

🍸 To change things up, you can leave out the olives and add a cup of grated cheese instead (or add the cheese with the olives too!). You can also swap out the oregano for rosemary or thyme or another herb if you prefer.

🍸 A Mediterranean gin such as Malfy works wonderfully with this recipe. Cut your bread on a **Meyer** cutting board, slather it with some butter and pair it with a **Martinez** (p. 235) and a bowl of our **Boozy Tomato Soup** (p. 47).

GINGREDIENTS

3 cups of all-purpose flour

1 ¼ teaspoons of Kosher salt

¾ teaspoon of fresh ground black pepper

½ teaspoon of active rapid rise yeast (also called instant yeast)

½ cup of pitted green olives, roughly chopped

½ cup of pitted Kalamata olives, roughly chopped

1 tablespoon fresh oregano, roughly chopped

2 cloves of garlic, minced

1 ¼ cups of water at room temperature

¼ cup of gin at room temperature

2 tablespoons of cornmeal

1 tablespoon of melted butter (for brushing on once it's cooked)

GINSTRUCTIONS

- In a large bowl, combine the flour, salt, pepper, yeast, olives, oregano, and garlic.

- Using a wooden spoon or your hand, add the water and gin and mix until a wet, sticky dough forms, about 30 seconds to a minute (We find our hands work best for this). Just be sure all the flour is incorporated, and you have a nice lump of dough.

- Cover the bowl tightly with plastic wrap and let it stand at room temperature for 18 - 24 hours. The surface should be dotted with bubbles, and it will have at least doubled in size.

- Prepare a skillet by lightly oiling a 10-inch cast-iron skillet and then sprinkling it with ground cornmeal (alternatively use a cast-iron Dutch oven).

- Working on a lightly floured surface, scrape the dough out of the bowl, sprinkle a tablespoon of flour on it to make it easier to handle, and then gently shape it into a round ball.

- Place the dough into the prepared skillet.

- Cover the skillet with a clean dish towel and let it stand at room temperature until the dough has doubled in size and does not readily spring back when you poke it with a finger, about 2 hours.

- Preheat the oven to 450°F. Place the pan into the oven and bake your bread until it's golden brown and sounds hollow when you tap it, about 30 - 40 minutes.

- Remove your bread from the oven, brush it with melted butter and give it a little sprinkle of Kosher salt or more cornmeal if you like. Slice and serve warm or cold.

"This was my first successful loaf of bread. Ever. It was easy and the rise was gorgeous. I will no doubt keep this in a frequent rotation. Excellent with olive oil and balsamic vinegar!"

Erica Goddard,
test cook

MEYER

Seaside Tomato Jam

**Serves: 2 to 4
(makes 1 cup)

Total Time: 30 minutes**

GINSPIRATIONS

This jam is amazing on a sandwich, drizzled on a salad, on a burger or over your favourite fish, chicken, or lamb dish - pretty much anything. It's crazy versatile and our guess is that you'll want to double or triple the recipe so that you have lots on hand.

If you don't have fresh oregano, you can use dried or switch it out for basil, thyme, or even rosemary or all! The red chili flakes really add a pop to the jam but if you aren't into spice, leave them out.

We used **Sheringham Distillery's Seaside Gin** for our jam. Spread it on a roast beef sandwich and pair with a **Seaside Martini** (p. 233) for a lovely lunch anytime.

GINGREDIENTS

1 tablespoon of extra-virgin olive oil

1 tablespoon of unsalted butter

1 small yellow onion, minced

2 cups or 1 pint of cherry or grape tomatoes, room temperature and cut in half

4 juniper berries, crushed

2 tablespoons of brown sugar

⅓ cup of **Sheringham Distillery Seaside Gin**

1 teaspoon of salt

¼ teaspoon of red chili flakes

1 tablespoon of balsamic vinegar

1 teaspoon of fresh oregano, basil, or thyme, chopped (or a mixture of all three)

GINSTRUCTIONS

- Slice the tomatoes in half.

- Add 1 tablespoon each of extra-virgin olive oil and butter to a medium-sized saucepan. Heat over medium-high heat until the butter foams.

- Add the minced onions and lower the heat to medium. Cook for 2 minutes to very slightly soften.

- Add the tomatoes and juniper berries and cook for 5 minutes.

- As the tomatoes start to break down, add the brown sugar, **Sheringham Distillery Seaside Gin**, salt, and red chili flakes.

- Cook for another 10 - 12 minutes, smashing down the tomatoes with a wooden spoon. The sauce should start to slightly thicken.

- Next, add the balsamic vinegar and fresh herbs, and stir to combine.

- Continue to cook for another 2 - 3 minutes and then turn off the heat.

- Pour your tomato jam into a clean glass mason jar or dish and let cool until ready to serve. It will thicken as it cools.

- If you make the jam in advance, store it in the fridge until ready to use. You can serve it at room temperature or slightly rewarmed if you wish. It will keep in the fridge for about a week.

it's been a gin
kind of day.

Raspberry Gin Jam

Makes: 4 jars of jam

**Total Time:
35 minutes**

GINSPIRATIONS

🍸 This jam is simply divine on your morning toast or served over ice cream. If you can't find fresh raspberries, frozen will do (but they aren't as tasty). Just be sure to thaw them completely before crushing.

🍸 The butter is technically optional but we highly recommend it as it stops the majority of the foam from forming, saving you from skimming in most cases.

🍸 The Fruit Fresh is citric acid. It stops your jam from turning brown as it sits over the next few months (if it lasts that long). We use the No Sugar Added pectin as we like to minimize how much sugar we add to our jam. We also add a couple of tablespoons of gin at the end to give the jam just a tiny bit more gin flavour that isn't cooked off.

🍸 If you don't have a water canner, a very large pot with a lid will do the job too, or you can pop your jars in the freezer instead. Be sure to leave a bit more headspace at the top of each jar to allow for expansion.

🍸 There are so many GINtastic gins you can use for this recipe. We used Whitley Neill Raspberry Gin because it enhances the raspberry flavour. Spread it on your morning toast for a delightful treat.

GINGREDIENTS

4 - 1 cup size mason jam jars with lids and screw bands

4 cups of raspberries, crushed

¼ teaspoon of butter (to reduce foaming)

1 cup + 2 tablespoons of gin

1 tablespoon of Fruit Fresh (citric acid), or ¼ cup of lemon juice

1 pkg BERNARDIN® No Sugar Needed Fruit Pectin (or other no sugar needed pectin)

1 cup granulated white sugar

GINSTRUCTIONS

• Place 4 clean mason jars on a rack in a boiling water canner or very large pot; cover the jars with water, and heat to a simmer (180°F). Set screw bands aside; heat lids in hot water, not boiling (180°F) - keep warm until ready to use.

• Crush raspberries one layer at a time. If desired, press the raspberries through a sieve to remove seeds before measuring out 4 cups. Add the crushed raspberries, butter, 1 cup of gin, and the Fruit Fresh (or lemon juice) into a large, deep stainless steel saucepan.

• Sprinkle the No Sugar Needed Fruit Pectin over the fruit mixture and then stir until it's dissolved. Bring the fruit mixture to a boil over high heat, stirring constantly.

• Once the fruit is boiling, add the sugar and return the mixture to a boil. Stirring constantly, boil for 3 minutes. Only start timing once your jam is boiling.

• Remove the jam from the heat and stir in 2 tablespoons of gin. Skim any foam from the surface. Quickly ladle the jam into a hot jar, leaving ¼-inch of headspace at the top of the jar.

• Wipe the jar rim to remove any jam residue. Place the jar lid on top to cover and then screw the band down until resistance is met, then increase to fingertip tight. Repeat with all 4 jars.

• Return the filled jars to the rack in the canner ensuring all the jars are covered by water. When the canner is filled, ensure that all jars are covered with at least 1-inch of water. Cover the canner pot and bring the water to a full rolling boil before starting the timer. Boil filled jars for 10 minutes.

• When the time is up, turn off the heat and remove the lid from the canner. Let the jars rest in the water for 5 minutes. Remove the jars from the water without tilting. Cool upright, undisturbed for 24 hours; DO NOT RETIGHTEN the screw bands.

• After cooling, check the jar seals. Sealed lids curve downward and have a dimple in the centre. Label and store your jam in a cool, dark place.

Made this GINspired recipe? Post your photo on Instagram and tag @the.gin.shop.ca

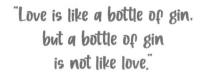

*"Love is like a bottle of gin,
but a bottle of gin
is not like love."*

The Magnetic Fields,
Love is Like a Bottle of Gin

Wild Blueberry & Gin Pancakes

Serves: 4

Total Time: 45 minutes, plus time for GINfusion to rest

GINSPIRATIONS

🍸 These are fat, fluffy, tasty little pillows of delight. Easy to make quickly and the recipe doubles nicely. We STRONGLY suggest you use real pure maple syrup. Using anything else is just wrong in our opinion. If you don't have pure maple syrup, a really good quality honey can do in a pinch.

🍸 You can use any berry with these pancakes. We prefer wild blueberries and love to use GINfused wild blueberries for an extra punch. However, raspberries and strawberries work well too (just remember to chop them up small). To infuse berries, simply place your berries in ½ cup of gin and let soak overnight. Strain the berries (and use them for sprinkling on your pancakes) and keep the infused gin to mix in the batter.

🍸 For this recipe, we used **Aviation Gin**. Pair these pancakes with a **Breakfast Martini** (p. 225) and it's a brunch made in Heaven.

GINGREDIENTS

GINfused Maple Syrup
½ cup of pure maple syrup
¼ cup of **Aviation Gin**

Pancakes
1 ½ cups of all-purpose flour
3 ½ teaspoons of baking powder
1 teaspoon of cinnamon
1 teaspoon of salt
1 tablespoon of granulated white sugar
1 ¼ cups of milk
1 large egg, room temperature
3 tablespoons of melted butter
¼ cup of **Aviation Gin**
½ cup of wild blueberries (*optional*)
Optional garnishes: GINfused maple syrup and/or whipped cream

GINSTRUCTIONS

- Make your GINfused maple syrup the day before and let it chill overnight. Combine ½ cup of pure maple syrup with ¼ cup of **Aviation Gin** in a small saucepan. Bring it to a rolling boil and let boil for 2 minutes. Pour your GINfused syrup into a small container, cover, and refrigerate overnight.
- To make the pancakes, whisk together the flour, baking powder, cinnamon, salt, and sugar in a large mixing bowl.
- Make a well in the centre and pour in the milk, egg, melted butter, and **Aviation Gin**. Whisk until smooth. If you prefer a thinner pancake and your batter is too thick, add more milk until it reaches the desired consistency.
- Heat a non-stick griddle or frying pan over medium-high heat. If you don't have a non-stick, use a tiny bit of oil to grease your pan. Sprinkle a few drops of water on your griddle - it should sizzle loudly. If it does, your griddle is hot enough. If it doesn't, continue to heat your griddle until a water droplet sizzles and evaporates quickly.
- When your griddle is hot, pour or scoop ¼ cup of batter onto the griddle for each pancake. Work in batches and do not overcrowd your griddle.
- Sprinkle a tablespoon of wild blueberries onto each pancake. Let cook until you see air bubbles pop on the top and the edges are slightly browned. Flip the pancakes and cook the other side until lightly browned.
- Place cooked pancakes on a warm plate in the oven to stay warm. Serve your pancakes hot with whipped cream and GINfused maple syrup.

Grilled Carrots with Gin Glaze

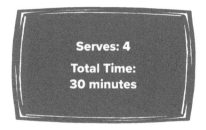

Serves: 4

Total Time:
30 minutes

GINSPIRATIONS

🍸 Carrots are a staple veggie in our homes. We're always trying to find new ways to prepare them. Gin-glazed carrots are seriously a yummy treat. They are almost like candy, they are so good.

🍸 Depending on the size of your carrots you can prepare them two ways: cut them in half lengthwise, or grill them whole. Thick carrots need to be cut down the middle, lengthwise, before grilling, otherwise, you run the risk of burning the thin ends while the thicker portion is still cooking. Thinner carrots do not need to be sliced down the middle and can be grilled whole.

🍸 Right before your carrots are finished you'll want to glaze them. Any sooner and you run the risk of burnt carrots. You want grill marks and a tiny bit of char...not char-b-q. If you want to play with the glaze, try adding a bit of sriracha for heat or cinnamon.

🍸 We used Boodles London Dry Gin in this recipe because of its coriander and caraway botanicals. Pair your carrots with grilled steak marinated in our **GINtastic Steak Marinade** (p. 89) and a **Gin Old Fashioned** (p. 233).

GINGREDIENTS

1 lb of carrots, peeled and sliced in half down the middle lengthwise

1 tablespoon of extra-virgin olive oil

1 teaspoon of Kosher salt

½ teaspoon of fresh ground black pepper

GIN Glaze

2 tablespoons of butter

¼ cup of brown sugar

2 tablespoons of liquid honey

¼ cup of gin

⅛ teaspoon salt (just a pinch)

GINSTRUCTIONS

• Preheat the grill for direct/indirect cooking.

• Peel the carrots and slice in half down the middle lengthwise (cut in quarters if really large carrots). You want long pieces to grill. Toss the carrots in olive oil, Kosher salt, and pepper.

• Place the carrots on direct heat and begin grilling, turning often to get all sides slightly charred. If they are cooking too fast (getting charred before they are fork tender), move to indirect heat to finish cooking. It should take about 15 - 20 minutes. Watch them carefully as you don't want little burnt sticks.

• Make the glaze as the carrots are cooking. In a small saucepan over medium heat, whisk together the butter, brown sugar, honey, gin, and salt. Whisk frequently until the brown sugar dissolves. Keep warm.

• Stick a fork in one carrot to ensure it is tender. Once your carrots are tender, brush the glaze on one side. Let them cook for one minute, then turn over and repeat on the other side. Remove the carrots from the grill and glaze one more time. Serve immediately.

fun fact:

It's been said that the royal family cleans their silverware with gin! A few drops of gin on a cotton pad can make your forks and spoons sparkle like a royal!

Soused Mashed Potatoes

Serves: 6

Total Time: 50 minutes

GINSPIRATIONS

🍸 Who doesn't love mashed potatoes?! Add some gin and you have a seriously GINtastic side dish.

🍸 The amount of liquid you add depends on how many potatoes you cook, so be sure to adjust up or down as needed. Start with half the amount of cream and gin if you think it might be too much liquid, then add more if need be. You don't want your potatoes watery.

🍸 These potatoes are potent so don't serve them to minors or non-gin lovers. Store any leftovers in the fridge. Try turning leftovers into potato pancakes or a topping for Shepherd's Pie.

🍸 We used Steinhart Classic London Dry Gin for this recipe. Pair your soused mashed potatoes with your favourite GINspired dishes such as **Spirited Roast Chicken** (p. 117) or **Pork Tenderloin with Mushrooms & Raging Gin Cream Sauce** (p. 93) and an **It's About Thyme Gin & Tonic** (p. 230).

GINGREDIENTS

2 lbs of russet or yellow potatoes, peeled and diced

1 teaspoon + ½ teaspoon of salt

½ cup of heavy whipping cream

⅓ cup of salted butter

2 garlic cloves, minced

1 tablespoon of fresh chives

1 teaspoon of fresh ground black pepper

¼ cup of gin

GINSTRUCTIONS

• Place the peeled and diced potatoes in a large saucepan. Cover the potatoes with cold water and add 1 teaspoon of salt to the water. Bring the pan to a boil and boil the potatoes for approximately 25 minutes or until they are soft and tender.

• Drain the potatoes and put them back into the pot on very low heat.

• Add the butter and allow it to melt. Add ¼ cup of cream.

• Mash the potatoes with a masher or whip with a hand mixer for extra creaminess. If they are dry, add the remaining ¼ cup of cream (you'll need to adjust your liquid level to the amount of potatoes). You want your potatoes to be thick and creamy, not watery.

• Stir in the minced garlic cloves, chives, ½ teaspoon of salt, and 1 teaspoon of fresh ground black pepper (or to taste). Stir in the gin. Serve hot with extra butter and chives for garnish.

"I like to have a Martini. Two at the very most. After three I'm under the table. After four I'm under my host."

Dorothy Parker

Dirty Martini Salsa

Makes: 2 cups of dip

Total Time: 10 minutes, plus time to chill

GINSPIRATIONS

This is for the olive lovers out there. Shaking and stirring are not required for this yummy salsa. This recipe is easily adjustable for a larger crowd and can absolutely be made the day before (in fact it's even better if it is). Serve it chilled with tortilla chips or raw veggies.

We used Tanqueray London Dry Gin for our salsa, but any traditional gin will do. Pair it with Gin Paloma and you are all set for happy hour.

GINGREDIENTS

4 oz can of chopped pimentos

2 tablespoons of gin

1 tablespoon of dry white vermouth

1 tablespoon of olive oil

Juice of ½ a large lime

Kosher salt and fresh ground black pepper

¾ cup of unstuffed, pitted olives of your choice, plus sliced olives for garnish

½ cup of pickled cocktail onions, plus some for garnish

1 tablespoon of olive brine

1 clove of garlic

GINSTRUCTIONS

- Put the pimentos, gin, vermouth, oil, lime juice, salt, and a few grinds of pepper in a food processor. Pulse until smooth, but still slightly chunky.

- Add the olives, onions, olive brine and garlic, and pulse until coarsely chopped. Taste and adjust salt and pepper as needed.

- Refrigerate for at least 1 hour or overnight.

- Garnish with sliced olives and a few cocktail onions. Serve with chips or raw veggies.

fun fact:

Every empty gin bottle is filled with a great story.

gINgenious Beef, Pork, & Lamb

gin is like pouring smiles on your brain.

BEST EVER BURGER WITH GIN MAYO

BLOODY MARY SLOW COOKER POT ROAST

TANGY & BOOZY BEEF STEW

GINNY STEAK PINWHEELS

SPICED STEAK WITH GIN

STEAK SALAD WITH CILANTRO LIME GIN DRESSING

GINTASTIC STEAK MARINADE

PORK LOIN ROAST WITH CREAMY GARLIC SUN-DRIED TOMATO GIN SAUCE

PORK CHOPS WITH GIN SAUCE

PORK TENDERLOIN WITH MUSHROOMS & RAGING GIN CREAM SAUCE

GIN & OREGANO MARINATED LEG OF LAMB

APRICOT & GIN GLAZED HAM

DRUNKEN LAMB PASTA

DRUNKEN ITALIAN NOODLES WITH SAUSAGE

CRANBERRY & GIN LEG OF LAMB

GRILLED GIN MARINATED LAMB CHOPS

BOOZY BLUEBERRY BBQ SAUCE

"Super easy, moist and delicious, especially great for a summer BBQ."

Julianne Oelke-Simonsen, test cook

Best Ever Burger with Gin Mayo

Serves: 4 to 6

Total Time: 15 minutes to mix, plus 1½ hours chilling, plus 20 minutes grilling and rest time

GINSPIRATIONS

The hamburger is a North American staple, but you've never had a burger until you've tried these GINfused burgers with gin mayo! Seriously, they are THAT good.

We highly suggest using the dried minced onion as it blends a bit nicer than fresh. If you do use fresh onion, be sure to mince it very finely. If your onion bits are too big, your burger may fall apart.

Chilling your burgers is important. First, chill the mixture and then chill it again after you make your patties. Adding the dimple in the centre of each raw burger is also important as it ensures a much more even cook.

How you garnish your burger is a completely personal choice, so make it your own. We can tell you that the gin BBQ mayo, cheese, and bacon are a must for the best-ever burger. We also highly suggest making some caramelized onions with **Aviation Gin** (see the **GINfused Sundried Tomato & Bacon Pinwheels** (p. 52) recipe for instructions).

We used **Aviation Gin** for our burgers. Pour yourself a **Serrano Cilantro G&T** (p. 232), grab your burger, and chill on the patio.

GINGREDIENTS

Burgers

1 ½ lbs of lean ground beef

1 large egg

¼ cup of Italian bread crumbs

1 tablespoon of dried minced onion (or finely minced fresh onion)

2 garlic cloves, minced (or 1 teaspoon of dried minced garlic)

1 tablespoon of Worcestershire sauce

2 tablespoons of **Aviation Gin**

1 teaspoon of Kosher salt

1 teaspoon of dried oregano

½ teaspoon of smoked paprika

½ teaspoon of fresh ground pepper

1 tablespoon of grainy Dijon mustard

Ginny BBQ Mayo

⅓ cup of mayonnaise

3 tablespoons of **Aviation Gin**

3 tablespoons of your favourite barbecue sauce

Garnish

Hamburger buns

Toppings such as cooked bacon, **Aviation Gin** caramelized onions, lettuce, tomato, cheese, and pickles

GINSTRUCTIONS

- Mix the mayonnaise, **Aviation Gin**, and barbecue sauce in a small bowl. Refrigerate until ready to use.

- Add the egg to a large bowl and whisk. Add the remaining burger GINgredients to the bowl and mix just until combined. Refrigerate for at least an hour.

- Remove the bowl from the fridge and form the meat mixture into equal patties. Make a ½-inch indentation or dimple in the middle of each patty with your thumb, knuckle, or measuring spoon (this will help the burgers cook evenly). Refrigerate your patties for another 15 minutes.

- Preheat an outdoor grill. Once hot, place the patties on the grill, reduce the temperature to medium, and close the cover. Cook until brown and slightly charred on one side, about 4 - 6 minutes. Flip the burgers and cook an additional 4 - 6 minutes, or to your preferred doneness. Don't flip the burgers a bunch of times as this can really dry them out. Once per side should be good.

- Add cheese if using; let melt. Remove the burgers to a plate, tent them with foil, and let rest for 5 minutes. Toast your hamburger buns if desired. Place a burger on a toasted bun, top with ginny mayo, bacon, and garnish as desired.

Bloody Mary
Slow Cooker Pot Roast

Serves: 4

**Total Time:
6 - 7 hours**

GINSPIRATIONS

- If you love a good Bloody Mary and you eat beef, this roast is for you! It's an easy and yummy dish. Good for a weeknight or Sunday dinner. Simply throw everything into your slow cooker and let it cook all day. When you are ready to eat, shred your beef and remove the fat.

- You may have noticed that the beef is not seared in a pan before it goes into the slow cooker. We have found this an unnecessary step as the roast is still juicy and delicious without the pre-sear. If you want to do it, go for it. But for those of us who are lazy, it works fine without the pre-sear.

- This recipe also works wonderfully with a boneless lamb roast.

- Serve this saucy beef over egg noodles or mashed potatoes. It goes well with a nice side salad or green beans too.

- For gin, we used a traditional London Dry gin such as Bombay Sapphire and paired it with an **It's About Thyme Gin & Tonic** (p. 230).

GINGREDIENTS

2 lbs of beef pot roast (such as a blade or sirloin tip roast)

Fresh ground salt and pepper

3 cups of passata sauce or 1 - 28 oz can of crushed tomatoes

1 large onion, diced

2 cloves of garlic, minced

½ cup of gin

2 tablespoons of Worcestershire sauce

5 generous dashes of hot sauce such as Tabasco (*optional*)

Juice of 1 lemon

½ teaspoon of celery salt

3 sprigs of fresh rosemary

5 dried juniper berries

GINSTRUCTIONS

- Remove the beef from the fridge about half an hour before you're planning to cook so it can come up to room temperature. Pat it dry with paper towels.

- Season it all over with freshly ground salt and pepper.

- Place the roast in a slow cooker.

- Add the passata, onion, garlic, gin, Worcestershire sauce, hot sauce, lemon juice, celery salt, rosemary sprigs, and juniper berries to the slow cooker.

- Season with salt and pepper, if desired.

- Cook for 5 - 6 hours on medium-high or 8 hours on low, or until the beef is tender and falls apart.

- Remove the beef from the sauce and gently shred. Remove any large chunks of fat as you work. Place the shredded beef back into the sauce. Serve over egg noodles or mashed potatoes.

fun fact:

During the plague, juniper was thought to be the best source of protection. Plague doctors filled their masks with juniper berries and victims would bathe in juniper oil.

Made this GINspired recipe? Post your photo on Instagram and tag @the.gin.shop.ca

Ginny Steak Pinwheels

Serves: 4 to 6

Total Time: 1 ½ hours, plus marinating time overnight

GINSPIRATIONS

These steak pinwheels are a bit on the fancy side, we admit. However, they are definitely worth the effort. Be sure to pound your steak flat so that it is easy to roll up. The resting period when it comes out of the oven is key, so don't skip that part.

If you aren't using these as appetizers and would like a bit of a sauce to drizzle over your pinwheels, we recommend you try the mushroom and onion gin cream sauce found in the **Pork Tenderloin with Mushrooms & Raging Gin Cream Sauce** (p. 93) recipe. They are a match made in Heaven.

We used a complex gin such as St.George's Botanivore Gin for this recipe. It has 19 different botanicals that all work in tandem. We paired it with a classic Dirty Martini.

GINGREDIENTS

¼ cup of olive oil

¼ cup of soy sauce

¼ cup of gin

¼ cup of Worcestershire sauce

1 tablespoon of Dijon mustard

1 tablespoon of lemon juice

1 clove of garlic, minced

1 teaspoon of Italian seasoning

½ teaspoon of ground black pepper

1 ½ lbs of steak, pounded to ½-inch thickness

1 clove of garlic, peeled

¼ teaspoon of salt

1 small onion, chopped

¼ cup of fine dry bread crumbs

1 cup of frozen spinach, thawed and squeezed dry, chopped

½ cup of crumbled feta cheese

GINSTRUCTIONS

- In a large resealable bag, combine the olive oil, soy sauce, gin, Worcestershire sauce, mustard, lemon juice, minced garlic, Italian seasoning, and pepper. Squeeze the bag to blend well.

- Ensure your steak is pounded to ½-inch thickness. Pierce the steak with a knife, making small slits about 1-inch apart. Place the steak into the bag, and seal. Refrigerate overnight to marinate.

- When you are ready to prepare your pinwheels, preheat the oven to 350°F.

- Crush the remaining clove of garlic on a cutting board with a large chef's knife. Sprinkle the salt over the garlic, and scrape with the flat side of the knife to make a paste.

- Remove the steak from the bag, and discard the marinade.

- Spread the garlic paste over the top side of the steak. Spread layers of chopped onion, bread crumbs, spinach, and finally, the cheese, over the garlic.

- Roll the steak up lengthwise, and secure with kitchen twine or toothpicks. Place the roll in a shallow glass baking dish lined with tin foil.

- Bake uncovered for 1 hour in the preheated oven, or until the internal temperature of the roll is at least 145°F in the centre. Let the steak roll stand for 5 minutes to set, then slice it into 1-inch slices to serve.

fun fact:

i only drink gin on days that end in y.

Spiced Steak with Gin

Serves: 3 to 4

Total Time: 1 hour and 15 minutes

GINSPIRATIONS

🍸 This recipe uses quite a few juniper berries but it is well worth it because they really deepen that gin flavour we love so much. You'll want to use one larger steak or 2 smaller steaks. Flank steak works best but any larger cut is wonderful.

🍸 To serve, you can either drizzle the sauce over the sliced beef or place it in a sauceboat and have everyone drizzle their own.

🍸 We used a traditional gin such as Beefeater for our steak and paired it with a classic Martini.

fun fact:

Juniper is packed with antioxidants and is known to do everything from fight infections to aid digestion.

GINGREDIENTS

2 teaspoons of juniper berries

1 ½ teaspoons of allspice berries

1 ½ teaspoons of black peppercorns

1 teaspoon of Kosher salt

1 ½ lbs of steak, trimmed

1 cup of beef broth

6 juniper berries

¾ cup of heavy cream

3 tablespoons of dry gin

1 tablespoon of olive oil

GINSTRUCTIONS

- Grind the 2 teaspoons of juniper berries, the allspice berries, and the peppercorns in a spice grinder until coarsely ground, then stir in the salt.

- Press the ground spices into both sides of the steak. Set aside to marinate at room temperature for 30 minutes.

- In a small saucepan, add the beef broth and the 6 juniper berries. Bring to a gentle simmer. Simmer until the broth has reduced by ¼, about 5 minutes.

- Stir in the cream and gin. Return to a simmer, and cook until reduced by half, about 10 minutes. Keep the sauce warm over very low heat.

- Preheat an outdoor grill for medium-high heat. Pour yourself a cocktail.

- Brush the steak with olive oil on both sides.

- Cook your steak on the preheated grill until it is cooked to your desired degree of doneness, about 4 minutes per side for medium. Place the steak on a plate, cover with tinfoil, and allow it to rest for 5 minutes.

- Slice the steak thinly and place it onto a serving dish. Remove the juniper berries from the gin sauce and discard. Pour the gin sauce over the steak slices and serve.

8Inspired

Tangy & Boozy Beef Stew

Serves: 4 to 6

Total Time: 8 - 10 hours

GINSPIRATIONS

Heather's mother used to make a version of this stew in the winter when they had outdoor picnics. She'd cart out her big pot of stew and put it over the open fire to keep warm. If you've never had an outdoor picnic in the middle of a snowy, cold Canadian winter, well you just haven't lived.

This stew is the perfect winter comfort food and you don't need a firepit to make it. It gets even better the next day, so make lots.

It's very easy to make this recipe. Simply throw everything into the slow cooker and let it cook. No need to brown the beef beforehand (you can if you want to, but it doesn't really need it).

We like to put it into the slow cooker in the morning and then go out and have a fun day on the slopes and then come home to supper ready to eat. Nothing could be easier.

We like the sauce the way it is because it makes for great dipping, but if you prefer a thicker sauce then either add more tomato paste (our preference) or the cornstarch slurry as mentioned in the GINstructions.

We used Steinhart's Classic Dry Gin because of its pleasant warming spiciness, with anise and white pepper. Pair your stew with a classic G&T using **Fever-Tree Indian Tonic**, and some crusty bread for dipping - winter comfort at its best.

GINGREDIENTS

2 lbs of stew beef, trimmed and cut into cubes
1 ½ cups of chopped carrots (approximately 2 - 3 large carrots)
1 large onion, chopped
2 cloves of garlic, minced (or 1 teaspoon of garlic powder)
1 - 8 oz can of tomato paste
¼ cup of brown sugar
¼ cup of white vinegar
1 tablespoon of Worcestershire sauce
½ cup of water
½ cup of gin
1 bay leaf
3 juniper berries, crushed
1 teaspoon of sea salt
½ teaspoon of fresh ground black pepper

GINSTRUCTIONS

- Trim and cut the stewing beef into cubes. Place the cubes into the bottom of a slow cooker or crock pot.
- Add the carrots, onions, and garlic on top of the beef.
- In a small bowl, whisk together the tomato paste, brown sugar, vinegar, Worcestershire sauce, water, and gin until well combined. Pour the mixture over the beef and vegetables.
- Add the bay leaf, juniper berries, and salt and pepper.
- Stir well to coat everything in the sauce.
- Cover tightly.
- Cook on low for 8 - 10 hours (for the best flavours) or high for 4 - 6 hours, stirring every few hours. The meat will fall apart and the vegetables will be super tender along with a tomatoey sauce when it's done.
- If your sauce is not as thick as you would like it, add another can of tomato paste the last hour of cooking OR make a slurry by combining 4 teaspoons of cornstarch with ¼ cup of cold water and stir that into your stew to thicken it (then let it cook for another half hour).
- Serve your stew alone, or over egg noodles or mashed potatoes.

fun fact:

gin drinkers are sassy, classy, and a little bit smart-assy.

Steak Salad with Cilantro Lime Gin Dressing

Serves: 4

Total Time: 30 minutes, plus time to chill the dressing

GINSPIRATIONS

🍸 This delectable salad makes a great meal any night of the week. It's quick to put together and filled with flavour.

🍸 You can add more **Tanqueray Rangpur Gin** to your dressing if you want, but remember that it isn't cooked off, so you'll only want to serve it to those who like gin (and who doesn't?!). If you want a creamier dressing, add a few tablespoons of sour cream. Be sure to chill the dressing before using it to allow time for the flavours to blend.

🍸 You can change your salad up by adding other veggies, changing the cheese, and, of course, using a different gin changes the dressing too.

🍸 We like to use **Tanqueray Rangpur Gin** for our salad because of its yummy limey flavour profile, and pair it with a Gin Margarita for a Mexican treat.

GINGREDIENTS

Cilantro Lime Gin Dressing

½ cup of extra-virgin olive oil

2 tablespoons of white wine vinegar

2 tablespoons of **Tanqueray Rangpur Gin** (or more to taste)

1 lime, juiced (about 2 tablespoons)

1 garlic clove, smashed

1 bunch of cilantro

½ teaspoon of sea salt or Kosher salt

½ teaspoon of fresh ground black pepper

2 tablespoons of sour cream (*optional* - it makes it into a creamy dressing rather than a vinaigrette)

Dry Rub

1 teaspoon of cumin

1 teaspoon of paprika

1 teaspoon of sea salt or Kosher salt

1 teaspoon of fresh ground black pepper

½ teaspoon of chili powder

¼ teaspoon of onion powder

¼ teaspoon of garlic powder

¼ teaspoon of dried oregano

Steak Fajita Salad

1 lb of steak (such as flank or sirloin)

2 tablespoons of olive oil, divided

1 red bell pepper, sliced

1 green bell pepper, sliced

1 medium onion, sliced

1 head romaine lettuce, chopped

1 pint of cherry or grape tomatoes, halved

2 avocados, sliced

4 tablespoons of queso fresco cheese, crumbled (*optional*)

Made this GINspired recipe? Post your photo on Instagram and tag @the.gin.shop.ca

ginspired 87

GINSTRUCTIONS

- Place all dressing ingredients into a blender, and blend until smooth. Place in the fridge to chill. It tastes best after chilling a few hours or overnight.

- Remove the steak from the fridge, remove packaging, and set it on a cutting board to come to room temperature while you prepare dry rub.

- To prepare the fajita dry rub, place all dry rub ingredients into a small bowl, then mix until thoroughly combined. Rub the fajita seasoning into both sides of the steak.

- Heat a 12-inch cast-iron skillet or grill pan over high heat. Add 1 tablespoon of oil to the pan. Let it heat up and then add the steak to the grill pan and sear 3 - 4 minutes per side for medium-rare. Remove the steak from the skillet and place it on a cutting board to rest while you cook the peppers and onions.

- Reduce the heat to medium-high, then add another tablespoon of oil to the skillet. Add the peppers and onions and toss them to coat in the fat and leftover fajita spices.

- Saute the vegetables, tossing frequently, until soft and charred in spots, 6 - 7 minutes. Remove the skillet from heat.

- Thinly slice the steak against the grain.

- Prepare the salad. Divide the lettuce between four bowls, then top each with half a sliced avocado and one-quarter of the tomatoes.

- Top each salad bowl with a quarter of the onions and peppers and a quarter of the steak. Sprinkle with cheese if using, and drizzle with the Cilantro Lime Gin Dressing to taste. Serve immediately.

"This recipe is fantastic! I LOVE big salads and this was one of the best I've ever made. I now have a bunch of new recipes to use: the whole works, just the steak and rub, just the yummy salad dressing, etc."

Susan Sirovyak, test cook

gINtastic Steak Marinade

Makes:
¾ cup of marinade

Total Time: 5 minutes,
plus time to marinate
and cook your steak

GINGREDIENTS

3 tablespoons of maple syrup (or granulated white sugar)

1 tablespoon of ground ginger (or 1 teaspoon of freshly grated)

3 cloves of garlic, crushed

2 tablespoons of gin

½ cup of soy sauce

GINSTRUCTIONS

- Whisk the maple syrup (or sugar), ginger, garlic, gin, and soy sauce together in a small bowl.

- Place the marinade in a large resealable plastic bag, add your steak and seal the bag tightly. Squish the bag a bit ensuring that all the meat is covered with the marinade.

- Marinate smaller steaks 3 - 4 hours, and larger ones 8 hours or overnight in the fridge.

- Remove your steak from the fridge 30 minutes before cooking.

- Grill your meat to your desired doneness using the extra marinade as a basting sauce.

- Remember to let your meat rest before serving.

GINSPIRATIONS

This is a super simple marinade that whips up in a jiffy and tastes oh-so-yummy. The trick is to ensure all of the steak is covered with the marinade, that you let it come to room temperature before grilling, AND that you let it rest when it comes off the grill. This will ensure a juicy and tasty steak every time.

We used Old Tom Gin because it goes so well with the maple syrup and soy sauce. Pair your steak with a cocktail made of gin mixed with a splash of **Fever-Tree Ginger Beer** and enjoy!

"Easy and quick. It brings your steak up to a new level."

Julianne Oelke-Simonsen, test cook

Pork Loin Roast with Creamy Garlic Sun-dried Tomato Gin Sauce

Serves: 4 to 6

Total Time:
1 ½ - 2 hours

GINSPIRATIONS

This just could be the best pork loin roast you will ever eat. Seriously - it's that good. Be sure to buy a loin roast, not a tenderloin. They are very different cuts of meat. We highly recommend using a meat thermometer to ensure your roast is cooked to your desired doneness without having to cut into it to make sure it is cooked (that just ruins it). We can tell you that once we started using a digital meat thermometer, life changed.

Change up your cream sauce by adding mushrooms or spinach if you want more veggies.

Serve your roast with egg noodles, mashed potatoes, or gnocchi for something different. The extra sauce goes wonderfully on just about anything. Add some green beans or a side salad and you have a meal fit for royalty. We used Dillon's Dry Gin for our sauce and paired it with a **Gimlet** (p. 235).

GINGREDIENTS

Roasted Garlic

4 cloves of garlic
1 teaspoon of olive oil

Pork Loin

1 pork loin roast, about 3 lbs
2 tablespoons of extra-virgin olive oil
2 tablespoons of Italian seasoning
1 teaspoon of garlic powder
1 teaspoon of Kosher salt
1 teaspoon of fresh ground pepper

Cream Sauce

¼ cup of butter
1 small onion, chopped
1 tablespoon of flour
¾ cup of heavy cream
½ cup of chicken broth
½ cup of gin
2 teaspoons of dried oregano
⅔ cup of Parmesan cheese, freshly grated
½ cup of sun-dried tomatoes, chopped
¼ teaspoon of cayenne pepper (*optional*)
Salt and pepper to taste

GINSTRUCTIONS

- Preheat the oven to 325°F.
- Remove the pork loin from the fridge and let it come to room temperature.

Roasted Garlic

- Peel each clove of garlic and place it on top of a piece of tin foil. Drizzle the garlic with olive oil. Fold up the tinfoil and form a foil pouch around the garlic.

Pork Loin

- Pat the pork loin dry with a paper towel. Drizzle with oil and rub all over.
- Place seasoning ingredients in a bowl and stir to combine. Sprinkle the seasoning all over the roast and rub it in gently.
- Place the pork loin fat side up in a roasting pan. Place the garlic pouch in the oven directly on the rack.
- Place the pork loin in the oven and roast it until the internal temperature registers between 145 - 160°F (approximately 1 hour and 10 minutes).
- Once your roast is at the desired temperature, remove it (and the garlic packet) from the oven, cover with tin foil and allow it to rest for 10 - 15 minutes.
- Open up your garlic packet and use a fork to smash the garlic. Set it aside.

Cream Sauce

- Prepare the cream sauce while the roast is resting.
- In a skillet, over medium-high heat, melt the butter and then add the onions. Cook the onions until they are translucent. Sprinkle the onions with flour and stir to combine.
- Add the cream, chicken broth, and gin to the skillet and stir well. Stir until your sauce thickens, scraping up any brown bits from the bottom of the pan.
- Add the oregano and grated cheese to the skillet and whisk the sauce until the cheese is completely melted, approximately 3 - 4 minutes.
- Reduce the heat and then add the smashed roasted garlic, sun-dried tomatoes, cayenne, salt, and pepper to taste.
- Simmer your sauce for 3 - 4 minutes or until the tomatoes are softened, stirring occasionally.
- Slice the pork loin into 1-inch pieces and drizzle the cream sauce over each slice.

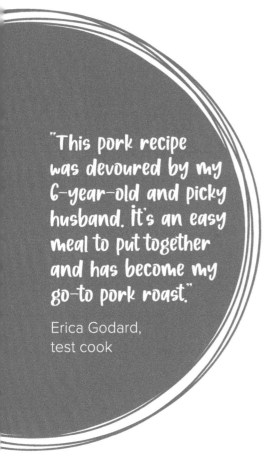

"This pork recipe was devoured by my 6-year-old and picky husband. It's an easy meal to put together and has become my go-to pork roast."

Erica Godard,
test cook

Pork Tenderloin with Mushrooms & Raging Gin Cream Sauce

Serves: 4

Total Time:
60 - 70 minutes

GINSPIRATIONS

🍸 This is the go-to pork tenderloin recipe for Heather's family. It's super juicy and tender. Honestly, it's also pretty hard to mess this recipe up, so she used it to teach her sons how to cook pork tenderloin when they were learning to cook.

🍸 The freshly squeezed citrus juices mixed with the **Raging Crow Caw-Caw-Phany Gin** over the spice mix does something wonderful to the pork. Your kitchen will smell divine.

🍸 Be sure to use pork tenderloin and not a loin roast. They are very different cuts of meat. You can use 1 or 2 small pork tenderloins, or one medium-large pork tenderloin OR you can double or even triple the ingredients for the seasonings and serve a crowd of people with very large tenderloins.

🍸 While you don't need the cream sauce (you can just use the juices in the pan), it really does make your pork that much better. It only takes a few minutes to create. If you don't like mushrooms, don't use them - an onion cream sauce works well too. Make sure your juniper berries are crushed or else remove them before serving.

🍸 For sides, a baked or mashed potato is perfect (especially if you have extra sauce) along with your favourite veggie, such as green beans, brussel sprouts, or peas.

🍸 For gin, we used **Raging Crow Caw-Caw-Phany Gin** because it is a strong traditional gin with 11 botanicals that pair wonderfully with the pork. Pair your pork tenderloin with a **Gin Old Fashioned** (p. 233) for a restaurant-worthy meal any time.

GINGREDIENTS

Pork Tenderloin

2 - ½ lb pork tenderloins or 1 - 1 lb pork tenderloin

1 tablespoon of olive oil

2 teaspoons of Italian seasoning

1 teaspoon of garlic powder

1 teaspoon of cumin

1 teaspoon of Kosher salt

1 teaspoon of chili powder

½ teaspoon of smoked paprika
(*optional*, but highly recommended)

¼ teaspoon of fresh ground black pepper

2 - 3 tablespoons of fresh lemon, lime, or orange juice
(or 1 tablespoon of each)

2 tablespoons of **Raging Crow Caw-Caw-Phany Gin**

Mushroom Cream Sauce

3 tablespoons of butter

1 medium onion, chopped

4 oz of mushrooms, chopped

½ cup of **Raging Crow Caw-Caw-Phany Gin**

½ cup of heavy cream

5 juniper berries, crushed

½ teaspoon of dried oregano

Salt and pepper to taste

Optional garnish: freshly chopped parsley

Made this GINspired recipe? Post your photo on Instagram and tag @the.gin.shop.ca

ginspired 93

GINSTRUCTIONS

- Take the pork tenderloins out of the fridge 20 minutes before you plan to cook them.

- Preheat the oven to 400°F and line a large baking dish with tinfoil.

- Pierce tenderloins all over with a fork. Rub oil onto all sides of the meat. Place the tenderloins into the prepared baking dish.

- Stir together the Italian seasoning, garlic powder, cumin, salt, chili powder, smoked paprika (if using), and black pepper. Sprinkle the mixture over tenderloin(s), patting it onto the surface of the meat on all sides.

- Drizzle lemon/lime/orange juice and **Raging Crow Caw-Caw-Phany Gin** over the top of each tenderloin.

- Bake for 40 - 50 minutes until the outside is browned and crispy and the centres are cooked through to desired doneness (you can take them out on the early side if you like the centres a little pink). Larger tenderloins could take up to 50 minutes or more, smaller tenderloins may only take 30 minutes. Use a meat thermometer to be sure.

- Remove the tenderloins from the oven and spoon juices from the dish all over the meat. Cover with tinfoil and rest in the baking dish for 5 - 10 minutes.

- Meanwhile, make your cream sauce. In a skillet, over medium-high heat, melt the butter and then add the diced onions and mushrooms. Cook the mixture until the onions are translucent and the mushrooms are starting to brown.

- Add the **Raging Crow Caw-Caw-Phany Gin** to the skillet, stirring to deglaze the pan (get all those brown bits up). Lower the heat to medium-low.

- Add the cream, juniper berries, and oregano, and stir to combine. Add salt and pepper to taste. Let the sauce cook for 3 - 4 minutes until well combined and thickened.

- Slice the pork into 1-inch pieces. Spoon the sauce over the slices or serve on the side, garnish with fresh chopped parsley if desired, and serve alongside fresh green beans or spring peas.

"Quick and easy and SO delicious.
Our family's go-to pork tenderloin recipe."

Jenny Wilson, test cook

Made this GINspired recipe? Post your photo on Instagram and tag @the.gin.shop.ca

Pork Chops with Gin Sauce

Serves: 2

Total Time: 15 minutes to prep, 2 hours or overnight for marinating, 10 minutes for cooking

GINSPIRATIONS

🍸 The longer you can let your pork chops marinate (up to overnight), the better they will be. Aside from the marinating time, this is a very quick and easy recipe to make for a weeknight supper. You can add more herbs if you prefer a stronger flavour or even change them up by replacing the rosemary with thyme or oregano.

🍸 If you prefer a thicker sauce, stir in additional crème fraîche or sour cream.

🍸 We used a traditional gin such as Tanqueray London Dry Gin because of its strong juniper profile. However, almost any gin will work. Pour yourself a Tom Collins and dig in.

GINGREDIENTS

½ cup of gin

4 juniper berries, crushed

2 - 6 oz pork chops, thick and boneless

2 garlic cloves, finely chopped

1 - 2 sprigs of rosemary, finely chopped

1 teaspoon of coriander seeds

3 tablespoons of olive oil

½ cup of apple juice

¼ cup of crème fraîche or sour cream

½ teaspoon each of salt and pepper (or to taste)

GINSTRUCTIONS

- Warm the gin in a small microwave-safe dish in the microwave for approximately 30 seconds. Do not let it boil. Add the crushed juniper berries to the warm gin. Leave to soak for 20 minutes.

- Trim the pork chops, leaving a little fat for flavour and to keep it moist. Pierce each chop with a fork in a few places. Place them in a sealable dish.

- Drain the juniper berries, reserving the gin.

- In a mini blender/food processor, combine the garlic, rosemary, and coriander seeds with the gin-soaked juniper berries, and 2 tablespoons of olive oil.

- Spread the mixture over the pork. Cover and marinate it for at least 2 hours but preferably overnight.

- When ready to cook, heat the remaining oil in a small cast-iron frying pan until very hot. Add the pork and cook it quickly on both sides until golden.

- Pour in the reserved gin. Cook it fast until reduced by half. Pour in the apple juice. Scrape the pan to loosen any brown bits. Bring to a boil and then reduce the heat to a low simmer.

- Cover the pork with a lid and simmer it for about 8 - 10 minutes (depending on the thickness of your pork chop it could be less or more) or until it's cooked through and the sauce is reduced but not too thick.

- Remove the pork to a warm plate to rest. Swirl the crème fraîche or sour cream into the sauce.

- Bring the sauce back to a boil and boil it rapidly for 1 - 2 minutes or until it's thickened slightly (it will be a thinner sauce). Season the sauce with salt and pepper. Taste and adjust to your preference. To serve, place each pork chop on a plate, drizzle with the sauce, and enjoy!

"A good heavy book holds you down. It's an anchor that keeps you from getting up and having another gin and tonic."

Roy Blount, Jr.

Gin & Oregano Marinated Leg of Lamb

Serves: 4 to 6

Total Time:
3 ½ hours - 4 ½ hours

GINSPIRATIONS

🍸 A leg of lamb is the dish to serve for special occasions or Sunday dinner. While it can be a pricier cut of meat, it is well worth the expense. Roasting a leg of lamb is actually fairly easy. Simply combine all the marinade ingredients. Slather that on the roast. Let it rest a little bit and then cook. Remember to let it rest for 15 minutes before carving and you are in for a very yummy treat.

🍸 You can use a bone-in or boneless roast. We prefer the bone-in because it's great for making stock and soup. If you aren't going to make stock, then a boneless roast is great.

🍸 For gin, we used Whitley Neill Original London Dry Gin. Pair your lamb with a **Cucumber Gimlet** (p. 227) and celebrate another amazing meal.

GINGREDIENTS

1 medium yellow onion, peeled

1 small apple, peeled and cored

Juice of 1 lemon

¼ cup of gin

¼ cup of olive oil, plus a bit more for drizzling

3 juniper berries

1 ½ teaspoons of Kosher salt

1 teaspoon of fresh ground pepper

½ cup of fresh oregano, roughly chopped

3 lbs leg of lamb

1 large red onion, peeled and chopped into large chunks

GINSTRUCTIONS

- In a food processor or blender, process the yellow onion, apple, lemon juice, gin, ¼ cup olive oil, juniper berries, salt and pepper to a smooth paste.

- Stir in the chopped oregano. Place the lamb in a roasting pan and cover the meat with the marinade, being sure to cover it well. Refrigerate for 2 hours.

- Preheat the oven to 350°F.

- Take the lamb out of the fridge and allow it to rest at room temperature for 30 minutes. Add the red onion chunks to the roasting pan and drizzle a little olive oil over it all.

- Roast for 25 minutes per pound for medium-rare or 30 minutes per pound for medium-well done. The internal temperature should be 130 to 135°F for medium or 140 to 145°F for medium-well (remembering that during the rest period it will keep rising).

- Remove the lamb from the oven and rest it in a warm place loosely covered with aluminium foil for 15 minutes. Carve and serve.

"I'm feeling supersonic. Give me gin and tonic."

Oasis, Supersonic

Grilled Gin Marinated Lamb Chops

Serves: 4
Total Time:
1 hour

GINSPIRATIONS

If at all possible, you'll want to grill these lamb chops. There is something about the BBQ that adds an extra layer of delicious flavour. The marinade is fairly basic to make so you can whip these chops up in no time for a quick weeknight or date night meal.

We used Hendrick's Gin in our marinade. Paired with a Gin Fizz, garlic roasted potatoes, and fresh spring peas, you'll be sure to impress your dinner companions.

GINGREDIENTS

8 lamb chops

Garlic powder

2 tablespoons of butter

2 tablespoons of Worcestershire sauce

2 tablespoons of lemon juice

¼ cup of gin

1 teaspoon of Kosher salt

Fresh ground pepper

Optional garnish: freshly chopped mint leaves

GINSTRUCTIONS

- Dry the lamb chops with a paper towel. Dust the lamb chops with a small amount of garlic powder on each side, rubbing it in to ensure they are well covered. Place the chops in a dish with a lid.

- Melt the butter in a small saucepan. Add the Worcestershire sauce, lemon juice, gin, and salt and pepper. Pour the liquid over the lamb chops.

- Allow to marinate for 30 minutes.

- Remove the chops from the marinade, reserving the liquid. On a preheated outdoor BBQ grill, cook the chops to desired doneness. Alternatively, broil the chops in the oven.

- When done, remove the chops from the heat and allow to rest 5 - 10 minutes after cooking.

- Meanwhile, simmer the remaining marinade in a small saucepan for approximately 10 minutes.

- Place 2 lamb chops on a plate and drizzle with the sauce before serving. Garnish with freshly chopped mint.

"I love how the botanicals in gin can pair well with so many different meats and flavour combinations!"

Cathy Leith, test cook

Made this GINspired recipe? Post your photo on Instagram and tag @the.gin.shop.ca

GINspired 97

apricot & Gin Glazed Ham

Serves: 4

**Total Time:
20 - 25 minutes**

GINGREDIENTS

4 tablespoons of gin

4 tablespoons of apricot jam

4 - 8 oz ham steaks

6 tablespoons of butter, softened

2 tablespoons of fresh parsley, chopped

¼ cup of ready-to-eat dried apricots, finely chopped

1 teaspoon of lemon juice (more to taste)

Ground black pepper

GINSTRUCTIONS

- Mix the gin and jam together. Brush the mixture over the ham steaks. Set aside for 10 minutes.

- Mix together the softened butter, parsley, finely chopped apricots, and lemon juice. Taste and adjust lemon juice to taste. Season with pepper and set aside.

- Preheat an outdoor grill to medium-high heat. BBQ the ham steaks on each side for approximately 2 - 3 minutes.

- Remove the ham steaks from the grill. Place a dollop of the apricot butter on each ham steak and let rest for 5 minutes. Serve immediately.

GINSPIRATIONS

- A ham steak is basically a thick slab of cooked ham. Most grocery stores sell them or you can buy a whole cooked ham and cut your own steaks. The ham is technically already cooked so it doesn't need long on the BBQ.

- The glaze, apricot butter, and that little bit of char from the BBQ takes this from plain ham to spectacular ham.

- We used Seventh Heaven Gin because of its apricot and almond notes. Pair your ham with a cocktail made of gin and **Fever-Tree Refreshingly Light Tonic** for a quick anytime supper.

fun fact:

British gin joints were some of the first places women drank alongside men. Good Catholics believed they were neglecting their children in favour of the spirit, giving it the nickname "Mother's Ruin".

gInspired 99

Drunken Lamb Pasta

Serves: 4

Total Time:
4 to 8 hours

GINSPIRATIONS

🍸 Lamb and pasta go hand in hand like gin and tonic. Adding lamb and gin to your sauce is a nice change from more traditional pasta sauce (you can also substitute ground beef if you prefer).

🍸 Spice your sauce as much or as little as you prefer. We tend to like it a bit more on the spicy side, but you do what works for you and your family.

🍸 While using a slow cooker really takes most of the work out for you (and is ridiculously easy to use), this recipe can also be made on the stovetop or in a cast-iron dutch oven and slowly simmered in the oven as well.

🍸 You'll want to use a stronger gin such as **Raging Crow Spruce Tip Gin**. While the alcohol cooks off, the stronger botanical flavour of the spruce is left behind and compliments the lamb wonderfully. Pair with a **Hiker's Martini (p. 228)** and serve with a crusty bread and Caesar salad for the full Italian experience.

Good friends offer advice. Real friends bring gin.

GINGREDIENTS

1 tablespoon of olive oil

1 ½ lbs of ground lamb

1 large onion, diced

4 oz of mushrooms, diced

2 carrots, peeled and diced

3 cloves of garlic, minced

1 - 28 oz can of crushed tomatoes

1 ½ cups of **Raging Crow Spruce Tip Gin**

1 teaspoon of dried oregano

1 teaspoon of dried rosemary

½ teaspoon of dried thyme

½ teaspoon of red pepper flakes
   (*optional*, add more or less to taste)

Salt and fresh ground pepper to taste

Egg noodles or linguine pasta

½ cup of freshly grated Pecorino Romano cheese
   (plus more for garnish)

Freshly chopped parsley

GINSTRUCTIONS

- Heat the oil in a skillet and then add the lamb. Cook the lamb until browned and cooked through.

- Remove the cooked lamb from the pan (leaving the drippings in the pan) and place it in a slow cooker/crockpot.

- In the same pan as you cooked the lamb, add in the diced onion and mushrooms, and cook for about 10 minutes to soften.

- Remove the mixture from the heat and add to the lamb in the slow cooker.

- Add in the carrots, garlic, crushed tomatoes, **Raging Crow Spruce Tip Gin**, and spices to the slow cooker. Place the cover on your slow cooker and allow the sauce to simmer on low for 6 - 8 hours or on high for 4 hours. Taste and adjust the spices if needed.

- When the sauce is just about done, cook your pasta according to the directions.

- Stir the cheese into the sauce.

- Place the cooked pasta in a large serving dish, add the sauce and stir well to coat and combine. Garnish your dish with freshly chopped parsley and more cheese.

Drunken Italian Noodles with Sausage

Serves: 3 to 4

Total Time: 35 minutes

GINSPIRATIONS

🍸 This is a wonderful weeknight meal that's quick and easy. Serve it with a nice salad and crusty bread and you'll have them asking for it again and again. If you are serving this recipe to minors, leave out the final splash of gin to the finished sauce.

🍸 You can make this as spicy as you like by adjusting the amount of the crushed red pepper flakes to your liking.

🍸 We used Piero Dry Gin because it has more of the Italian herb aromatics. Pair your dinner with a Gin Fizz and dig in.

GINGREDIENTS

Olive oil

1 lb of Italian sausage

1 large onion, chopped

1 ½ teaspoons of salt

1 teaspoon of Italian seasoning

¼ teaspoon of crushed red pepper flakes (*optional*)

½ teaspoon of cracked black pepper

1 red bell pepper, cored and thinly sliced

1 yellow bell pepper, cored and thinly sliced

1 orange bell pepper, cored and thinly sliced

4 cloves of garlic, minced

½ cup of gin

1 - 28 oz can of diced tomatoes with juice

2 tablespoons of fresh parsley, chopped

¼ cup of fresh basil leaves, chopped

8 oz of egg noodles, uncooked

Optional garnish: shaved Parmesan cheese

fun fact:

When buying gin from small distilleries was banned in the Gin Act of early 18th century London, people avoided detection by using the first vending machine called the Puss N Mew to buy their gin.

GINSTRUCTIONS

- Place a large, heavy-bottom pan or braising pot over medium-high heat.

- Add about 2 tablespoons of olive oil. Once the oil is hot, crumble the spicy Italian sausage into the pan in small chunks (you want to keep the sausage fairly chunky). Brown the sausage in the oil.

- Once the crumbled sausage is fully cooked and browned, remove it from the pan (leaving the drippings in the pan) and place it into a small bowl. Set aside.

- Next, reduce your heat to medium and add the chopped onion into the pan with the sausage drippings. Cook the onions for roughly 5 minutes or so, allowing them to caramelize and become golden. Stir often to keep them from burning (add a touch more olive oil, if necessary). Reduce the heat if necessary.

- Once the onion is golden, add the salt, Italian seasoning, red pepper flakes, and cracked black pepper to the pan. Stir to combine.

- Reduce the heat to medium-low, add the sliced bell peppers, and sauté with the onion for about 2 minutes until slightly tender.

- Add in the garlic. Once it becomes aromatic, add in the gin and allow it to reduce for a few moments.

- Add the diced tomatoes with their juice and return the browned spicy Italian sausage back into the pan.

- Gently fold the mixture to combine. Allow it to simmer for about 3 - 4 minutes to blend the flavours, then turn the heat off.

- To finish the sauce, drizzle in about 2 - 3 good tablespoons of olive oil to create a silky, rich flavour. Add the chopped parsley and about half of the chopped basil. Add another splash of gin, if desired. Stir and keep warm while you prepare the noodles.

- Prepare the egg noodles according to instructions on the package. Drain the noodles very well, and add them directly into the sauce, using tongs to gently toss and combine the noodles with the sauce.

- Check the seasoning to see if you need to add any additional salt or pepper or spice. Serve in bowls and garnish with a sprinkle of the remaining basil and top with shaved Parmesan.

Cranberry & Gin Leg of Lamb

Serves: 4 to 6
Total Time:
2 ½ hours - 3 hours

GINSPIRATIONS

- This is probably the easiest leg of lamb you'll ever make. The garlic infuses the meat nicely while the gin, rosemary, and cranberry sauce add a wonderful boost of flavour.
- We don't really have any alternatives for this recipe. Just go make it.
- We used a rosemary-infused Gordon's gin for our lamb roast. Pair your roast with a Gibson Martini and relax and enjoy.

fun fact:
gin is
liquid sanity.

GINGREDIENTS

3 lbs leg of lamb
3 cloves garlic, sliced
Salt and fresh ground pepper
½ cup of butter, divided
2 onions, roughly chopped
2 cups of beef broth, divided
⅓ cup of gin
3 tablespoons of cranberry sauce
3 sprigs fresh rosemary, 2 chopped and leave one whole
Optional garnish: chopped fresh parsley

GINSTRUCTIONS

- Preheat the oven to 350°F.
- Make incisions in the leg of lamb and insert slices of garlic into the cuts. Rub the lamb with salt and pepper.
- Melt ¼ cup of the butter in a large skillet and brown both sides of the lamb. Remove the lamb from the skillet (leaving the drippings in the pan) and place it in a roasting pan.
- Add the chopped onions to the lamb drippings in the skillet and saute gently for a few minutes. Once the onions are translucent, add 1 cup of beef broth and deglaze the pan (being sure to scrape up all those yummy bits on the bottom).
- Add the gin, cranberry sauce, and chopped rosemary. Stir to combine. Scrape the bottom of the pan to loosen any meaty bits.
- Simmer the sauce for a few minutes until the cranberry sauce is melted. Pour this mixture over the lamb. Place the last rosemary sprig on top of the lamb.
- Cover the roast with a lid or tin foil and place in the oven. Roast for 25 minutes per pound for medium-rare or 30 minutes per pound for medium-well done. The internal temperature should be 130 to 135°F for medium or 140 to 145°F for medium-well (remembering that during the rest period it will keep rising). Baste occasionally during cooking. If the lamb juices look like they are drying out at any time you can add another ¼ cup of stock.
- Remove the lamb from the oven. Place it on a cutting board and loosely cover it with aluminium foil. Allow the roast to rest for 15 minutes.
- To make the sauce, place the roasting pan on top of the stove on a burner. Heat the drippings to a simmer and then add the remaining ¼ cup butter and ½ cup of beef broth.
- Bring it to a boil and then turn the heat down to a simmer, scraping all the meaty bits from the pan.
- To serve, carve the lamb, pour the sauce over each slice, and garnish with freshly chopped parsley.

Boozy Blueberry BBQ Sauce

Makes: 2 ½ cups

Total Time:
45 minutes

GINSPIRATIONS

🍸 Being Canadian, we both love everything that uses wild blueberries (you may have noticed that). Heather used to go blueberry picking as a child and distinctly remembers plopping herself down into a patch and eating just as many as went into her bucket. The black bears and black flies aside, it was always a day to remember and enjoy. Now she just buys wild blueberries at the local berry farm - it's much safer.

🍸 If you've never had blueberry bbq sauce, you seriously don't know what you are missing. It's not something you can find in the grocery store. It's super easy to make and is amazing on any pork such as ribs or tenderloin. It works great on chicken thighs too.

🍸 If you use frozen blueberries, please thaw them completely and then drain the liquid off (keep it for another recipe). If you don't, you'll need to cook your sauce much longer or it will be watery. And you don't want watery BBQ sauce.

🍸 If you aren't into spice, leave out the jalapeno or remove its seeds. You can also cut back on the crushed red pepper flakes, but keep some as it adds a really nice flavour to the sauce.

🍸 You'll want a strong gin for this recipe. We used Monkey 47 and it is delicious! Use this sauce for your next rib cookout and pair it with a **Berry Tasty Gin Smash** (p. 226), some potato salad and grilled corn on the cob.

GINGREDIENTS

1 tablespoon of olive oil

1 small onion, diced

2 cloves garlic, minced

3 ½ cups of fresh or frozen wild blueberries (if using frozen berries, be sure to thaw and drain well)

1 cup of ketchup

½ cup of brown sugar, firmly packed

½ cup of apple cider vinegar

½ cup of gin

1 jalapeño, seeded and diced (*optional*), or leave the seeds in for extra heat

1 teaspoon of Kosher salt

½ teaspoon of fresh ground black pepper

1 teaspoon of crushed red pepper flakes

2 small or 1 large bay leaf

GINSTRUCTIONS

• In a large saucepan, heat the olive oil over medium heat. Add the onions and garlic and sauté until translucent and fragrant.

• If you are using frozen berries, be sure to thaw them completely and DRAIN them. If you don't, your sauce will be watery.

• Add the remaining GINgredients. Bring to a low simmer and cook down for approximately 30 minutes, until the sauce is thickened and syrupy.

• Remove the bay leaves and let cool slightly.

• Using an immersion blender, purée your sauce until smooth (or leave a few chunks if you prefer). Alternatively, transfer to a blender and purée if you do not have an immersion blender.

• Store in an airtight container in the fridge for up to 5 days.

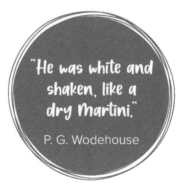

"He was white and shaken, like a dry martini."

P. G. Wodehouse

Made this GINspired recipe? Post your photo on Instagram and tag @the.gin.shop.ca

Unimaginable Poultry

Perfect for gin lovers and curious imbibers

GIN & TONIC CHICKEN KABOBS

GIN IN THE LIME IN THE COCONUT CHICKEN

GAME DAY GINNY LEMON CHICKEN WINGS

FUNDY MARY CHICKEN

MAD CHICKEN

SPIRITED ROAST CHICKEN

CHICKEN WITH JUNIPER BERRIES & GIN

SMASHED CHICKEN BREAST WITH GINNY MUSHROOMS

ONE-POT MEDITERRANEAN CHICKEN & LEMON GIN RICE

LEMON CHICKEN PASTA WITH RICOTTA, PEAS, & GIN

GIN-BRINED CHICKEN OR TURKEY

MARTINI CHICKEN

TURKEY & GREEN APPLE SALAD WITH GINTY DRESSING

Gin & Tonic Chicken Kabobs

Serves: 4

Total Time: 3 hours

GINGREDIENTS

3 ⅓ lbs of boneless, skinless chicken breasts

¼ cup of gin

½ cup of **Fever-Tree Lemon Tonic Water**

2 tablespoons of olive oil

¼ cup of fresh squeezed lime juice (approximately 2 limes)

1 tablespoon of lime zest

¼ cup of fresh mint, minced

¼ teaspoon of salt

½ teaspoon of fresh ground pepper

½ teaspoon of ground coriander

1 large red onion, quartered

GINSPIRATIONS

Who doesn't love a good kabob? And these ones are super simple with the hint of G&T. The tonic you use will really change the flavour of this recipe so be choosy. We suggest **Fever-Tree Lemon Tonic** if you can find it.

Feel free to add other veggies to your kabobs like mushrooms or cherry tomatoes. We suggest you make separate veggie kabobs as they tend to cook at a different rate than the chicken/onion ones do. Just brush any leftover marinade over them. Do not soak your veggies in the marinade.

For gin, we used a citrus gin such as Beefeater. Pair your kabobs with a **Cucumber Gimlet** (p. 227) and serve with rice and our **Mixed Greens with GINaigrette** (p. 49) for a wonderful summer meal on the patio.

GINSTRUCTIONS

- Cut the boneless skinless chicken into 2-inch cubes and place it in a large bowl or plastic resealable bag.

- Pour the gin and tonic over the chicken and squish it all up to mix. Add olive oil, lime juice, lime zest, mint, salt, pepper, and coriander, and squish it all up again.

- Seal the bag or cover the bowl. Place in the fridge and marinate for 1 - 3 hours. The gin is strong, so do not marinate overnight or your chicken will be dry.

- Soak 8 - 10 bamboo skewers in water for at least 30 minutes.

- Cut the red onion into chunks. Separate the onion layers so that you have a piece approximately 1-inch by 1-inch by ⅛-inch (depending on the thickness of each onion layer).

- Skewer the kabobs starting with the onion piece and then a chicken cube. Continue alternating between red onion and chicken cubes, being sure to leave a few inches of skewer at each end. Set the skewers on a large platter. Preheat your grill to 375°F.

- Grill your kabobs on medium heat (or broil) for 10 minutes or until the onions begin to brown slightly and the chicken reaches an internal temperature of 165°F. Turn the skewers to ensure even cooking. They will cook fairly quickly depending on the size of your chicken cubes and the temperature you use. Remove from the heat and serve!

"The gin really works well in this recipe to tenderize and flavour the chicken."

Maggie Richards, test cook

gin in the Lime in the Coconut Chicken

> We have an open-door policy. Show up with gin and we'll let you in.

GINSPIRATIONS

🍸 Let's add some gin in the lime in the coconut! While you are at it, add some chicken too for one scrumptious meal.

🍸 Make sure you use a full-fat coconut milk for this recipe. Not all coconut milks are created equal and you want a thick one for a nice thick and creamy sauce. While the sauce should reduce down and get thicker as you simmer it, it is not supposed to be as thick as gravy so keep that in mind. It's sauce, not gravy.

🍸 A pinch of turmeric adds a nice golden colour. You can also add a chopped red or green chili if you really want to spice it up.

🍸 Garnish with more chopped cilantro, red pepper flakes, toasted coconut, or even a splash more gin if you aren't serving this dish to minors. If you are serving minors, the alcohol in the recipe evaporates during cooking.

🍸 We like to use a lime or citrus flavour infused gin such as Malfy with this recipe. It really kicks it up a notch. We recommend pairing this chicken with a **Berry Tasty Gin Smash** (p. 226) and serving with rice.

GINGREDIENTS

4 skinless, boneless chicken breasts or equivalent in boneless thighs (about 1½ lbs)
¼ teaspoon of Kosher salt
¼ teaspoon of fresh ground pepper
1 tablespoon of coconut oil (may need a tiny bit more)
½ cup of onion, diced
2 teaspoons of all-purpose flour
1 cup of gin
2 tablespoons of fresh lime juice (about one large lime)
1 tablespoon of fresh cilantro, chopped
¼ - ½ teaspoon of red pepper flakes (*optional*)
½ cup of full-fat coconut milk
Pinch of turmeric powder (*optional* – for colour)
Optional garnishes: chopped cilantro, red pepper flakes, toasted coconut and/or a splash of gin)

GINSTRUCTIONS

- Place the chicken breasts between two pieces of parchment paper and pound them down to make them an even thickness. This helps the chicken cook evenly and makes it more tender. Sprinkle each side of each chicken breast with salt and pepper.
- Heat the coconut oil in a large skillet (cast-iron works best) over medium-high heat. Add the chicken breasts and cook each side for approximately 5 - 7 minutes or until browned on each side.
- Remove the chicken from the skillet and set aside on a plate. The chicken doesn't need to be fully cooked yet as you'll be returning it to the pan to heat shortly.
- Turn the heat down to medium-low. Add a little more oil to the pan if needed along with the diced onion. Sauté until soft and starting to brown. Sprinkle the onion with 2 teaspoons of flour. Stir well and cook for approximately 20 - 30 seconds.
- Add the gin. Stir the mixture well, scraping up any brown bits. The gin sauce will thicken slightly. Add the lime juice, cilantro, and red pepper flakes. Bring the mixture to a simmer for about 5 minutes to reduce the sauce down. Add the coconut milk and turmeric (if using).
- Bring to a simmer again for about 5 minutes. Once the sauce thickens and reduces slightly, add the chicken back into the skillet. Allow everything to cook for another 5 - 10 minutes or until the chicken is cooked all the way through.
- Serve with rice or cauliflower rice and spoon the sauce over everything. Add extra cilantro, chili flakes, or toasted coconut for garnish if desired.

Made this GINspired recipe? Post your photo on Instagram and tag @the.gin.shop.ca

Game Day Ginny Lemon Chicken Wings

Serves: 4

Total Time: 30 minutes

GINSPIRATIONS

🍸 Take your game day wings to the next level with these yummy morsels. Simply toss your wings in the gin, lemon and brown sugar mixture, bake, and serve with the dipping sauce.

🍸 For the dipping sauce, you can use the one here OR if you are in a hurry, a good ranch dressing with a spot of gin goes a long way too.

🍸 We used a lemony gin such as Malfy gin for our wings. Pair with a Gin Spritz, spiked with prosecco, red vermouth, and **Fever-Tree Sparkling Pink Grapefruit**. Serve with some raw veggies and your game day or happy hour is complete.

fun fact:

The best way to taste a new gin is at room temperature, diluted with an equal measure of water. This reveals both qualities and flaws.

GINGREDIENTS

Wings

4 lbs of chicken wings, at room temperature

Zest and juice of 1 lemon

¼ cup of gin

1 cup of brown sugar

¼ cup of olive oil

2 teaspoons of Kosher salt, divided

Fresh ground pepper

Dipping Sauce

½ cup of full-fat sour cream

½ cup of mayonnaise

2 cloves of garlic

¼ cup of fresh cilantro, chopped

1 tablespoon of extra-virgin olive oil

2 tablespoons of gin

2 tablespoons of fresh lemon juice

Salt to taste

GINSTRUCTIONS

- Preheat the oven to 425°F. Line a baking sheet with non-stick tinfoil.
- Whisk together the lemon zest and juice, brown sugar, olive oil, 1 teaspoon of Kosher salt, and a dash of fresh ground pepper. Add the wings to the mixture and toss, making sure they are completely coated.
- Place the wings on the foil in a single layer. Bake them for 20 minutes or until golden and crispy, turning halfway through. Give them a light sprinkle of Kosher salt when they come out of the oven.
- To make the dipping sauce, add all ingredients to a food processor. Mix until smooth. Alternatively, whisk all the dipping sauce GINgredients together in a bowl until well combined. Serve the wings with the dipping sauce on the side.

Fundy Mary Chicken

Serves: 4

**Total Time:
30 minutes**

GINSPIRATIONS

This chicken has everything a good Bloody Mary should have - tomatoes, celery salt, celery, spice, and, of course, gin. It's a fairly quick and easy dish for any night of the week.

You can spice it up as much or as little as you like. Add some diced chilies or chopped jalapeño if you want a bit more of a kick.

We used **Fundy Gin** made by **Still Fired Distilleries** for this recipe. Pair this chicken with a **Fundy Peach Gin & Tonic (p. 229)** and serve it over rice or pasta along with a tossed salad for a complete meal.

GINGREDIENTS

4 boneless skinless chicken thighs or breasts (about 1 lb)

½ teaspoon of celery salt

¼ teaspoon of fresh ground pepper

2 tablespoons of butter

1 tablespoon of olive oil

2 celery stalks, thinly sliced

1 - 14.5 oz can of diced tomatoes, undrained

⅓ cup of **Still Fired Distillery - Fundy Gin** (or more to taste)

1 teaspoon of grated lime zest

2 tablespoons of freshly squeezed lime juice (approximately 1 large lime)

1 teaspoon of Worcestershire sauce

4 lime wedges or 2 additional tablespoons of freshly squeezed lime juice

1 tablespoon of chopped celery leaves (or fresh parsley)

Optional garnishes: hot pepper sauce and celery salt

GINSTRUCTIONS

- Pound the chicken thighs slightly with a meat mallet to uniform thickness; sprinkle with celery salt and fresh ground pepper.

- In a large skillet, heat butter and oil over medium heat; brown the chicken on both sides. We use our **Meyer** skillet for this recipe as it helps the chicken cook evenly.

- Remove the chicken from the skillet and keep warm (keeping the juices in the pan). In the same skillet, add the celery and cook for 3 - 4 minutes or until tender.

- Return the chicken to the pan. Add the tomatoes, Fundy Gin, lime zest, lime juice, and Worcestershire sauce.

- Bring to a boil. Reduce the heat and cover. Simmer, covered, for 8 - 10 minutes or until the chicken is cooked through.

- When done, squeeze a lime over each piece of chicken and garnish it with celery leaves. If desired, top with a hot pepper sauce and a sprinkle of celery salt for a true Bloody Mary experience. Serve over rice or pasta.

fun fact:

Gin and tomato juice was all the rage as a hangover cure in New York City in 1928, years before the vodka-based Bloody Mary made its debut at the King Cole Room in the St. Regis Hotel.

Mad Chicken

Serves: 4

**Total Time:
30 - 40 minutes**

GINSPIRATIONS

🍸 This will be your go-to meal for a quick weeknight meal. Chicken thighs are generally a fairly good price so it's an economical recipe too. If you don't have boneless chicken thighs, bone-in with skin-on thighs or chicken breasts work well too — simply ensure that you cook them longer.

🍸 If you don't like cilantro, you can totally use parsley or dill instead.

🍸 For gin, we used **Mad Lab Gin6**. It's a unique blend of juniper, coriander, lime zest, cucumber, bay leaf, and dill that goes wonderfully with this recipe. Pair your chicken with a **Mad Martini** (p. 234).

"This chicken is so shockingly easy and delicious. It is a perfect mid-week, two working parents kind of meal where you actually get a lovely meal."

Erica Godard, test cook

GINGREDIENTS

1 large or 2 small apples (Granny Smith or Cortland apples work well)

1 lb of boneless, skinless chicken thighs (or chicken breasts)

2 tablespoons of extra-virgin olive oil

2 tablespoons of **Mad Lab Gin6**

2 tablespoons of fresh cilantro, dill, or parsley, chopped, divided

2 garlic of cloves, minced

1 teaspoon of whole coriander seeds, smashed

4 juniper berries, smashed

1 teaspoon of honey

½ teaspoon of Kosher salt

½ teaspoon of fresh ground black pepper

GINSTRUCTIONS

- Preheat the oven to 400°F. Grease or line a 9 x 13-inch baking pan.

- Peel and core the apples and thinly slice (between ⅛- and ¼-inch is fine). Spread the apples in the baking pan, evenly covering the bottom of the pan.

- Lightly smash the juniper berries and coriander seeds.

- In a large bowl, whisk together the olive oil, **Mad Lab Gin6**, 1 tablespoon of chopped cilantro, garlic, coriander, juniper berries, honey, salt, and pepper.

- Add the chicken and toss together gently. Note: If you are using chicken breasts, you may want to slice them in half or pound them slightly thinner.

- Spread the chicken out into one layer over the apples in the pan. Pour any remaining spices and liquid over the top.

- Place in the oven and roast until the chicken is cooked through and the apples are softened, about 20 - 30 minutes, depending on the thickness of your chicken.

- Turn on your broiler. Broil the chicken for 2 - 3 minutes until the tops are nicely browned. Take out of the oven and let rest 2 - 3 minutes before serving.

- Garnish with the remaining tablespoon of cilantro and serve, being sure to spoon some apples and juice over your chicken.

Spirited Roast Chicken

Serves: 3 to 4

**Total Time:
2 hours**

GINSPIRATIONS

- Injecting chicken can be a tiny bit challenging if you have never done it before. You DO need a flavour injector but it is well worth the purchase. Once you've injected a chicken, you will be injecting it with all sorts of yummy flavourings.

- Play with the injection sauce. Add some spice if you like (just make sure it is a liquid). The sugar or maple syrup is optional so leave it out if you wish.

- If your chicken is on the larger size, you may need to double the injection and seasoning amounts to ensure full coverage.

- The chicken drippings make a wonderful gravy, especially if you add another splash of gin to finish it.

- We used Seventh Heaven Gin for our spirited chicken. It adds a delicious apricot flavour. However, you can also try a gin with thyme or rosemary as well. Pair your chicken with a **Martinez** (p. 235), **Soused Mashed Potatoes** (p. 75) or a rice pilaf, and a veggie of your choice for a lovely dinner any time.

"I never realized how easy it is to inject a chicken before; this recipe opened up a whole new world of flavour for me."

Cathy Leith, test cook

GINGREDIENTS

1 whole chicken, 3 - 4 lbs

2 tablespoons of all-purpose flour

1 teaspoon of poultry seasoning

Salt and pepper to taste

¼ cup of butter, softened

Injection Sauce

1 teaspoon of garlic powder

¼ cup of gin

½ cup of butter melted

1 teaspoon of brown sugar or maple syrup (*optional*)

GINSTRUCTIONS

- Preheat the oven to 325°F.

- Prepare your chicken by washing it thoroughly. Pat the chicken dry with a paper towel, making sure it's dry.

- Prepare the butter gin sauce by combining the garlic powder, gin, melted butter, and brown sugar in a deep bowl.

- Inject the chicken: Insert your flavour injector into the sauce and fill your injector. Take the needle and insert it just under the skin of the chicken, slowly pushing it into opposite sides, without tampering with the skin. Then, inject the sauce until you begin to experience back-pressure. Continue injecting your sauce while withdrawing the needle. Start first with the wings and drumsticks and then move onto the breast. Try to limit the number of injection holes to avoid having a high number of holes in your chicken (and losing your sauce).

- Once all the sauce has been injected, season your chicken first with the flour, then poultry seasoning, and salt and pepper. Carefully rub the softened butter over the skin.

- Cook the chicken at 325°F until it reaches an internal temperature of 165°F, basting occasionally.

- If the skin starts to get too browned partway through cooking, cover your chicken with tin foil or a cut-up paper bag. Don't use a lid, as you still need the air movement.

- Once the chicken is cooked, take it out of the oven and let it rest 10 minutes before carving.

Chicken with Juniper Berries & Gin

Serves: 4

**Total Time:
30 minutes**

GINSPIRATIONS

You can use boneless, skinless, or bone-in chicken for this recipe. Both work wonderfully. Be sure to crush your juniper berries or else remove them before serving.

If you love mushrooms, we highly recommend adding some sliced mushrooms to your sauce when you add the onions. They cook down beautifully and go well in the sauce.

We suggest using a traditional gin strong in juniper such as Tanqueray London Dry Gin for this chicken recipe. Pair it with an **It's About Thyme Gin & Tonic** (p. 230), **Soused Mashed Potatoes** (p. 75) or gnocchi, and green beans for a scrumptious dinner.

GINGREDIENTS

8 chicken thighs or 4 chicken breasts

3 tablespoons of all-purpose flour

Salt and pepper, to taste

1 tablespoon of olive oil

1 tablespoon of butter

1 small onion, diced

⅔ cup of chicken broth

⅓ cup of gin

6 juniper berries, lightly crushed

1 tablespoon of fresh tarragon

2 tablespoons of crème fraîche or sour cream

GINSTRUCTIONS

- Season the flour with salt and pepper in a large shallow dish. Add the chicken and dredge until coated with the seasoned flour.

- Heat the oil and butter in a large deep skillet (cast-iron is best) on medium-high heat. Place the chicken (skin down, if it has skin) in the hot skillet and cook for about 5 minutes until it's nicely browned.

- Lower the heat to medium and then add the onion and sauté for a minute or two.

- Add the chicken broth, gin, juniper berries, and tarragon to the skillet. Cover and simmer for about 15 minutes or until the chicken is cooked through. Remove the chicken from the skillet and keep warm.

- Add the crème fraîche or sour cream into the sauce in the skillet and stir to combine. Cook for 2 - 3 minutes, allowing your sauce to thicken. When ready to serve, pour the sauce over your chicken or serve alongside in a small bowl.

fun fact:

The Philippines has the world's highest per-capita gin consumption, with an estimated 25 million cases consumed annually.

Smashed Chicken Breast with Ginny Mushrooms

Serves: 4

Total Time:
45 minutes

The house may not be tidy but the gin is always neat.

GINSPIRATIONS

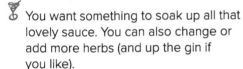 For a hearty anytime meal, this is it. The chicken with the mushroom gin sauce goes really well with many sides such as **Soused Mashed Potatoes** (p. 75), rice, or gnocchi.

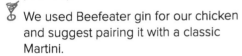 You want something to soak up all that lovely sauce. You can also change or add more herbs (and up the gin if you like).

We used Beefeater gin for our chicken and suggest pairing it with a classic Martini.

GINGREDIENTS

1 tablespoon of olive oil

3 + 1 tablespoons of butter

4 skinless, boneless chicken breasts, pounded to an even thinness

Salt and fresh ground pepper to taste

8 - 10 fresh white or brown mushrooms, sliced

1 large onion, diced

2 cloves of garlic, sliced

⅓ cup of gin

½ cup of chicken broth

4 juniper berries, crushed (or more if you want a stronger flavour)

½ teaspoon of ground thyme

Optional garnish: freshly chopped or dried parsley

GINSTRUCTIONS

- In a large skillet, heat olive oil and 3 tablespoons of butter over medium heat.

- Ensure your chicken breasts are pounded to an even thickness (in other words, smashed). Season the chicken with salt and fresh ground pepper. Add to the skillet and brown both sides.

- Reduce the heat, cover, and cook for another 10 minutes, or until the chicken juices run clear. Remove the chicken from the skillet (keeping the juices in the pan) and keep warm.

- Add the mushrooms, chopped onion, and garlic to the skillet. Cook until tender and most of the water is cooked out of the mushrooms. Stir in the gin and chicken broth. Add the juniper berries and thyme. Cook the mixture for another 5 minutes until the sauce is reduced and slightly thickened. Taste and add more seasoning if required.

- Add the remaining 1 tablespoon of butter and stir until melted. Add the chicken back into the skillet to reheat (approximately 2 minutes), spooning the sauce over each piece.

- Place each chicken breast on a plate, spoon the sauce over it, garnish with fresh chopped parsley, and serve.

One-Pot Mediterranean Chicken & Lemon Gin Rice

Serves: 4

Total Time:
1 ½ hours

GINSPIRATIONS

🍸 This may just be the best chicken and rice dish you've ever had. It's easy, lemony, and oh-so-yummy. It's baked in the oven in just one pan, making cleaning up a snap.

🍸 The rice gets the double whammy of the chicken stock plus the juices of the cooking chicken for extra deep flavour. Add the lemon gin and you will seriously have them begging you to make this dish often.

🍸 We prefer to use boneless chicken thighs as they are quick and easy. However, you can use bone-in thighs too, just adjust the cooking time a tiny bit. Chicken breast tends to dry out, so if you use them, don't put them in the pan until the rice has cooked for 20 minutes.

🍸 The liquid to rice ratio is important. Rice baked in the oven requires a lot more liquid than when it's cooked on the stove. And when you add chicken on top of the rice, it drops the liquid so you need to take that into account.

🍸 We used a lemon gin such as Gordon's Sicilian Lemon Gin because it really adds to the lemony flavour. Pair this one-pot wonder with a **Gin Hard Seltzer** (p. 229) and serve with fresh peas or a Greek salad.

GINGREDIENTS

Chicken and Marinade

2 lbs of boneless chicken thighs

2 tablespoons of fresh lemon zest + 4 tablespoons of lemon juice (approximately 2 lemons)

1 tablespoon of fresh oregano, chopped (or dried oregano)

4 cloves of garlic, minced

½ teaspoon of sea salt

Rice

1 tablespoon of extra-virgin olive oil

1 tablespoon of butter

1 small onion, finely diced

1 cup of uncooked long grain rice

2 cups of chicken broth

½ cup of lemon gin

1 tablespoon of dried oregano

¾ teaspoon of sea salt

½ teaspoon of fresh ground pepper

Garnishes

Finely chopped fresh parsley or oregano (*optional*)

Fresh lemon juice and zest (highly recommended)

GINSTRUCTIONS

- Combine the chicken thighs and marinade ingredients in a sealable plastic bag and let marinate in the fridge for at least 20 minutes but preferably overnight.

- Preheat the oven to 350°F. Remove the chicken from the marinade, reserving the marinade (you'll be using it later).

- Heat 1 tablespoon of olive oil in a deep, heavy-based skillet (cast-iron is best) over medium-high heat. Add the chicken to the skillet and cook quickly on each side just until seared. Remove the chicken from the pan and set aside.

- Add and melt 1 tablespoon of butter to the skillet over medium-high heat. Add the onion to the butter and sauté for a few minutes until translucent.

- Add the remaining rice ingredients and the reserved marinade to the pan. Let the liquid come to a simmer and let it simmer for 30 seconds.

- Place the seared chicken thighs on top of the rice and then place a lid on the skillet (or cover it with tinfoil if you don't have a lid that fits).

- Place the skillet in the hot oven and bake for 35 minutes. Then remove the lid and bake for a further 10 minutes, or until all the liquid is absorbed and the rice is tender (45 minutes in total).

- Remove the pan from the oven and allow it to rest for 5 - 10 minutes before serving. Garnish this one-pot meal with freshly chopped parsley or oregano, a squeeze of fresh lemon juice, and freshly grated lemon zest.

fun fact:

Centuries before the birth of gin, juniper was already being imported to Britain from the Mediterranean. It's considered the best in the world.

Lemon Chicken Pasta with Ricotta, Peas, & Gin

Serves: 4
Total Time: 30 minutes

GINSPIRATIONS

You will LOVE LOVE LOVE this scrumptious lemony pea ricotta pasta. We swear. Try to use fresh peas if you can, especially those first spring peas...yummy. You can totally make this recipe with chicken or without. For a quick weekday meal, we would usually grab a rotisserie chicken from the grocery store and tear it apart. But you can also use any leftover cooked chicken.

You can use any type of pasta (fresh or dried) but we find a penne or fusilli work best to hold the sauce.

The bacon is totally optional for garnish but we highly recommend adding it if you have it. You can also up the gin amount to your preference.

We used a lovely lemony gin, Whitley Neill's Lemongrass & Ginger Gin for this recipe. Pair with a **White Lady** (p. 236), a fresh green salad, and a crusty bread and you'll have the most amazing meal. Promise.

GINGREDIENTS

Sauce

1 clove of garlic
⅓ cup of fresh parsley
1 teaspoon of dried oregano
1 teaspoon of fresh thyme, or ½ teaspoon dried thyme
1 ½ cups of peas, frozen and thawed, or use fresh
¼ - ½ cup of gin (to taste)
15 oz tub of ricotta cheese
1 tablespoon of lemon zest (1 large lemon)
3 - 4 tablespoons of fresh squeezed lemon juice (to taste)
¼ cup of good extra-virgin olive oil
2 teaspoons of Kosher salt
¾ teaspoon of fresh ground pepper

Assemble

1 lb of pasta (penne, fusilli, or macaroni)
1 cup of peas (fresh is best)
Rotisserie chicken (chopped) or cooked chopped chicken (*optional*)
½ cup of grated Parmesan cheese
1 - 4 tablespoons of olive oil, to drizzle
Optional garnishes: crushed red pepper (to taste), crumbled cooked bacon, Parmesan cheese, freshly chopped parsley

GINSTRUCTIONS

- Cook your pasta according to the directions until it's al dente. When the pasta is al dente, drain and then return it to the same pot. Drizzle with a touch of olive oil and stir. Set aside.

- Meanwhile, make the ricotta pea sauce. In a food processor or blender, add garlic, parsley, oregano, and thyme. Pulse or blend until the parsley and garlic are finely chopped.

- Add 1 ½ cups of peas, as well as the gin, ricotta, lemon zest and juice, ¼ cup of olive oil, 2 teaspoons of Kosher salt, and fresh ground black pepper. Pulse until the mixture comes together but still has some texture to it, it shouldn't be completely smooth.

- Add the ricotta mixture to the pasta and toss to combine. Add the remaining cup of peas and chopped chicken, if you are using it. Add ½ cup of grated Parmesan cheese and a few drizzles of olive oil. Toss to combine. Add a few shakes of crushed red pepper if you like. Stir.

- Divide the pasta into 4 bowls. Garnish each with crumbled cooked bacon, more Parmesan, a touch more gin, and freshly chopped parsley, and serve.

Gin-Brined Chicken or Turkey

Serves: 4 to 6

Total Time: 2 hours, plus 24 hours for brining

GINSPIRATIONS

🍸 This amazing gin brine makes chicken unbelievably juicy, tender, and flavourful. Once you've tasted this, you will never want to eat normal chicken again! The downside is adding a cup of gin into your chicken can make it expensive, so you may want to save this recipe for a special occasion or celebration.

🍸 A brine for poultry should be approximately 2 teaspoons of salt for every 7 tablespoons of water (this is called a 10% brine).

🍸 For turkey or a larger chicken, increase the quantities of water and salt proportionately to the weight (and gin if you don't mind the expense!).

🍸 Your chicken should be completely submerged in the brine in a non-metallic container and kept cold in the fridge or a garage in winter if it's cold enough. We've also been known to use a larger plastic cooler for a larger chicken or turkey and added some ice cubes to keep it cold when it doesn't fit in the fridge. Adding a heavy plate on top of the bird helps keep it submerged too.

🍸 Most of the work for this recipe is done in the brining and roasting. You'll have a moist and flavourful chicken when all is said and done. Plus, the drippings make an amazing gravy.

🍸 Use a gin with thyme and lemon botanicals such as The Botanist or infuse your own gin. Pair your chicken with a **Chef's Little Helper** (p. 227), roasted potatoes, and veggies for an amazing special occasion treat.

GINGREDIENTS

Brining

1 chicken (roughly 3 - 4 lbs)

12 cups of water

1 cup of sea salt

1 lemon, quartered

1 cup of gin

2 limes, halved

A few sprigs of fresh thyme

4 bay leaves

1 teaspoon of peppercorns or
    ½ teaspoon of fresh ground black pepper

6 juniper berries, lightly crushed

Roasting

2 tablespoons of all-purpose flour

Fresh ground pepper to taste

¼ cup of butter, softened

A few sprigs of fresh thyme

GINSTRUCTIONS

Brining

- Mix together the water, gin, and salt in a large non-metallic container (big enough to hold the brine and chicken) and stir until the salt is dissolved.
- Add the chicken and ensure it is completely submerged, add more water if not. Squeeze in the juice of the lemons and limes and then add them into the water around the chicken. Add all the other brine ingredients to the container.
- Place a plate over the chicken to keep it all submerged, if need be. Cover and store for 24 hours in the fridge if possible, or a similarly cold place.

Roasting

- Preheat the oven to 325°F.
- Remove the chicken from the brine and pat dry. Place it in a roasting pan. Remove the herbs, limes, and lemons from the brine and stuff it all into the cavity of the chicken.
- Season your chicken first with the flour, and then fresh ground pepper. Carefully rub the softened butter over the skin. Top with fresh sprigs of thyme.
- Place in the oven and cook the chicken at 325°F until it reaches an internal temperature of 165°F, basting occasionally. Usually it will take about an hour and a half or so to cook.
- If the skin starts to get too browned partway through cooking, cover your chicken with tin foil or a cut-up paper bag. Don't use a lid, as you still need the air movement.
- Once the chicken is cooked, take it out of the oven and let it rest 10 minutes before carving.

fun fact:

The juniper berry is actually not a berry at all. It's a female seed cone, a highly-evolved pinecone with fleshy and merged scales that give it the appearance of a berry.

Martini Chicken

Serves: 4

Total Time: 30 minutes

GINSPIRATIONS

🍸 Here is a yummy chicken recipe that cooks up in a jiffy. You can increase the gin and olives if you like or take a walk on the wild side and add a dash of hot sauce.

🍸 We used a stronger gin, Monkey 47, to ensure a lovely strong botanical flavour. Pair your chicken with a Dirty Martini (of course), add a nice side salad and some crusty bread, and enjoy!

GINGREDIENTS

4 skinless, boneless chicken breasts, pounded thin

Cornstarch for dusting

½ teaspoon of salt

½ teaspoon of ground black pepper

2 tablespoons of olive oil

2 tablespoons of butter

3 cloves of garlic, chopped

¼ cup of pimento-stuffed green olives, sliced

¼ cup of gin

1 tablespoon of dry vermouth

1 teaspoon of lemon juice

GINSTRUCTIONS

- Pat the chicken dry with paper towels. Dust both sides of each chicken breast with cornstarch and season with salt and pepper.

- Heat the olive oil in a large skillet over medium-high heat.

- Place the chicken in the skillet and cook until browned on both sides. Cover and cook for another 10 minutes, or until the chicken juices run clear. Remove from the pan, set aside, and keep warm.

- Reduce heat to medium and add the butter and garlic to the skillet. Cook and stir mixture until garlic is fragrant, about 2 - 3 minutes.

- Add in the olives, gin, vermouth, and lemon juice. Stir to combine, being sure to scrape any bits from the pan.

- Add the chicken back into the pan, toss to coat in sauce, and re-heat for 2 - 3 minutes. Once reheated, divide the chicken over 4 plates, pour a little sauce on each breast, and serve.

fun fact:

Dukes Bar in Mayfair's Dukes Hotel is often cited as home of the best Martini in the world. Drinks are mixed on a tableside trolley, and the bar maintains a strict two-Martini limit.

Turkey & Green Apple Salad with GINty Dressing

Serves: 4

Total Time: 20 minutes

GINSPIRATIONS

🍸 If you ever have loads of leftover turkey (or chicken) and you are tired of the same old recipes for leftovers, give this salad a try. It's quick to pull together and is a refreshing change from the usual salads. You can also change things up and turn it all into a wonderful sandwich by using the turkey-apple mixture on bread with the goat cheese and mixed greens on top. Yum!

🍸 We used Barr Hill Gin (Caledonia Spirits) for our salad because its juniper botanicals are perfectly balanced by the raw honey. Pair this recipe with a Bee's Knees and enjoy your leftovers in a new way.

Laughter is the best medicine, or gin...whatever.

GINGREDIENTS

Dressing

¼ cup of fresh mint

1 small shallot

Juice of ½ large lemon (about 2 tablespoons)

2 tablespoons of gin

1 tablespoon of honey

¾ cup of olive oil

Salad

3 cups of leftover cooked turkey or chicken, diced

2 large Granny Smith apples, cored and thinly sliced

2 green onions, chopped

⅓ cup of pistachios, chopped

Mixed salad greens for 4 servings

Crumbled goat cheese (*optional*)

GINSTRUCTIONS

- Make the dressing: In a food processor, pulse together mint, shallot, lemon juice, gin, and honey until everything is finely minced. With the food processor still running, slowly drizzle in the oil. Pulse until well combined.

- Core and slice the apples. Finely chop the green onions.

- In a large bowl, toss together the turkey, apples, green onions, 4 tablespoons of chopped pistachios, and ½ cup of the dressing. Mix to combine.

- Divide the mixed greens evenly among 4 plates. Drizzle each plate with the remaining dressing.

- Top each salad with about 1 cup of turkey-apple mixture. Garnish with remaining pistachios and crumbled goat cheese (if using).

Chili, Lime, &
Gin Oysters.
find recipe on
page 140.

gINdescribable fish & seafood

you're the gin to my tonic.

GINTASTIC CILANTRO LIME SHRIMP

LOBSTER RAVIOLI ALLA GIN

TIPSY ASIAN SHRIMP

GINNY SHRIMP COCKTAIL

CHILI, LIME, & GIN OYSTERS

MARTINI MUSSEL MADNESS

CRAB & LOBSTER CAKES & A TALE OF TWO GINNY SAUCES

PAN-FRIED HADDOCK WITH GIN SAUCE

DRUNKEN LOBSTER

ROMEO'S PAN-SEARED SCALLOPS & GINNY ASPARAGUS RISOTTO

MARTINI MAHI-MAHI

PHENOMENAL GIN & TONIC BATTERED FISH

G&T BOOZY FISH TACOS

GIN-GLAZED FISH

ReGINerate [verb]:
the use of a juniper-based
spirit to rejuvenate and restore
the body. More frequently
experienced on the weekend.

gINtastic Cilantro Lime Shrimp

Serves: 2 to 3

Total Time: 30 minutes

GINSPIRATIONS

This recipe is a shrimp staple in Heather's family. It's quick and easy and oh-so-tasty any time of year.

Be warned, the shrimp cook FAST! Be careful not to overcook them - over-cooked shrimp are rubbery, tough, and just blah. So don't do it. Cook the shrimp, stirring frequently, until the shrimp are nice and pink and opaque. Then, get them out of the skillet!

There is a bit of sauce in the pan at the end. You can either cook it longer and reduce it down to get it a tiny bit thicker OR simply pour it over your rice or noodles.

You can use shrimp with tails on or off. We are tail off girls but the choice is yours.

If you like your shrimp a bit spicier, add more red pepper flakes. If you don't like spice, don't use the red pepper flakes at all (though even a tiny pinch adds so much flavour).

For gin, we used a lime-infused gin such as 3 Lacs - Lime and Basilic. Pair your meal with a **Serrano Cilantro G&T** (p. 232).

Note that we used a **Meyer** non-stick fry pan in the photo for this recipe.

GINGREDIENTS

1 lb of shrimp, shelled and deveined

2 + 1 tablespoons of olive oil

4 cloves of garlic, minced

⅛ teaspoon of red pepper flakes (*optional*)

1 tablespoon of cilantro, chopped

1 teaspoon of honey

3 tablespoons of fresh lime juice (approximately 1½ limes)

1 teaspoon of lime zest

½ teaspoon of salt (or to taste)

½ teaspoon of fresh ground pepper (or to taste)

¼ cup of gin

Optional garnishes: chopped cilantro, lime slices

GINSTRUCTIONS

- Peel and devein the shrimp, leaving the tails on or off to your preference.

- In a medium-sized bowl (or a large resealable plastic bag), combine 2 tablespoons of olive oil, garlic, red pepper flakes, cilantro, honey, lime juice, lime zest, salt, and pepper. Give it a good whisk (or squish) to combine all the ingredients.

- Add the uncooked shrimp and toss to ensure all the shrimp are covered with the marinade. Put the bowl (or bag) in the fridge and let the shrimp marinate for 15 to 20 minutes. Don't go longer than 20 minutes.

- When you are ready to cook, heat 1 tablespoon of olive oil in a cast-iron skillet over medium-high heat. Using a slotted spoon remove the shrimp from the marinade.

- Add the drained shrimp to the hot oil and cook quickly for 2 minutes, flip, and then add the marinade to the skillet. Let it cook for 30 seconds and then add the gin to the skillet. It will sizzle and steam. Scrape up any bits on the bottom of the pan to deglaze it and continue cooking for about 2 minutes or until the shrimp are opaque and orange-pink. Do not overcook!

- Adjust the seasoning, if necessary. Remove the shrimp from the pan and cook the sauce a minute or two longer to reduce, if desired OR use the sauce the way it is and pour it onto your rice or noodles.

- Serve immediately over rice, rice noodles, or zucchini noodles, topped with additional cilantro and garnished with lime slices.

Lobster Ravioli alla Gin

Serves: 4

Total Time:
1 and ½ hours

GINSPIRATIONS

Many years ago, Heather had lobster ravioli for the very first time. It was served with a white cream sauce that she wasn't a fan of, BUT she remembers thinking "why have I never had lobster ravioli before?" and "why isn't there a red sauce option?" Since then, she's tried it at many restaurants and made it her mission to create her own perfect lobster ravioli AND creamy red gin sauce. It's been worth the effort.

Making your own ravioli isn't difficult - it's just finicky and time-consuming. So, if you choose to use a store-bought ravioli for a quick weeknight meal, who are we to judge (hey, we've done it too). Using premade fresh pasta dough sheets also speeds up the process. Or, if you are great at making your own homemade pasta dough, go for it. We highly suggest purchasing a ravioli maker if you plan to make ravioli from scratch often.

The deliciously creamy tomato gin sauce honestly goes with just about any pasta. Try it with penne or tortellini or any kind of ravioli. Plus, you can totally make it meatless if you choose. If you prefer a spicier sauce, add more chili flakes.

We add a tiny splash of gin to the sauce at the end for an extra ginny flavour, but that is totally optional and not recommended if you are serving the sauce to minors.

For gin, we used **Tanqueray No. TEN Gin**. The citrus-forward flavour of this premium gin goes wonderfully with this dish. Pair your lobster ravioli alla gin with a **No. TEN Martini** (p. 223) for an upscale restaurant quality meal at home.

GINGREDIENTS

Lobster Ravioli

Fresh ready-to-use pasta dough sheets (either bought or homemade)

7 oz of cooked cold lobster meat, drained and patted dry (or shrimp or crab)

1 ½ cups of ricotta cheese

2 tablespoons of **Tanqueray No. TEN Gin**

6 or 7 sun-dried tomatoes (about ½ a cup)

1 small bunch of fresh parsley

½ teaspoon of lemon zest

¼ teaspoon of salt

¼ teaspoon of fresh ground pepper

Egg wash: **1 beaten large egg + 1 tablespoon of water**

Creamy Rosé Gin Sauce

2 tablespoons of extra-virgin olive oil

1 tablespoon of butter

1 small onion, diced

3 cloves of garlic, minced

1 tablespoon of Italian herbs (or 1 teaspoon of each oregano, basil, and thyme)

¼ teaspoon of red pepper chili flakes

½ cup + 1 tablespoon of **Tanqueray No. TEN Gin**

1 - 28 oz can of crushed tomatoes, no salt added

½ - 1 teaspoon of salt (adjust to your taste)

½ cup of heavy whipping cream

½ teaspoon of fresh ground pepper

½ cup of freshly grated Parmesan cheese (plus more for garnish)

2 tablespoons of fresh basil, chopped (plus more for garnish)

Made this GINspired recipe? Post your photo on Instagram and tag @the.gin.shop.ca

GINSTRUCTIONS

Ravioli

- Pulse together the ricotta, **Tanqueray No. TEN Gin**, and sun-dried tomatoes in a food processor until smooth and creamy (there might still be small chunks of tomato but that's ok).

- Add the parsley and lemon zest and pulse until combined and then transfer to a bowl. Finely chop the lobster meat then add it to a bowl with the rest of the ricotta filling mixture.

- Line a baking sheet with parchment paper.

- To make your ravioli, start one inch from the short edge of the fresh pasta sheet and spoon your lobster mixture, 1 tablespoon at a time, down the length of the sheet, spacing about 1" apart. Brush the dough and the top of your filling with egg wash and cover them with a second sheet of dough. The egg wash will help the dough stay in place, bonding the two layers.

- Press around each mound to seal, then press outward toward the edges, pushing out any air pockets. The most important part of this step is getting the air out of the ravioli when you seal it, otherwise, it might burst in the water or cook unevenly.

- Using a sharp knife or pizza cutter, cut each ravioli into a two-inch square. Arrange them on the prepared baking sheet.

- **Tip:** Use a ravioli maker to make this process much easier. You can also make smaller ravioli if you prefer.

- The ravioli can be made up to three hours in advance, just be sure to loosely cover them with plastic wrap.

Creamy Rosé Gin Sauce

- Heat the olive oil and butter in a large saucepan over medium heat. Add the onion and garlic and cook, stirring frequently, until sweated and slightly softened, about 3 - 4 minutes.

- Add the herbs and red pepper flakes and cook for another minute. Add the **Tanqueray No. TEN Gin** and cook for 3 minutes. Add the crushed tomatoes and ½ teaspoon of salt. Stir and cook for 7 - 8 minutes or until a touch of oil starts to show on the top.

- Stir in the heavy whipping cream and fresh ground pepper. Mix well. Taste and adjust the salt and pepper. Cook for 1 - 2 minutes and then remove the pan from the heat. Add ½ cup of freshly grated Parmesan cheese and a tablespoon of **Tanqueray No. TEN Gin** (optional). Stir to combine.

- When you are ready to cook your ravioli, bring a large pot of salted water to a boil. Add the ravioli, being careful not to crowd the pot. Cook the ravioli for around 3 - 4 minutes or until they float to the surface.

- Remove with a slotted spoon and add to the sauce and toss gently to ensure your pasta is coated. Add a touch of pasta water if your sauce is too thick.

- Divide the ravioli onto 4 plates and garnish with freshly grated Parmesan cheese and a sprinkle of fresh basil.

fun fact:

By 1743, England was drinking 2.2 gallons of gin per person per year.

Made this GINspired recipe? Post your photo on Instagram and tag @the.gin.shop.ca

Tipsy Asian Shrimp

Serves: 2
**Total Time:
20 minutes**

*maybe she's born
with it.
maybe it's
bucketloads of gin.*

GINSPIRATIONS

You can make this super simple shrimp recipe in minutes! The key is to have it all ready to go before you start cooking. Feel free to add more veggies if you like. Be sure to add the gin at the end or it will all evaporate and you won't have much of a sauce.

For gin, we used something with a hint of ginger such as Loop. Pair your shrimp with a **Club Quarantine (p. 228)** and serve over hot rice for a quick meal any time.

GINGREDIENTS

½ lb of large raw shrimp, peeled and deveined

1 tablespoon of vegetable oil (peanut is best)

2 teaspoons of white pepper

3 cloves garlic, sliced

2 teaspoons of fresh ginger, grated or minced

2 green onions, thinly sliced on a bias

½ cup of fresh or freshly thawed green peas

2 tablespoons of soy sauce

2 tablespoons of gin

GINSTRUCTIONS

- Have ALL the ingredients ready. This dish MUST be done very quickly and over very high heat.

- Peel and devein the shrimp. Slice the garlic and green onions. Grate the ginger. Be sure your peas are thawed if you are using frozen.

- Heat the wok or frying pan until very hot.

- Add the oil and garlic to the hot pan. Add in the shrimp, and cook it all for a minute.

- Add the white pepper, ginger, the green onions, and peas, still at high heat.

- Toss for a moment until the shrimp changes colour from a grey to a bright orange-pink.

- When the shrimp are cooked to your taste (this should only take a moment), add the soy sauce and the gin to the pan. It should make a great sizzling sound.

- Put a lid on the pan immediately, and turn off the heat.

- Wait one minute and then serve hot over white rice.

Ginny Shrimp Cocktail

Serves: 4
Total Time:
1 hour and 15 minutes

GINSPIRATIONS

 Shrimp cocktail is a staple for appetizers and get-togethers. We've been known to eat it for a main meal too. It's SO good. This method of cooking the shrimp takes a bit longer, but it is well worth it. Of course, you could just cook your shrimp the usual way (in a pot of salted boiling water), but this way adds so much more flavour.

Whether you leave the tails on or off is a personal choice. We prefer to take the entire shell - tails and all - off, because picking that tail off as you go to eat a shrimp can be annoying. However, for a crowd, leaving the tail on makes for a very pretty presentation.

We highly suggest you keep the stock for making either chowder or our **Romeo's Pan-Seared Scallops & Ginny Asparagus Risotto** (p. 151).

A gin with a peppery flavour such as Cotswold Dry Gin works wonderfully with this shrimp recipe. Pair your shrimp cocktail with a gin and **Fever-Tree Mediterranean Tonic Water** and either serve in individual glasses (we like to use Martini glasses) or a larger bowl for a crowd. The sauce can be served either in each glass or in a bowl on the side.

GINGREDIENTS

Cocktail Sauce

1 cup of ketchup
2 ½ teaspoons of prepared horseradish
½ teaspoon of Tabasco sauce
1 tablespoon of gin
½ teaspoon of celery salt
1 tablespoon of freshly squeezed lemon juice

Shrimp

1 ½ lbs of unpeeled raw jumbo shrimp
8 cups of water
1 tablespoon of salt
1 cup of dry vermouth
1 tablespoon of whole peppercorns
1 tablespoon of coriander seeds
2 bay leaves
1 small onion, diced
4 sprigs of fresh tarragon
1 lemon, halved
Optional garnish: fresh parsley

GINSTRUCTIONS

- Mix together the ketchup, horseradish, Tabasco, gin, celery salt, and lemon juice. Taste and adjust Tabasco, gin or celery salt if needed. Chill until ready to serve.
- Peel and devein the shrimp, leaving the tails attached if desired. Save the peels. Place the peeled shrimp in a bowl and refrigerate until needed.
- Place the shrimp peels into a large pot.
- Add water, 1 tablespoon of salt, vermouth, peppercorns, coriander seeds, bay leaves, onion, tarragon, and lemon. Bring to a boil, then reduce heat and simmer uncovered for 20 minutes.
- Remove the pot from heat and let sit 30 minutes more, then strain the broth through into a fresh pot.
- Bring the stock to a boil. Add shrimp and cover. Leave for 3 minutes. Check and see if the shrimp are opaque and pinky-orange. If not, cook for another minute or 2 until they are.
- Remove from the heat and drain.
- Fill a bowl with ice water and add the shrimp. Leave the shrimp for 3 minutes to chill and stop the cooking process.
- Remove the shrimp from the ice water and then chill in the fridge until ready to serve.
- To serve, place shrimp in individual pretty glasses and add a dollop of sauce, or serve the shrimp in a larger bowl with the sauce on the side for a larger crowd. Garnish with fresh parsley if desired.

Chili, Lime, & Gin Oysters

Serves: 3 to 4

**Total Time:
2 hours**

GINGREDIENTS

Juice of 1 large lime

1 teaspoon of lime zest, finely grated

¼ cup of gin

½ teaspoon of ground ginger

1 teaspoon of Mirin

1 teaspoon of white granulated sugar

½ of a red chili pepper

2 dozen oysters

GINSTRUCTIONS

- Place all the drizzle ingredients in a jar, cover with lid, and shake vigorously.

- Shuck each oyster.

- Drizzle a teaspoon of sauce over each oyster just before serving.

- Alternatively, for a more intense flavour, drizzle the sauce over the oysters one hour before serving.

GINSPIRATIONS

- Oysters are a big deal here in the Maritimes. And there are many varieties and hundreds of ways to serve them. If you are looking to spice up your oysters and add some ginny fun, look no further. Your guests will gobble these up. Warning - the sauce is potent and spicy. If it is too spicy for you, remove the seeds from the chilli pepper before chopping (or omit altogether), or if it is too alcoholic, hold back on half the gin.

- For a more intense flavour, drizzle the sauce on each oyster and let sit for 1 hour before serving.

- Wondering what Mirin is? It's a subtly sweet Japanese rice wine that is used in many Asian dishes. It's similar to sake, but has more sugar and a lower alcohol content and you can buy it in the grocery store. In a pinch, if you don't have Mirin, you can also use a teaspoon of rice vinegar, though you'll need to counteract the sourness with an additional ¼ teaspoon of sugar if you do.

- You'll want to use a more limey gin such as Whitley Neill Brazilian Lime. Pair your oysters with a classic Martini and let the party beGIN!

I make gin disappear. What's your superpower?

fun fact:
London Dry gin
doesn't need to be made
in London – it's a broad
style guideline rather than
a legal indicator.

Martini Mussel Madness

Serves: 4

Total Time:
1 hour

GINSPIRATIONS

🍸 Mussels are a staple where Heather lives. In fact, PEI blue mussels are world-famous – if you can get some we highly suggest you snatch them up.

🍸 As someone who has cooked many, many mussels, Heather can tell you that the trick to NOT overcooking your mussels is to try and cook them in a deep skillet in one single layer. DO NOT use a big pot and just dump them all in on top of each other. If you do, the bottom ones will be overcooked and the top ones will be undercooked. Using a deep skillet (such as the **Meyer** one we used in the photo) prevents this from happening. At most, you want two layers. Cook them in batches to keep them to one to two layers.

🍸 Be sure to save the sauce or juices for dipping. It's meant to be thin - it's mostly melted butter and gin after all. Dip each mussel in it and then you can also dip your bread in it. Yummyyy! Save any extra sauce to make chowder or risotto.

🍸 Adding gin to your mussels really gives them a unique taste. Traditionally, wine or beer is used to steam mussels, so why not gin?! Give it a try. We used Monkey 47 with our mussels, but you could also use a gin with a strong citrus note. Pair your mussels with a **Gimlet** (p. 235). As a gin lover, we just know this will be your new favourite mussel recipe.

GINGREDIENTS

3 lbs of mussels (about 4 dozen)

1 cup of fresh parsley, packed

¾ cup of pitted green olives or olives with pimentos

3 tablespoons of olive brine

3 - 4 cloves of garlic, minced

¼ cup of olive oil

1 lemon, zested and juiced

¼ cup of butter, plus 3 tablespoons

2 small onions, chopped

1 teaspoon of salt

½ teaspoon of fresh ground pepper

½ cup of gin

¼ cup of dry vermouth

GINSTRUCTIONS

- Wash, debeard, and scrub the mussels as follows: Place the mussels in a colander in the sink and run cool water over them. Using your hands or a clean scrubbing brush, rub off any debris like seaweed, sand, barnacles, or mud spots that could be on the shell. Use a knife to gently remove any beards. If you find any mussels with open shells, lightly tap that mussel against the side of the sink. If it closes, keep it. If it stays open, discard (DO NOT EAT).

- Set the mussels aside.

- Using a food processor, finely chop the parsley, olives, olive brine, garlic, and lemon zest. Pour in ¼ cup of olive oil and the lemon juice and process into a pesto.

- In a large, deep skillet with a tight-fitting lid, melt ¼ cup of butter over medium-high heat.

- Add the onions and cook until softened, 5 - 6 minutes. Season the onions with salt and pepper. Stir in the pesto.

- Add the gin and vermouth. Stir and cook until reduced, about 1 minute.

- Add the mussels in one layer if possible, cover and steam until opened, 6 - 8 minutes. Remove from heat. Discard any unopened mussels.

- Add the remaining 3 tablespoons of butter to the mussels and shake the pan to melt it into the sauce (this is a thin sauce).

- Using a slotted spoon, scoop out the mussels and place them in a serving dish. Pour the sauce into a separate dish for dipping. Serve with the bread for mopping.

- To eat, remove a mussel from the shell, dip it in the sauce and pop it in your mouth!

Crab & Lobster Cakes & a Tale of Two Ginny Sauces

Serves: 4 to 6

Total Time:
2 and ½ hours

GINSPIRATIONS

🍸 Everyone has a favourite style of crab cake recipe. You can use either crab or lobster for these cakes, but the combination is amazing. Living where Heather does (Prince Edward Island), she tends to have more lobster on hand than crab so sometimes her cakes are lobster cakes, sometimes they are crab cakes, but most often they are a combination of both.

🍸 If you are from somewhere in the world that is also famous for crab cakes, chances are this recipe is very different from yours. We use mashed potatoes in our cakes because we are also famous for our potatoes on Prince Edward Island. It's a match made in heaven.

🍸 If you have leftover mashed potatoes, it's a great way to use them up. Just be sure to warm your potatoes up before making your cakes. If you want a slightly spicier crab cake, adding a drop of sriracha or some smoked paprika is also nice.

🍸 These cakes freeze well, uncooked. When you are ready to serve them, simply remove the cakes from the freezer and thaw. Then, sauté and bake as described above.

🍸 The sauce you choose is up to you. Some people love aioli and others are more into ketchup. Give both a try! You can also spice your sauce up by adding more sriracha or gin. If you don't have dill, try cilantro instead.

🍸 For gin, a lemony dill gin such as **romeo's gin** is wonderful. Serve 2 cakes per person along with the dipping sauce of choice on the side, and a fresh green salad. Pair your cakes with a romeo's G&T for a tale worth telling.

GINGREDIENTS

Crab and Lobster Cakes

2 - 3 medium-sized potatoes, peeled (enough to make 2 cups of mashed potatoes)

1 egg, beaten

1 tablespoon of mayonnaise

1 tablespoon of gin

1 teaspoon of Old Bay Seasoning

1 teaspoon of fresh parsley, minced

½ teaspoon of fresh ground pepper (or to taste)

2 green onions, chopped (approximately 1½ tablespoons)

2 tablespoons of celery, finely chopped (approximately 1 celery rib)

2 tablespoons of red pepper, finely chopped

12 oz of cooked crab and/or lobster (fresh or frozen), drained, patted dry, and cut into bite-sized chunks

½ to 1 cup of fresh bread crumbs

¾ cup of finely ground seasoned bread crumbs (for dredging)

1 - 2 tablespoons of olive oil

2 tablespoons of butter (for dotting each patty)

1 lemon, cut in quarters

Ginny White Dipping Sauce (Lemon, Dill, Gin Aioli)

½ cup of mayonnaise

1 tablespoon of freshly squeezed lemon juice

1 tablespoon of Dijon mustard

1 tablespoon of gin

2 teaspoons of dried dill weed or 1 tablespoon of fresh dill weed

¼ teaspoon of lemon zest

⅛ teaspoon of sea salt

⅛ teaspoon of fresh ground pepper

Ginny Red Dipping Sauce

¼ cup of mayonnaise

¼ cup of ketchup

1 tablespoon of freshly squeezed lemon juice

1 tablespoon of gin

⅛ teaspoon of fresh ground pepper

GINSTRUCTIONS

Crab & Lobster Cakes

- *NOTE: Your cakes need to chill for 1 hour, so be sure to allow enough time for chilling.*

- Peel and dice the potatoes. Place them in a medium-sized saucepan and cover with water. Bring the potatoes to a boil and cook until very tender. Drain.

- Place the warm potatoes in a large bowl and mash well. Add the beaten egg and stir until combined. Add the mayonnaise and gin. Stir.

- Add the Old Bay Seasoning, parsley, and fresh ground pepper. Stir. Add the chopped green onions, celery, and red pepper. Stir well and ensure it is all combined.

- Drain and pat dry the crab and lobster (you don't want soggy patties). Add the crab and lobster to the mixture and mix well.

- Add just enough of the fresh bread crumbs so that the mixture holds together and can be formed into patties (usually this is about ½ cup, but could be slightly more).

- Using a ¼ cup measuring cup, take one scoop of the crab/lobster mixture, place it in your hand and form it into a round patty. Continue to make patties until all the mixture is gone.

- Place the seasoned bread crumbs in a large shallow dish. Dredge both sides of each patty in the bread crumbs until it is completely covered on all sides.

- Place the patties on a parchment paper-lined baking sheet. Place the baking sheet in the fridge and chill for 1 hour to allow the flavours to blend and for the patties to become firm (so they won't break apart when sautéed).

- Preheat the oven to 375°F.

- Heat the olive oil in a large skillet (cast-iron is best) over medium-high heat. When the oil is hot, reduce the heat to medium and add the patties. Sauté 2 - 3 minutes on each side, until golden brown.

- Transfer the browned cakes to a fresh parchment paper-lined baking sheet. Dab each cake with a dot of butter (approximately ½ teaspoon each). Squeeze lemon juice over each cake. Bake in the oven for 6 - 7 minutes to finish the cooking process and allow the cakes to become firm and the butter to melt into the cake.

- Remove from the oven and let rest for 2 minutes before serving. Serve with lemon wedges and dipping sauce of your choice.

Ginny White Dipping Sauce (for the traditionalist)

- In a small mixing bowl, whisk together all the ingredients. Place covered in the refrigerator for at least one hour before serving (stores up to a week).

Ginny Red Dipping Sauce (for the ketchup lovers)

- Combine the mayonnaise and ketchup in a bowl. Add the lemon juice, gin, and pepper, mix until pink in colour and combined. Place covered in the refrigerator for at least one hour before serving (stores up to a week).

Pan-fried Haddock with Gin Sauce

> **Serves: 2**
>
> **Total Time:**
> **35 minutes**

GINSPIRATIONS

🍸 Haddock is a light and versatile fish that tastes even more amazing with gin! Be sure to start with a quality piece of fish. Living by the ocean, Heather gets hers fresh. If you can't get your fish fresh, at least make sure it is flash frozen and from a reputable source (i.e., preferably NOT a box). Thaw it completely before you start to cook.

🍸 Some version of this recipe is made at Heather's house almost weekly. Sometimes they leave out the olives and add more lemon. Sometimes she adds more gin. Sometimes she adds more chili pepper and sometimes she uses different fresh herbs. Make it your own.

🍸 Dredging the fish in flour and then the egg, adds a lovely little crispy outside without a heavy batter.

🍸 We used Sipsmith Gin for this dish. Pair your fish with a G&T made with **Fever-Tree Lemon Tonic** and serve with rice, cauliflower rice, or simply lots of veggies.

GINGREDIENTS

Fish

3 fillets of fresh haddock

½ teaspoon of Kosher salt

½ teaspoon of fresh ground pepper

2 tablespoons of all-purpose flour

1 large egg, beaten

3 tablespoons of butter

Sauce

2 tablespoons of extra-virgin olive oil

1 medium onion, chopped

2 cloves of garlic, minced

¼ cup of gin

½ cup of cherry or grape tomatoes, cut in half

¼ cup of Kalamata olives

1 tablespoon of red chili pepper, chopped, or
   1 teaspoon of red chili pepper flakes (*optional*)

¼ teaspoon of salt (or to taste)

½ teaspoon of fresh ground pepper

¼ cup of chicken stock

1 tablespoon of freshly squeezed lemon juice

1 tablespoon of butter

1 tablespoon of freshly parsley, chopped

1 tablespoon of freshly basil, chopped

    Made this GINspired recipe? Post your photo on Instagram and tag @the.gin.shop.ca

GINSTRUCTIONS

- Pat your fish dry with paper towels. Season the fish on both sides with salt and pepper and then dredge in the flour, ensuring both sides are dusted well.

- Beat an egg and then coat the fish with the egg wash on both sides. In a large frying pan (cast-iron is best), melt 3 tablespoons of butter on medium-heat.

- Add the fish to the frying pan (we love to use a stainless-steel **Meyer** frying pan) and fry on each side until golden brown and cooked through, approximately 3 - 4 minutes on each side. Be careful not to overcook. Remove the fish from the pan and keep warm.

- In the same frying pan, heat the extra-virgin olive oil. Add the chopped onions to the oil and cook for 2 - 3 minutes until translucent.

- Add minced garlic and cook for one more minute. Add the gin and scrape up all the bits (deglaze). Add the tomatoes, olives, red chili pepper (if using), salt, and pepper and cook for 2 - 3 minutes.

- Add the chicken stock and let it reduce by half (3 - 4 minutes). Add the lemon juice and 1 tablespoon of butter. Stir until combined. Sprinkle the sauce with fresh parsley and basil. Taste the sauce and adjust the seasonings if required.

- Return the fish to the pan to briefly reheat and get coated with the sauce, approximately one minute. To serve, place the fish on each plate and spoon the sauce over each piece.

"This haddock recipe is amazing!"

Louise Boudreau, test cook

Drunken Lobster

Serves: 4

Total Time: 45 minutes

GINSPIRATIONS

🍸 Lobster is a Maritime staple. Drunken lobster is even better than plain lobster. This boozy garlic gin butter is amazing to dip your lobster in or brush it on a lobster tail and give it a quick grill on the BBQ.

🍸 There are some tricks to cooking lobster well. First of all, NEVER cook a lobster with its claw bands on. Remove the bands. Always. If you don't, your lobster will not taste good.

🍸 The second thing is that your water should taste like the sea. That means either you use sea water or put in enough salt that it tastes like the sea. Always taste your water before boiling it. If you don't cringe when you taste it, there isn't enough salt.

🍸 Don't overcrowd your lobster in the pot either. Smaller batches are better. Generally, cook only a max of 6 lobsters at a time, unless you have a massive pot.

🍸 To eat your lobster, remove all the meat from the shell and dip it in the boozy butter. Any leftover butter is great for dipping a roll or crusty piece of bread.

🍸 We used Sipsmith Lemon Drizzle Gin for our butter. Pair your lobster with a **Seaside Martini** (p. 233), potato salad, coleslaw, and a roll for the perfect Maritime drunken lobster feast.

GINGREDIENTS

4 - 1 ¼ to 1 ½ lb live lobsters (bands removed)

1 cup of sea salt

16 cups of water OR sea-water for boiling (omit salt in that case)

Boozy Butter

2 cups of salted butter

2 juniper berries, finely crushed

1 tablespoon of fresh tarragon, chopped

1 tablespoon of fresh parsley, chopped

3 garlic cloves, finely minced

⅛ teaspoon of red pepper chili flakes

¼ cup of gin

2 tablespoons of freshly squeezed lemon juice

GINSTRUCTIONS

- Choose a pot large enough to hold all the lobsters comfortably, you don't want to crowd them. Fill the pot with 16 cups of water or thereabout.

- Add the sea salt to the water. Taste the water. Does it taste like the sea? If yes, continue. If not, add a touch more salt until it does.

- Bring the water to a rolling boil. Remove any bands from the lobsters' claws.

- Add the live lobsters to the water one at a time and start timing immediately. Cover and cook for 10 - 12 minutes (a smaller lobster cooks in closer to 10 minutes, a pound and a half lobster takes 12 minutes). Cooked lobsters will turn bright red, but that's not the best indicator of doneness, especially for large lobsters, so be sure to use the recommended times.

- Using tongs, remove the lobsters from the water and place on a large tray. Let the lobsters rest for 5 minutes or so after cooking to allow the meat to absorb some of the moisture in the shell.

- Make your boozy butter. Melt the butter in a saucepan on medium-low heat. Once it's melted, add the remaining butter GINgredients to the pan. Stir and let cook for 2 minutes. Add more gin if desired.

- To serve, divide the butter into half-cup sized ramekins and serve alongside the lobster for dipping. Crack your lobster, dip the meat in the boozy butter, and feast!

Romeo's Pan-Seared Scallops & Ginny Asparagus Risotto

Serves: 4

Total Time:
1 hour

GINSPIRATIONS

🍸 The beauty of risotto is that it takes on whatever flavour you add to it, whether from the broth, gin, or vegetables. You can truly make it your own. If you don't like asparagus, try spring peas. If you don't eat mushrooms, leave them out. You can also switch the scallops for shrimp or other seafood if you like.

🍸 Making risotto requires your full attention but it is SO worth it. While not hard to make, there are some definite tricks to creating a creamy, delicious meal.

🍸 Give yourself 30 - 35 minutes for the risotto. Never rinse risotto before cooking or it will lose all its starchiness. Prep all your ingredients first. You cannot leave the risotto while you're stirring and adding the broth, so having to stop mid-way through to grab ingredients that you want to add at the end will just cause you stress. Never stop stirring. Make sure your broth is hot but not boiling. It will make all the difference in the world.

🍸 The ratio of broth to risotto is 4:1. If you need to double the recipe remember that tip.

🍸 Don't skip toasting the risotto in the fat, or the addition of the gin before adding your broth. It's a chemistry thing that is important for flavour.

🍸 For gin, we used **romeo's gin** for its blend of juniper, cucumber, dill, lavender, almond and lemon which goes amazingly in this recipe. Pair your risotto with a **Spa Water Caesar** (p. 234) using **romeo's gin** for a delicious dish any day of the week.

GINGREDIENTS

1 lb of fresh MSC-certified scallops, patted very dry

1 small bunch of asparagus, tough ends removed, sliced into ½-inch pieces

4 cups of low-salt broth (chicken or vegetable)

2 tablespoons of extra-virgin olive oil

1 small onion, diced (about ½ cup)

2 garlic cloves, minced

½ cup of mushrooms, chopped

1 cup of risotto rice

½ cup + 2 tablespoons of **romeo's gin**

1 teaspoon of salt, plus ½ teaspoon more for the scallops

½ teaspoon of fresh ground pepper, plus ½ teaspoon more for the scallops

1 tablespoon of fresh thyme

½ cup of fresh Parmesan cheese, finely grated

2 tablespoons of a high-heat oil (such as avocado or canola) + 1 tablespoon of butter

1 + 2 tablespoons of butter

Optional garnishes: grated fresh Parmesan cheese and fresh thyme, drizzle of romeo's gin if desired

fun fact:

The earliest mention of the word 'cocktail' in reference to a drink was on March 20th, 1798 in the London Morning Post and Gazetteer. In the newspaper's satirical account, the beverage was consumed by Pitt the Younger at the Axe and Gate Tavern on the corner of Downing Street and Whitehall, which was later torn down to expand the Prime Minister's residence.

GINSTRUCTIONS

- Remove the scallops from the refrigerator and set them on the counter while you prepare the risotto. Pat them dry with paper towels (change the paper towels if needed to get them as dry as possible) and set aside.

- In a steamer or saucepan, steam the asparagus pieces for 2 minutes, rinse in cold water, and set aside.

- In a new saucepan, gently heat the chicken broth and keep it nearby on a low simmer (this is VERY important, as your broth must be warm).

- Heat a large, deep skillet over medium heat and then add the olive oil, onion, garlic, and mushrooms. Cook for approximately 5 minutes, stirring occasionally with a wooden spoon.

- Move the onion and mushroom mixture to the edge of the skillet and add 1 tablespoon of butter to the middle of the pan.

- Add the risotto and stir to combine. Slightly toast the risotto by cooking it a minute or two. Add ½ cup of **romeo's gin** and stir until completely absorbed by the ingredients.

- Pour yourself a cocktail. Making risotto can take a while.

- Season the risotto with salt and pepper. Add ½ cup of hot broth to the risotto and stir until absorbed. Continue adding the broth, ½ cup at a time, and stirring until it's all absorbed. Be patient, this can take a while. Keep stirring - do not leave the stove!

- If the risotto seems to be burning, turn your heat down. If it's not absorbing each ½ cup of hot liquid within 3 - 4 minutes, turn your heat up a bit. The idea is that each ½ cup of broth is stirred in and absorbed in a few minutes, but it shouldn't take more than five minutes.

- When you have 1 - 2 cups of broth left, add the asparagus pieces and stir them into the risotto.

- Add the remaining broth ½ cup at a time, stirring until it's all absorbed. Never stop stirring! Taste the risotto for seasoning, adding more salt and pepper as necessary.

- When all the liquid is absorbed, and the risotto is al dente or "to the tooth" (firm but not crunchy) turn off the heat. Add a tablespoon of fresh thyme, 2 tablespoons of butter, 2 tablespoons of **romeo's gin**, and the Parmesan cheese. Stir to combine, cover, and set aside while you cook the scallops.

- Heat a cast-iron skillet over high heat. Add 2 tablespoons of a high-heat oil such as avocado or canola and 1 tablespoon of butter to the pan.

- Season one side of the scallops with salt and pepper. Place them seasoned side down in the hot skillet. Season the other side with more salt and pepper.

- After 2 minutes, gently turn over the scallops with tongs. If the scallop does not easily release from the pan, let it sit for a few more seconds. It should easily release with a nice, brown crispiness on the cooked side.

- Cook the scallops for another 2 - 3 minutes. DO NOT OVERCOOK! Scallops cook quickly. If desired, add another pat of butter to the pan and spoon the buttery oil over the tops.

- Divide the risotto into 4 bowls. Place a few scallops on top of the risotto. Garnish with more grated Parmesan cheese, fresh thyme, and a drizzle of **romeo's gin**.

Martini Mahi-Mahi

Serves: 4

**Total Time:
45 minutes**

GINSPIRATIONS

🍸 A fishy Martini? Not exactly, but close. This recipe has all the classic components of a traditional dirty Martini but with fish. What's not to like?

🍸 You can use any fish for this recipe, but a flaky white fish such as mahi-mahi or halibut tends to work best.

🍸 The olive sauce is thin but it drizzles wonderfully and adds the salty olive goodness you want in a good Martini.

🍸 We used Tanqueray London Dry Gin for our fish and paired it with a **Chef's Little Helper** (p. 227).

I love water, especially when it's frozen and surrounded by gin.

GINGREDIENTS

4 boned, skinned mahi-mahi fillets (6 oz each) or any white fish, such as halibut or haddock

1 teaspoon of Kosher salt

½ teaspoon of fresh ground pepper + more for garnish

Martini Marinade

½ cup of gin

¼ cup of sweet vermouth

1 tablespoon of lemon zest, freshly grated

3 garlic cloves, peeled and lightly crushed

Olive Sauce

2 tablespoons of extra-virgin olive oil

2 tablespoons of fresh lemon juice, plus lemon wedges for garnish

¾ cup of chicken broth

1 ½ cups of pimento-stuffed green olives, chopped

¼ cup of gin

2 tablespoons of unsalted butter

GINSTRUCTIONS

• In a large resealable plastic bag, add all the marinade GINgredients. Squish it around until the marinade is well combined.

• Pat the fish dry and then season both sides with salt and pepper. Place the fish in the resealable plastic bag with the marinade. Seal the bag and marinate in the fridge for 20 minutes.

• When ready, drain the fish, being sure to save the garlic and discard the marinade. Pat the fish and garlic with paper towels to avoid dripping alcohol near the heat.

• Heat the olive oil in a large cast-iron frying pan over medium-high heat. Add the fish and garlic to the hot pan and cook until the fish is browned on one side, 3 - 4 minutes.

• Turn the fish over and cook until it's cooked through but still moist in the centre, 2 - 3 minutes more. Transfer the fish to a warm platter, leaving garlic in the pan.

• Pour the lemon juice and chicken broth into the pan and stir to pick up brown bits. Stir in the olives and gin. Simmer until reduced by half, about 3 minutes. Stir in the butter until melted. This creates a thin sauce.

• To serve, plate the fish and drizzle the olive and garlic sauce over each piece. Garnish with fresh ground pepper and lemon wedges.

Phenomenal Gin & Tonic Battered Fish

Serves: 2

**Total Time:
45 minutes**

GINSPIRATIONS

A phenomenal deep-fried, battered fish can be life-altering, but it can also be intimidating. Deep frying is a skill. You don't want your fish under or overdone or greasy. And you definitely don't want your batter falling off.

Be sure your fish is DRY to start with. Then, dredge it in the seasoned corn-starch, then dip it in the batter. Dry fish is critical to the batter not falling off. This batter is thick. Don't be tempted to add more liquid.

Follow our tips about the oil. If your oil is too hot or too cold or too crowded, your fish will suffer.

Once you have perfected deep frying, then you can play with the batter a bit. Add in ¼ teaspoon of cayenne pepper or a dash of hot sauce to make this recipe spicy. Or try adding different spices like curry powder or turmeric, or changing up the gin or tonic for different variations.

We used Malfy, a lovely Mediterranean gin. Pair your phenomenal fish with chips (french fries), a side of coleslaw, and a classic gin and tonic, using **Fever-Tree Mediterranean Tonic Water**.

GINGREDIENTS

Fish

2 teaspoons (1 packet) of traditional dry yeast

⅛ teaspoon of salt

⅛ teaspoon of white granulated sugar

1 cup of **Fever-Tree Mediterranean Tonic Water** (room temperature)

1 cup of all-purpose flour

1 tablespoon of garlic powder

1 tablespoon of paprika

¼ cup of gin

1 teaspoon of balsamic vinegar

¼ cup of cornstarch

1 teaspoon of Kosher salt

½ teaspoon of fresh ground pepper

4 cod, hake, or haddock fillets skinned, pin-boned

Canola oil for frying

Ginny Tartar Sauce

1 cup of mayonnaise

2 teaspoons of sweet relish

1 teaspoon of yellow mustard

1 teaspoon of fresh lemon juice

2 teaspoons of gin

Life is basically all the stuff you do between that first cup of coffee and that first glass of gin!

GINSTRUCTIONS

- Make your batter. In a large bowl, mix the yeast, salt, and sugar until well combined. Pour the **Fever-Tree Mediterranean Tonic Water** into the yeast mixture and gently stir.

- Whisk in the flour, garlic powder, paprika, gin, and vinegar. Leave the mixture to ferment – it is ready to use when the mixture starts to bubble. Your batter will be thick.

- Preheat your cooking oil in a deep fryer or large dutch oven (3 - 4 inches deep). A thermometer should read 365°F by the time you are ready to fry the fish. If the oil begins to smoke, it's too hot and a sign that the oil is breaking down, which affects the flavour so let it drop down to 365°F to 375°F.

- In a shallow dish, add the cornstarch, salt, and pepper. Pat the fish dry with paper towels. Dredge a piece of fish in the seasoned cornstarch ensuring both sides are well dusted.

- Dip the fish in the batter, being careful to shake off any excess. Repeat with each piece of fish until all pieces are battered.

- Once the fish is coated, plunge it carefully into the hot oil. Work in small batches. Do not overload your pot or the temperature will drop and you may have greasy fish. Cook the fish until it floats and is golden brown and crispy, usually 5 - 8 minutes. The fish will stop steaming.

- Watch the temperature of the oil carefully, if the temperature is too low you'll end up with greasy fish, and too high will cook the outside before the inside is done. Maintaining the oil temperature is crucial. Keep your oil 365°F to 375°F max.

- Remove the fish from the oil with a slotted spoon and place on a wire drying rack (NOT paper towel) on top of a baking sheet to catch the drips. When you put it on paper towels, the crust will steam from below, leading to soggy bottoms and a coating that is more likely to fall off.

- Sprinkle your hot fish with a pinch of salt if desired. Place the baking sheet with the wire rack and fish in the oven to stay warm while you make the tartar sauce.

- To make the tartar sauce, place all the GINgredients in a small bowl and whisk together until well combined.

- Serve your phenomenal fish immediately with the tartar sauce, a squeeze of lemon, chips (aka fries), and coleslaw. YUMMY!!!

G&T Boozy Fish Tacos

Serves: 4

Total Time: 1 hour (plus chilling time for the slaw)

GINSPIRATIONS

🍸 If you've never had a fish taco, today is the day you need to have one. If you have had fish tacos, you KNOW how amazing they can be. Add gin and tonic to the mix and it's serious taco heaven.

🍸 This fish taco recipe uses gin and **Fever-Tree Lemon Tonic Water**. Make sure it is ICE COLD. It will ensure your fish pieces are crispy. You could also use our **Phenomenal Gin & Tonic Fish Batter** (p. 154) which uses a different batter method. Fish tacos are usually a bit faster to make so we've given you another batter option.

🍸 Review the deep-frying rules and tips from p. 154. Hot oil but not too hot. Don't overcook your fish. Rest cooked fish on a wire rack NOT a paper towel or dish-towel.

🍸 No fish taco would be complete without a boozy slaw and avocado mash. You could also use our **Boozy Guacamole** (p. 58) recipe for an extra ginny hit. If you aren't a fan of avocado, you can leave it out but it makes your tacos that much yummier.

🍸 If you want your slaw or mash a bit spicier, add some red chili flakes or even a small diced chili for some extra kick.

🍸 For gin, anything with lime and cilantro is a hit such as **Tanqueray Rangpur**. Pair your tacos with a Gin Margarita and dive in!

GINGREDIENTS

Boozy Coleslaw

½ cup of sour cream

½ cup of mayonnaise

¼ cup of gin

Zest and juice of 1 lime

1 teaspoon of white sugar

½ teaspoon of celery seeds

½ teaspoon of sea salt

½ teaspoon of fresh ground pepper

1 package of coleslaw cabbage mix
(or 2 cups finely chopped or grated cabbage)

Fish

1 lb of white fish fillets, such as haddock/cod
(cut into pieces or strips)

1 cup + ¼ cup of all-purpose flour
(plus a little extra for dusting fish)

Salt and pepper to taste

⅓ cup of cornstarch

2 teaspoons of baking powder

¼ teaspoon of sea salt

1 ¼ cups of ice-cold **Fever-Tree Lemon Tonic Water**

¼ cup of ice-cold gin

Oil for deep frying

Avocado Mash

2 ripe avocados

2 tablespoons of finely chopped cilantro

1 tablespoon of fresh lime juice

¼ teaspoon of sea salt

¼ teaspoon of fresh ground pepper

Tortillas & Toppings

8 small tortillas

Finely chopped cilantro

Shredded lettuce

Squeeze of lime juice

GINSTRUCTIONS

Coleslaw

- Make the coleslaw a few hours ahead. In a large bowl, whisk together the sour cream, mayonnaise, gin, and lime zest and juice. Add the sugar, celery seeds, salt, and pepper and stir until well combined. Taste and adjust seasoning as you like.

- Add the coleslaw cabbage mix (or chopped cabbage). Toss to combine. Cover and refrigerate for at least 4 hours. The coleslaw can also be made the day before as it lasts well in the fridge and the flavours blend more the longer it sits.

- Preheat your cooking oil in a deep fryer or large dutch oven (3 - 4 inches deep). A thermometer should read 365°F by the time you are ready to fry the fish. If the oil begins to smoke it's too hot and a sign that the oil is breaking down, which affects the flavour so let it drop down to 365°F to 375°F.

Fish

- Start by placing ¼ cup of all-purpose flour into a shallow bowl and season it with salt and pepper. Lightly dust both sides of the fish pieces with the seasoned flour.

- In a new large bowl, add 1 cup of flour, cornstarch, baking powder, and salt and gently stir to combine.

- Make a well in the centre of the flour mixture and quickly pour in the ice-cold **Fever-Tree Lemon Tonic Water** and gin into the flour. Whisk together until smooth.

- Dunk the dusted fish pieces into the batter. Once the fish is coated, plunge it carefully into the hot oil. Work in small batches. Do not overload your pot or the temperature will drop and you may have greasy fish.

- Cook the fish until it floats and is a light to medium golden brown in colour and crispy, usually 3 - 5 minutes for small pieces. The fish will stop steaming.

- Watch the temperature of the oil carefully. If the temperature is too low, you'll end up with greasy fish, and too high will cook the outside before the inside is done. Maintaining the oil temperature is crucial. Keep your oil 365°F to 375°F max.

- Remove the fish from the oil with a slotted spoon and place on a wire drying rack (NOT paper towel) on top of a baking sheet to catch the drips. When you put it on paper towels, the crust will steam from below, leading to soggy bottoms and a coating that is more likely to fall off. Sprinkle your hot fish with a pinch of salt if desired.

Avocado Mash

- Mash the avocados with the cilantro, lime juice, salt, and pepper, leaving some texture in the avocado.

- Prepare your tortillas. Preheat a cast-iron frying pan. Taking one tortilla at a time, gently fry each tortilla on both sides (about a minute on each side). It should puff up and go a little crispy. Place each warmed tortilla onto a kitchen towel and gently fold in half. Repeat this process until all your tortillas are done.

- To serve, take a tortilla, add a scoop of the coleslaw, some crisp fish and top with shredded lettuce and avocado mash. Garnish with a sprinkle of chopped cilantro and a little squeeze of lime juice.

gin-glazed fish

Serves: 2

**Total Time:
25 minutes**

GINGREDIENTS

2 juniper berries

½ teaspoon of coriander seeds

¼ cup of gin

¼ cup of apricot jam

2 fillets of any fish, skinless (about 6 oz each)

2 tablespoons of cornstarch

¼ teaspoon of salt

¼ teaspoon of fresh ground pepper

1 tablespoon of salted butter

GINSPIRATIONS

- The amazing thing about this glaze is that it works with any type of fish. However, if you use salmon, you won't want to dust it with cornstarch. The cornstarch is intended for any skinless fish fillet. It adds a tiny bit of crispness that goes wonderfully with the glaze.

- If you don't have apricot jam, try plum or blueberry jam. Marmalade works well too, depending on the gin you use. It will change the flavour in a whole new way. If you like a saucier fish, double the glaze recipe.

- We used Seventh Heaven Gin for our fish. Pair the recipe with a gin and **Fever-Tree Aromatic Tonic Water**. Serve the fish with coleslaw, tossed salad, or rice and veggies.

GINSTRUCTIONS

- Place the juniper berries and coriander seeds in a resealable freezer bag or mortar. Using a pestle, mallet, or rolling pin, coarsely crush the berries and seeds. Transfer the crushed seeds and berries to a small saucepan.

- Add the gin and jam to the saucepan. Bring the mixture to a boil over medium-high heat, stirring often, until it's reduced to about 3 tablespoons, approximately 3 - 5 minutes. Strain the glaze into a small bowl.

- Pat the fish dry and dredge it in the cornstarch ensuring both sides are dusted well. Season it with salt and pepper.

- In a medium-sized cast-iron skillet, melt the butter over medium-high heat. Add the fish and cook until browned, 2 - 3 minutes per side. Add the remaining glaze to the skillet and cook for 1 minute, tossing the fish until covered in the glaze.

- Divide the fish over two plates and drizzle each piece with the juices from the pan.

fun fact:

Gin was popularized in England following the accession of William of Orange in 1688. Gin provided an alternative to French brandy at a time of both political and religious conflict between Britain and France.

Made this GINspired recipe? Post your photo on Instagram and tag @the.gin.shop.ca

gINcredulous Desserts

Smile. There's gin.

KAZUKI NEGRONI BROWNIES

DEATH BY CHOCOLATE RASPBERRY
   GIN BROWNIES

CINNAGIN APPLE SQUARES

CHAI OATMEAL CHOCOLATE CHIP
   COOKIES

DRUNKEN BLUEBERRY CHEESECAKE

NO-BAKE BLIMEY CHEESECAKE

DARK CHOCOLATE & GIN TRUFFLES

DARK CHOCOLATE, PEANUT BUTTER, &
   GIN LAVA CAKES

BLUEBERRY & GIN COBBLER

FLOURLESS CHOCOLATE
   RASPBERRY TORTE

BERRY GINTERESTING TART

BOOZY CARROT CAKE

VANILLA GIN CUSTARD

GINGERBREAD CAKE

GIN, LEMON, & COCONUT CAKE

LEMON RASPBERRY GIN TRIFLE

APPLE PIE À LA GIN

KEY LIME PIE WITH A TWIST

GIN PIE PASTRY DOUGH

SCRUMPTIOUS PUMPKIN PECAN CAKE

GIN & TONIC LOAF

TOFFEE GIN BANANA BREAD

DREAMY SEVILLA ORANGE GIN CAKE

WHITE CHOCOLATE GIN FUDGE

EMPRESS CUPCAKES

GIN CARAMEL PEANUT BUTTER CUPS

GINNY SNACK'N CAKE

BOOZY CHOCOLATE SAUCE

CARAMEL GIN SAUCE

G&T ICE CREAM

BOOZY CHOCOLATE ICE CREAM

GINFUSED WILD BLUEBERRY PIE FILLING

Kazuki Negroni Brownies

Serves: 9
Total Time: 1 hour

GINSPIRATIONS

🍸 A classic Negroni cocktail in a brownie? Heck yes!!! A perfect balance of sweet and tart, with just a hint of orange, these brownies will surprise and delight you while tempting your tastebuds.

🍸 You can eat them warm or cold and, believe it or not, they taste even better the next day (though they probably won't last that long). Feel free to add nuts if that is your preference.

🍸 Store them at room temperature in an air-tight container for up to 3 days, or freeze them for a treat another day.

🍸 For gin, we used **Sheringham Distillery's** award-winning **Kazuki Gin**. The cherry blossom and yuzu peel notes go wonderfully in this recipe. Serve this up on your plate, with a scoop of vanilla bean ice cream, and pair it with a **Kazuki Negroni** (p. 231) for a truly delectable dessert.

I just want to drink gin, travel, and take naps.

GINGREDIENTS

2 tablespoons of **Sheringham Distillery Kazuki Gin**

2 tablespoons of Campari

2 tablespoons of sweet vermouth

1 tablespoon of orange zest

4 oz of unsweetened chocolate

¾ cup of unsalted butter

2 cups of white granulated sugar

3 eggs, room temperature

2 cups of all-purpose flour

⅓ cup of chocolate chips or chunks

Optional garnish: orange zest and/or **Boozy Chocolate Sauce** (p. 213)

GINSTRUCTIONS

- Preheat the oven to 350°F and grease a 9 x 9-inch square baking pan.

- In a small bowl, make your Negroni by adding the **Sheringham Distillery Kazuki Gin**, Campari, and vermouth. Stir in the orange zest and let rest (you can also soak the orange zest in the Negroni for a few hours).

- In a large microwavable bowl, add chocolate and butter. Microwave for 2 minutes or until the butter is melted. Remove from the microwave and stir until the chocolate is completely melted and the mixture is smooth and shiny.

- Add the sugar and mix well. Blend in the eggs 1 at a time. Add the Negroni including the soaked orange zest. Gently fold in the flour.

- Spread the brownie mixture into the baking pan. Sprinkle the chocolate chips or chunks over everything.

- Bake for 30 - 35 minutes or until the edges start to crack. If you like a gooier brownie, cook it less; if you prefer a more cake-like brownie, cook it a few minutes more.

- Do not overcook. Remove from the oven and let cool (it will continue to cook and set as it cools). Once cool, garnish with orange zest and cut into squares.

Death by Chocolate Raspberry Gin Brownies

Serves: 9

Total Time: 1 hour, plus a day for the GINfusion to rest

GINSPIRATIONS

🍸 You'll never go back to your old brownie recipe again. These decadent little squares of heaven might just blow your mind. It took a lot of trial and error to get these babies just perfect. While you don't NEED the sauce, you'll want it. Warm, it is like the best hot fudge sauce ever and cold it is like a yummy ganache frosting on your brownie. Either way, it really makes this brownie pop.

🍸 These brownies are amazing warm and, believe it or not, they taste even better the next day. Store them at room temperature in an air-tight container for up to 3 days, or freeze them for a treat another day.

🍸 For the sauce, we recommend using our **Raspberry Gin Jam** (p. 68), but any raspberry jam will do in a pinch. Extra sauce can be stored in the fridge and easily warmed up for ice cream or as a wonderful fruit dip.

🍸 We used Gordon's Bramble Gin for this recipe because of its berry notes, but if you don't have a berry botanical, use a more neutral gin. Serve this up on your plate and pair it with **Larry's White London** (p. 235) for a true death-by-chocolate experience.

GINGREDIENTS

1 cup of fresh raspberries

¼ cup of gin

4 oz of unsweetened chocolate, chopped

¾ cup of butter

2 cups of white granulated sugar

3 large eggs, room temperature

1 teaspoon of reserved raspberry-infused gin

1 cup of all-purpose flour

½ teaspoon of baking powder

⅓ cup of semi-sweet or dark chocolate chips

Optional Chocolate Raspberry Sauce

1 cup of heavy whipping cream

3 tablespoons of raspberry jam
(try our **Raspberry Gin Jam** (p. 68) for an extra kick)

3 oz of dark chocolate, chopped

2 tablespoons of the reserved raspberry-infused gin

GINSTRUCTIONS

- The day before, prepare your GINfusion by placing the fresh raspberries and gin in a sealable jar or bowl. Let stand at least overnight (give it a shake occasionally to make sure all the berries get infused with the gin).

- When you are ready to make your brownies, start by preheating the oven to 350°F and greasing a 9 x 9-inch square baking pan.

- Remove the raspberries from the gin, reserving the infused liquid. Keep the raspberries at hand, as you'll be using them shortly.

- In a large microwavable bowl, add chocolate and butter. Microwave for 2 minutes or until the butter is melted. Remove from the microwave and stir until the chocolate is completely melted and the mixture is smooth and shiny. Add the sugar and mix well. Blend in the eggs 1 at a time.

- Add a teaspoon of the reserved raspberry-infused gin and stir. Gently fold in the flour and baking powder.

- Spread the brownie mixture into the baking pan. Sprinkle the gin-infused raspberries over the top of the batter. Gently push them down a tiny bit into the batter but not totally submerged. Sprinkle chocolate chips over everything.

- Bake for 30 - 35 minutes or until the edges start to crack. If you like a gooier brownie, cook it less; if you prefer a more cake-like brownie, cook it a few minutes more. Do not overcook. Remove from the oven and let rest (they will continue to cook and set).

- Make your Chocolate Raspberry Sauce by placing the cream, jam, and chocolate in a microwave-safe glass bowl. Microwave for 1 minute or until the cream is hot but not boiling. Remove from the microwave and stir mixture until the chocolate is melted and the jam is blended well into the sauce. Add the raspberry-infused gin and gently stir until combined.

- Drizzle the sauce over your brownies and enjoy warm or cold. For an extra special treat, add a scoop of vanilla ice cream and drizzle the sauce over it as well.

fun fact:

The first cocktail listed in the first British book to contain cocktail recipes – William Terrington's Cooling Cups and Dainty Drinks – was a gin cocktail made with ginger syrup, orange curaçao, and bitters.

CinnaGin Apple Squares

Serves: 9

Total Time:
45 minutes

GINSPIRATIONS

 This recipe originated with an apple square recipe Heather's mother and grandmother used to make. It is SO easy and quick to prepare and everyone LOVES it. We decided to take it to the next level with cinnamon gin and the glaze.

While you don't NEED the glaze, if you aren't serving this to minors, you'll want it. You may be tempted to add more apple or cinnamon to the recipe. we urge you not to, as too much apple will water down your batter (believe us, we've done it). And, too much cinnamon overpowers the other flavours.

These squares are best served fresh out of the oven (slightly cooled first), but they are also great at room temperature or the next day. They rarely make it to the next day, but you can also drizzle your glaze over it all and put them in the fridge for later if you so choose. They freeze well – just don't add the glaze until you actually serve them.

Be sure to use cinnamon-infused gin as this makes all the difference. You can easily infuse your own or buy a cinnamon gin such as Old Curiosity Distillery's Christmas Gin. This yummy dessert pairs nicely with a **Canadian Tuxedo** (p. 226).

GINGREDIENTS

1 cup of all-purpose flour

1 teaspoon of baking powder

¼ teaspoon of salt

¼ teaspoon of cinnamon

⅛ teaspoon of ground nutmeg

¼ cup of butter, melted

½ cup of brown sugar

½ cup of white granulated sugar

1 large egg, room temperature

1 tablespoon of cinnamon-infused gin

1 small apple, peeled and finely chopped

¼ cup (approx.) of cinnamon sugar

Glaze *(optional)*

2 tablespoons of cinnamon-infused gin (see Pro Tip below)

1 tablespoon of milk

¼ to ½ cup of powdered icing sugar

GINSTRUCTIONS

- Preheat the oven to 350° F. Grease an 8 x 8-inch square baking pan.

- In a small bowl, combine flour, baking powder, salt, cinnamon, and nutmeg. Set aside.

- In a larger bowl, combine melted butter with the brown and white sugars. Beat in the egg and cinnamon-infused gin until smooth and creamy.

- **Pro Tip:** To infuse your own gin, add 1 cup of gin to a mason jar along with a couple of cinnamon sticks. Let sit for a few days before using. Give your jar a shake once a day. The longer it sits, the better it tastes (makes a great gift too).

- Fold in the dry ingredients (flour mixture) just until combined. Fold in the diced apple. Your mixture will be thick. Scrape the mixture into your greased pan and spread as evenly as possible. Sprinkle the top with cinnamon sugar.

- Bake for 30 minutes or until a toothpick comes out clean and the edges are slightly browned. Let cool for 10 minutes.

- Prepare the glaze by mixing cinnamon gin, milk, and powdered icing sugar until the powdered icing sugar is dissolved and it is at the thickness you desire. Start with ¼ cup of powdered icing sugar and then add more if needed. Your glaze should run off your spoon but not be watery.

- Cut your cake into 9 squares, place a square on a plate and drizzle it with the glaze. Serve warm.

"This recipe is a HUGE hit. It's a very special dessert that you can serve your family on a weeknight or even serve at a gala. Quick, delicious, and fun to make!"

Susan Epstein, test cook

Chai Oatmeal Chocolate Chip Cookies

**Serves: 12
(2 dozen cookies)**

Total Time: 1 hour, plus chilling/cooling time

GINSPIRATIONS

🍸 These are Heather's go-to cookies. She makes them the most out of all the cookies in her recipe box. Many years ago she combined a few of her favourite recipes to come up with this one. She loves chai tea and drinks it every day. She also loves a good chocolate chip cookie and a good oatmeal cookie, so this Chai Oatmeal Chocolate Chip Cookie recipe was born. Add gin and booya - cookie heaven!

🍸 These cookies are slightly crispy on the outside and rich and chewy on the inside. They are what we call a 'sturdy' cookie that goes well in lunchboxes. They also freeze really well.

🍸 Infusing your butter with chai does something amazing and we urge you not to skip this step. If you want to really up your cookie game, use a chocolate chai tea or an extra bold chai tea. You can thank us now.

🍸 It's important to note that you won't taste the gin really. What it does do is BOOST the flavour of the chai and the chocolate. Yes, you could leave it out - but why would you?

🍸 We use an infused gin for our cookies - usually a cinnamon or toffee infusion but ideally if you have a chocolate gin such as Lord's Chocolate Gin, it is amazing. Pair these yummy cookies with a Chocolate Martini for a delicious treat anytime.

GINGREDIENTS

1 cup of unsalted butter

4 tablespoons of good quality loose leaf chai tea or 4 teabags

1 ¾ cups of all-purpose flour

2 ½ cups of rolled oats (NOT instant or quick)

1 teaspoon of baking soda

1 teaspoon of salt

1 teaspoon of ground cinnamon

⅔ cup of white granulated sugar

1 ½ cups of brown sugar

2 large eggs, room temperature

2 teaspoons of gin (preferably toffee or cinnamon-infused)

¾ cup of chocolate chips

GINSTRUCTIONS

• Take your eggs out of the fridge to come to room temperature while you prepare the butter.

• In a small saucepan over medium heat, combine the butter and tea until the butter is completely melted. Reduce the heat to low, and allow the mixture to simmer for 10 minutes, stirring occasionally.

• After 10 minutes, strain the tea from the melted butter using a tea strainer (or whatever you have on hand) or remove the teabags if you used those instead. Discard the tea and place the butter in the fridge to cool for about 15 minutes (or until room temperature but not solid – there might be bits on the bottom just starting to solidify).

• Place the flour, oats, baking soda, salt, and cinnamon in a large bowl. Stir to combine and then set aside.

• In a large mixing bowl of an electric stand mixer, combine the cooled butter with the white and brown sugars, eggs, and gin. Beat on medium for a minute or 2 ensuring all the sugar is dissolved. The batter will appear quite moist. Add the dry ingredients to the bowl and stir just until combined. Stir in the chocolate chips.

If you walk a mile in my shoes you'll end up in a gin bar.

- Place the bowl with the dough in the fridge to chill for an hour or 2 (you can also chill overnight). Do not skip this step! It's important that the mixture firm up and the flavours blend.

- Preheat the oven to 375°F. Line a cookie sheet with parchment paper and set aside.

- When you are ready to bake your cookies, take the dough out of the fridge. Using a large cookie dough scoop, drop the dough by the spoonful onto your prepared cookie sheet. You can also form into balls by hand if you prefer. Use a fork to gently squish the balls down slightly. (Note: You should get at least 2 dozen large cookies, but if you make them smaller you could easily get 3 dozen).

- Bake your cookies in the oven for approximately 15 minutes, depending on your oven, or until slightly golden brown. They will come out looking like they're not fully cooked but they'll be beautiful and chewy once cooled. Allow the cookies to cool a few minutes and then transfer them to a wire cooling rack to finish cooling.

Made this GINspired recipe? Post your photo on Instagram and tag @the.gin.shop.ca

GINspired 167

Drunken Blueberry Cheesecake

Serves: 10-12

Total Time: 3 ½ hours, plus overnight chilling

GINSPIRATIONS

- We love baked cheesecake but we don't like the whole water bath process. It can be tricky and you can still end up with a cracked cheesecake. This Drunken Blueberry Cheesecake is ultra creamy and swirled with fresh ginny wild blueberry sauce. It's baked to perfection with no water bath and no fuss! It also uses our **GINfused Wild Blueberry Pie Filling** (p. 220) which is AHMAZING.

- You can switch up the flavours by changing the pie filling flavour and, of course, the gin.

- Be sure to let the cheesecake rest in the warm oven an hour after the baking time. This helps you avoid the whole water bath process. Also, chill your cheesecake overnight. It helps it set and the flavours to blend really wonderfully.

- We used **Empress 1908** for this recipe. The purple colour and citrus go perfectly. Pair a slice of your cheesecake with a **Club Quarantine** (p. 228) for the ultimate drunken blueberry cheesecake experience.

GINGREDIENTS

Crust

2 ½ cups of graham cracker crumbs

1 tablespoon of white granulated sugar

1 teaspoon of pumpkin pie spice

⅓ cup of melted butter

Filling

3 - 8 oz packages of full-fat cream cheese, room temperature

2 cups of full-fat sour cream

1 ½ cups of white granulated sugar

4 large eggs, room temperature

1 tablespoon of **Empress 1908 Gin**

1 batch of **GINfused Wild Blueberry Pie Filling** (p. 220)
  (or 1 - 21 oz can of blueberry pie filling +
  ¼ cup of gin stirred in)

Ginny Whipped Cream *(optional)*

1 cup of heavy whipping cream

1 tablespoon of **Empress 1908 Gin**

3 - 4 tablespoons of powdered icing sugar

GINSTRUCTIONS

- If you haven't already done so, make your **GINfused Wild Blueberry Pie Filling** (p. 220) and allow it to completely cool.

- Preheat the oven to 325°F and line a 9-inch springform pan with parchment paper.

- Stir together graham cracker crumbs, sugar, and pumpkin pie spice. Add the melted butter and stir until it looks like wet sand. Press the mixture into the bottom of the pan and ½-inch up the sides.

- Bake for 10 - 12 minutes, just until dry. Do not brown. Remove from the oven to cool. Reduce the oven temperature to 275°F.

- In a large bowl of a stand mixer, beat the cream cheese until smooth. Add the sour cream, sugar, eggs, and gin and beat until creamy and smooth.

- Pour half of the filling into another bowl. Stir in ½ cup of the blueberry pie filling. Pour the blueberry cheesecake filling into the prepared crust.

- Carefully pour the remaining plain cheesecake filling over the blueberry filling to cover it in an even layer. Spread to smooth.

- Drop teaspoons of the **GINfused Wild Blueberry Pie Filling** over the top of the cheesecake and using a knife, gently swirl it through the cheesecake batter. Reserve the remaining pie filling for serving.

- Bake at 275°F for 1 ½ - 2 hours, until the outer 2 inches are set and the centre is still somewhat jiggly. Turn the oven off and let the cake sit in the warm oven for 1 more hour.

- Remove the cheesecake from the oven and set on the counter to cool to room temperature. Once cooled, place in the fridge and chill at least 8 hours or overnight before serving.

- To make the ginny whipped cream, in a cold bowl of a stand mixer, whip the cream on high until firm peaks form. Add the gin and powdered icing sugar. Whip until stiff peaks form.

- To serve, spoon the remaining **GINfused Wild Blueberry Pie Filling** over the cheesecake and pipe ginny whipped cream around the edges.

fun fact:

at one time, there was a working gin still in one out of every four habitable structures in London.

Made this GINspired recipe? Post your photo on Instagram and tag @the.gin.shop.ca

No-Bake Blimey Cheesecake

Serves: 12
Total Time: 1 hour, plus overnight chilling

GINSPIRATIONS

- In the summer, when it's way too hot to bake, we like to have this light and delicious ginny no-bake cheesecake. It's a snap to whip up and chills in the fridge overnight, so you can make it the evening before when the daytime temp is a bit cooler (hopefully).

- We're not fans of gelatine in cheese-cake - it feels like cheating so we made sure this one doesn't have it.

- If you don't want lime, you can substi-tute lemon or orange zest and juice instead.

- If you really want to make your cake fancy, try mixing a couple of tea-spoons of gin into some lemon or lime curd and then drizzling that over your cheesecake along with the ginny whipped cream. Seriously decadent. Keep this dessert in the fridge.

- We used **Tanqueray Rangpur** gin for this recipe. Pair a slice with a **Rangpur Citrus Spritz** (p. 224) for a delectable summer treat.

a true friend reaches for your hand...and puts a glass of gin in it.

GINGREDIENTS

Crust
1 - 10.5 oz box of digestive cookies
½ cup of butter, melted

Cake
4 oz of white chocolate, chopped
2 - 8 oz packages of full-fat cream cheese, softened
½ cup of powdered icing sugar
¼ cup of gin
1 teaspoon of lime zest
1 tablespoon of lime juice
1 teaspoon of vanilla
1 ¼ cups of heavy whipping cream

Topping
½ cup of heavy whipping cream
2 tablespoons of powdered icing sugar
2 teaspoons of gin
1 teaspoon of lime zest (plus more for garnish)
Optional garnish: lime zest, lime slices, or candied limes

GINSTRUCTIONS

Make the Crust
- Grease the sides and bottom of an 8-inch springform pan.
- In a food processor, add the cookies and pulse until finely crushed. Add the melted butter and process until it comes together. Press the biscuit crumb into the bottom of the springform pan and make sure it's firmly pressed down. Refrigerate for now.

Make the Cake
- Place the white chocolate in a microwave-safe bowl and microwave just until melted (approximately 1 - 2 minutes). In the bowl of an electric stand mixer, add the cream cheese. Beat until creamy and smooth.
- Add the powdered icing sugar, gin, lime zest and juice, and vanilla and beat until well combined and creamy smooth. Fold the melted chocolate into the cream cheese mixture.
- In a separate bowl, whip the 1 ¼ cups of cream until firm peaks form and it holds its shape. Gently fold the whipped cream into the cream cheese mixture. Spread the batter on top of the cookie layer and even it out with a spatula. Refrigerate overnight.

Make the Topping
- In a cold bowl of a stand mixer, whip the cream on high until firm peaks form. Add the powdered icing sugar, gin, and lime zest. Whip until stiff peaks form. Pipe the topping onto the cheesecake and garnish it with lime zest and lime slices, if desired.

Home is
where the gin is.

Dark Chocolate & Gin Truffles

Makes 24 to 36 truffles

Total Time: 40 minutes, plus chilling time

GINSPIRATIONS

🍸 These are little balls of heaven. They are potent so do not feed to minors or teatotallers.

🍸 They actually taste even better a day or 2 after you make them and last in the freezer for a good month. We prefer to store ours in the freezer but they are good in the fridge too.

🍸 Play with different flavour add-ins. You can even divide the base truffle mix into 2 bowls and try 2 different flavours. If you aren't using any added flavour, you can increase the gin amount a tiny bit. But again, these are potent so don't go too crazy.

🍸 These truffles are amazing without garnish but if you feel the need for something more, a simple roll in cocoa powder does the trick. If you want to go fancy, you can dip them in chocolate, but this seems to decrease the ginny flavour a bit.

🍸 Yes, this recipe uses a lot of chocolate but you also get lots of delicious truffles in return. They make a wonderful gift for the gin-lovers in your life.

🍸 We used a citrusy gin in this recipe such as **Sheringham Distillery's Kazuki Gin** but any gin really is amazing. You can totally change the flavour depending on the gin you use and the flavours you add. Pair this treat with a **Kazuki Negroni** (p. 231) and you are all set.

GINGREDIENTS

14 oz of dark chocolate, roughly chopped

½ cup of heavy whipping cream

¼ cup of gin

Optional flavours:

> 1 tablespoon of fresh juice and 1 teaspoon of lime, lemon, or orange zest
>
> 1 tablespoon of raspberries, strawberries or blueberries, crushed
>
> 1 teaspoon of peppermint extract
>
> 1 tablespoon of any jam
>
> 1 tablespoon of any **Fever-Tree** mixer

Optional garnishes: cocoa powder, coconut, chocolate for dipping

GINSTRUCTIONS

- Gently melt the chopped chocolate in a bowl over a pan of simmering water (double boiler if you have one). Don't allow the bowl to touch the water. Remove the bowl from the heat and stir in the heavy whipping cream and gin.

- Add in your flavouring of choice - for example, the lime juice and zest or a spot of jam. Mix until totally combined and smooth.

- Pop the mixture into the fridge uncovered for 1 - 2 hours.

- Remove the bowl from the fridge and with clean hands, form the chocolate into small, walnut-sized balls (a small cookie scoop works well for this too). Note: If your chocolate is too hard, you may need to let it rest a bit to come closer to room temperature before shaping it into balls. Be warned, it's a messy job, but well worth it.

- Place the truffles on a parchment paper or silicone-lined baking sheet. If they aren't too melty, you can now roll them in a bit of cocoa powder or coconut before popping the entire baking sheet back into the fridge for 2 hours or the freezer for 1 hour.

- Once they are chilled a second time, they are ready to eat as is or dip them in additional melted chocolate, if desired.

- Store your truffles in the fridge or freezer. Let them sit for a minute or 2 out of the fridge before eating.

Dark Chocolate, Peanut Butter, & Gin Lava Cakes

Serves: 4
Total Time: 30 minutes

GINSPIRATIONS

- We like to whip up these lava cakes when we're in a hurry for an impressive dessert that takes next to no time to make. You can't go wrong with a decadent lava cake. Add some peanut butter and gin and WOAH baby...these might just blow your guests' (and your family's) minds.

- If you don't like peanut butter or just want to change things up, replace it with some **Raspberry Gin Jam (p. 68)** or leave it out totally for a pure chocolatey treat. Or go crazy and make peanut butter AND jam lava cakes.

- You can prepare your batter and ramekins ahead of time and keep them in the fridge until you are ready to bake. Just be sure to cover them with plastic wrap so that they don't form a skin. When you are ready, simply uncover and bake.

- The trick to a perfect lava cake is cooking it for exactly 13 minutes. But if your oven is on the hotter or cooler side, you'll need to adjust slightly. You want the centres still soft when you take them out of the oven. Then, let it rest a minute before attempting to invert and plate it. Go slow and gentle and before you know it, you'll have an impressive little cake just waiting to be devoured.

- Be sure to serve your lava cakes warm from the oven or else you won't have the lava goodness pour out when you cut into it.

- Adding the gin really gives the chocolate a serious flavour boost so don't leave that out. We used Beefeater because we love its spicy and fruity aroma. Pair your lava cakes with a **Gin Hard Seltzer (p. 229)** and ice cream, then crack the cake open for some gooey peanut butter and chocolate decadence.

GINGREDIENTS

Butter and cocoa powder for greasing and dusting

4 oz of good quality dark chocolate (65% or higher), roughly chopped

½ cup of butter

1 cup of powdered icing sugar

2 large whole eggs + 2 egg yolks, room temperature

2 teaspoons of gin

6 tablespoons of all-purpose flour

4 teaspoons of peanut butter

Optional garnishes: powdered icing sugar, vanilla ice cream or whipped cream, berries

GINSTRUCTIONS

- Take the eggs out of the fridge at least a half-hour before you start making your lava cakes to allow them to come to room temperature. Preheat the oven to 425°F.

- Generously butter (grease) 4 ramekins or custard cups (they should be ¾ to 1 cup size). Dust each buttered cup with cocoa powder and knock out any extra. The inside of each cup should be fully greased and dusted with cocoa powder. This ensures that your lava cakes release easily.

i wish i loved exercise as much as i love gin and chocolate.

- In a large microwave-safe bowl, add the chocolate and butter. Microwave for 1 minute or until the butter is melted. Remove from the microwave and whisk until the chocolate is completely melted and looks silky smooth. Add 1 cup of powdered icing sugar and mix well.

- Add the whole eggs 1 at a time, blending well after each addition. Add the egg yolks and blend well until the batter is glossy and smooth. Stir in the gin. Stir in the flour and stir the batter until it is silky smooth and completely combined.

- Divide half the batter evenly between the 4 ramekins. Add 1 teaspoon of peanut butter to the middle of each cup on top of the batter.

- Divide the remaining batter evenly between the 4 ramekins and place on top of the peanut butter, being sure to cover the peanut butter well. You should now have a layer of chocolate batter on the bottom, a dollop of peanut butter in the middle, and another layer of chocolate batter on the top.

- Bake for 13 minutes, or until the sides are firm but the centres are still soft. Do not overcook or you won't have lava! Remove from the oven and let stand for 1 minute.

- Carefully run a small butter knife around the edges of the cakes to loosen them from the ramekins. Then, very delicately place a dessert plate over the top of the cake and invert both. The ramekin is now upside down on your plate. VERY slowly lift the ramekin off the plate, leaving the lava cake resting gently on the plate. Do not rush or you will break your cake open.

- Once all your lava cakes are removed from the ramekins and plated, dust each with some powdered icing sugar and garnish with vanilla ice cream or whipped cream and serve!

Made this GINspired recipe? Post your photo on Instagram and tag @the.gin.shop.ca

Blueberry & Gin Cobbler

Serves: 9 to 10
Total Time: 1 hour

GINSPIRATIONS

🍸 You are in for a real treat. This dessert is SO easy to put together and the result is super delicious. It's not made like a traditional cobbler, but the result is just about the same.

🍸 While you can use a can of blueberry filling plus gin, we highly recommend you make your own **GINfused Wild Blueberry Pie Filling** (p. 220) and have it on hand. You can also use different flavours such as raspberry, mixed berry, or cherry. They all work well and infuse nicely with the gin.

🍸 Be sure you layer your dessert in the exact order of the GINgredients. The magic happens because of the order everything gets layered. Fresh blueberries work best, but you can also use frozen in a pinch.

🍸 Use a gin with more berry aromatics if you can such as Greenall's Blueberry Gin. Pair your cobbler with a **Pump Up the Jam** (p. 230) and some vanilla ice cream.

GINGREDIENTS

2 ½ cups of **GINfused Wild Blueberry Pie Filling** (p. 220)
    (or 1 - 21 oz can of blueberry pie filling + ¼ cup of gin stirred in)

1 large can of crushed pineapple, drained well (*optional*)

¼ cup of shredded coconut

1 cup of fresh or frozen wild blueberries, divided

¼ cup of gin

1 box of yellow cake mix

¾ cup of butter, cold

GINSTRUCTIONS

• Preheat the oven to 375°F. Grease a 9 x 13-inch cake pan.

• Spread the pie filling on the bottom of the dish. Next, spread the crushed pineapple (if using) over the pie filling and then top with the shredded coconut.

• Sprinkle ¾ cup of the fresh blueberries over the mixture. Drizzle the gin over everything. Evenly sprinkle the dry cake mix over the top.

• Thinly slice the butter and place the sliced butter pieces over the dry cake mix, making sure you cover the entire dish (small gaps are ok). Alternatively, you can also melt the butter and drizzle it instead, but we find the best results with sliced cold butter.

• Sprinkle the remaining blueberries over the butter.

• Bake for 40 - 45 minutes or until the top is a deep golden brown.

• Serve warm with vanilla ice cream.

fun fact:

Much like other spirits and wine, gin comes in many different flavours, textures, strengths, and tones. Try different gins to find your perfect tipple!

flourless Chocolate Raspberry Torte

Serves: 10 to 12

Total Time: 1¼ hour, plus time to let the GINfusion rest

GINSPIRATIONS

- This is a fairly easy and yet super impressive, decadent, deeply chocolaty dessert. You will want to make this a go-to dessert for potlucks and parties. It tastes even better the next day.

- You can make it totally from scratch or skip a few steps by using previously infused raspberry gin or even using our **Raspberry Gin Jam (p. 68)** in your filling.

- The main torte has only 5 GINgredients and takes a couple of minutes to mix together. If you want to change things up, use different berries or try swirling peanut butter into the middle layer instead of the raspberry filling. You'll just need to warm the peanut butter up slightly first so that it swirls in ok.

- There are tons of options for garnish as well. Use the ganache if you want a mind-blowing chocolate experience or simply dust your torte with powdered icing sugar and serve it alone. The choice is yours.

- You can make this recipe in advance, and store it in the fridge, tightly wrapped, for up to 3 days. To store longer, let it cool completely, press a sheet of plastic on top of the torte, place in an airtight container, and freeze it for up to 3 months. Do not garnish with ganache if you are freezing it. Let it thaw overnight in the fridge before garnishing.

- We used **Whitley Neill Raspberry Gin** for extra raspberry flavour. Pair this dreamy, decadent dessert with a Chocolate Martini for a chocolaty tastegasm.

GINGREDIENTS

Raspberry-Infused Gin

1 cup of fresh raspberries

1 cup of gin

OR a good quality raspberry gin

Filling

1 cup of raspberries, fresh or frozen

¼ cup of white granulated sugar

¼ cup of gin

OR

½ cup of **Raspberry Gin Jam (p. 68)** or raspberry jam mixed with ¼ cup of gin

Torte

9 oz of good-quality dark chocolate (65% or higher), chopped

1 cup + 2 tablespoons (9 oz) of unsalted butter

1 ½ cups of white granulated sugar

7 large eggs, room temperature

¼ cup of raspberry-infused gin

Ganache

½ cup of heavy whipping cream

2 tablespoons of salted butter

4 oz of dark chocolate, roughly chopped

2 tablespoons of raspberry-infused gin

Optional Garnishes

Fresh raspberries

Few sprigs of fresh mint leaves

Powdered icing sugar

Whipped cream or vanilla ice cream

Made this GINspired recipe? Post your photo on Instagram and tag @the.gin.shop.ca

fun fact:

Nearly all juniper used in gin is picked wild: almost none is cultivated.

GINSTRUCTIONS

Infuse the Raspberry Gin (the day before)

- Place the raspberries in a mason jar. Squish them up a bit with a spoon. Pour the gin over the raspberries. Place a tight lid on the jar. Give it a good shake to combine and let sit overnight (or longer) in the fridge.
- Take the eggs out of the fridge at least a half-hour before you start making your torte to allow them to come to room temperature.

Filling

- In a small saucepan, add the raspberries, granulated sugar, and gin. Cook on medium heat, stirring until the sugar is dissolved and you have a thick, jam-like consistency, usually 3 - 4 minutes. Set aside and leave to cool.

Torte

- Preheat the oven to 375°F. Grease and line a 9-inch springform pan (or an 8-inch pan if you want a taller torte) with parchment paper. Grease the parchment paper as well.
- Add the chocolate and butter to a large microwave-safe bowl (or double boiler), and melt together in the microwave (or on the stovetop), until the chocolate is almost completely melted.
- Remove from the microwave and stir until your butter and chocolate are smooth, silky, and totally melted. Stir in the sugar, then let the mixture cool for a few minutes. Add the eggs, 1 at a time, fully combining between each addition.
- After all the eggs are added, continue to stir until the batter becomes thick, glossy, and utterly gorgeous. Stir in the raspberry-infused gin.
- Pour half the batter into the prepared pan. Dollop the raspberry filling over the batter. Use a knife to swirl it into the batter.
- Add the remaining batter on top. If any raspberry filling floats to the top, swirl it into the batter as well.
- Bake 30 - 35 minutes until the torte jiggles slightly in the middle but is not completely set. It will be puffed up and look like a baked brownie around the edges and be jiggly in the centre. Begin checking at the 30-minute mark to ensure the torte does not overbake.
- Let cool in the pan. It will sink so don't be alarmed.

Ganache

- While the torte is cooling. In a small saucepan, gently heat the whipping cream and butter, stirring with a wooden spoon or whisk all the time until the mixture comes to a simmer.
- Take the pot off the heat, add the dark chocolate, and stir or whisk until the chocolate has melted and you have a thick, glossy sauce. Stir in the raspberry-infused gin. Set aside to slightly cool.

Assemble

- Once your torte is cooled, remove it from the pan and place it on a serving plate. Pour the ganache over the top and garnish with fresh raspberries and a few fresh mint leaves. Or, if you aren't using the ganache, simply dust with powdered icing sugar.
- Cut into wedges and serve alone or with vanilla ice cream, whipped cream, or anything else your heart desires.

Berry GINteresting Tart

GINSPIRATIONS

🍸 If you are looking for the perfect no-bake dessert, this is it. This white chocolaty, ginny tart is incredibly creamy and rich and yet is also super quick and easy to make. You can use any berry you like to switch the flavour up.

🍸 Using the sweeter digestive cookie crumbs really does add that extra little something, though you can use graham crumbs too.

🍸 You'd think that chocolate over berries would be super heavy, and while it is rich, the gin goes wonderfully with the white chocolate and really deepens the flavours.

🍸 We used New Holland Blue Haven Blueberry Gin. Pair your creamy slice with some fresh whipped cream and a **Berry Tasty Gin Smash** (p. 226) for a decadent treat everyone will think you spent hours and hours making. We won't tell if you won't.

GINGREDIENTS

Crust

3 cups of digestive cookie crumbs or graham cracker crumbs

¼ cup of white granulated sugar

½ cup of unsalted butter, melted

Filling

12 oz of white chocolate, chopped

½ cup of heavy whipping cream

¼ cup of unsalted butter

¼ cup of gin

2 cups of fresh berries (raspberries, wild blueberries, strawberries, blackberries, etc.)

GINSTRUCTIONS

- Wash and dry your berries. If using larger berries, such as strawberries, slice or chop into smaller pieces. Set aside.

- Make the crust. Stir together the cookie crumbs or graham crumbs and sugar. Add the melted butter and mix until all the crumbs are moist.

- Press the mixture into the bottom and up the sides of an ungreased 9-inch fluted tart tin with a loose base. Refrigerate while you prepare the filling (no need to bake this one).

- Place the white chocolate, heavy whipping cream, and butter in a large microwave-safe bowl. Heat in 20-second intervals, stirring after each one, until the chocolate is melted and smooth. Stir in the gin.

- Take the crust out of the fridge and gently place the berries onto the bottom of the crust. Carefully pour the white chocolate gin filling on top.

- Place back in the fridge and chill until firm for at least 2 hours.

- Garnish with a few fresh berries and serve with whipped cream if desired.

I'm a GINvincible force of nature.

Boozy Carrot Cake

I tried to say no to gin...but it's 40% stronger than me!

Serves: 10 to 12

Total Time: 2 ½ hours, plus time for the GINfusion to rest

GINSPIRATIONS

🍸 Heather has never really loved carrot cake or traditional cream cheese frosting, however, she has people in her life who LOVE carrot cake (aka Larry) and request it for dessert. So she was determined to make a carrot cake that she loved too. And this is it. There have been many many people who tell us this is the best carrot cake they've ever had. Even Heather can devour this gin-soaked cake in a heartbeat

🍸 It's super moist and flavourful and the frosting is to die for. Once you add gin and chocolate to your cream cheese frosting, you'll never go back. This is a much lighter and fluffier frosting than a traditional cream cheese frosting.

🍸 You can add raisins or nuts into the cake itself if you like, however, it doesn't need it.

🍸 If you prefer, you can bake this recipe as 24 cupcakes or in a 9 x 13 baking pan instead. Just be sure to adjust your baking time.

🍸 Unfrosted, the cake freezes well too. Store any leftover cake in the fridge (and have it for breakfast).

🍸 Infusing your gin with grated carrot really boosts all the flavours of this cake. The cinnamon-infused gin in the cake, syrup, and frosting complements it all nicely.

🍸 Try using a gin with ginger aromatics such as Cotswolds Ginger Gin to really make this gin-soaked cake shine. Serve your cake with a **Gin Hard Seltzer** (p. 229) and be prepared to serve seconds.

GINGREDIENTS

Carrot-Infused Gin

1 carrot, finely grated
¼ cup of gin

Cake

2 ¼ cups of all-purpose flour
2 teaspoons of baking powder
1 teaspoon of baking soda
1 ½ teaspoons of ground cinnamon
½ teaspoon of ground ginger
¼ teaspoon of ground nutmeg
⅛ teaspoon of ground cloves
½ teaspoon of salt
¾ cup of vegetable oil
4 large eggs, room temperature
1 ½ cups of light brown sugar, lightly packed
½ cup of white granulated sugar
½ cup of sour cream
½ cup of crushed pineapple, including the juice
Juice and zest from 1 clementine orange (or a small orange)
¼ cup of carrot-infused gin (plus the gin-soaked carrot)
1 tablespoon of cinnamon-infused gin
3 cups grated carrots, lightly packed
Optional add ins:
    ½ cup of chopped nuts (pecans or walnuts are best)
    ½ cup of raisins

Ginny Syrup

¼ cup of white granulated sugar
¼ cup of water
2 tablespoons of cinnamon-infused gin

Cream Cheese Frosting

3 oz of white chocolate, roughly chopped
8 oz package brick-style, full-fat cream cheese, softened to room temperature
½ cup of unsalted butter, softened to room temperature
1 tablespoon of cinnamon-infused gin (or more to taste)
2 - 3 cups of powdered icing sugar

Optional Garnishes

Crushed pecans

Orange zest

GINSTRUCTIONS

- Infuse your carrot gin at least 1 day prior to making your cake (or use carrot-infused gin if you can find it). In a small mason jar, add the finely grated carrots. Pour the gin over. Seal the jar tightly and give it a good shake. You'll be using all of it in the recipe.
- If you don't have cinnamon-infused gin, you'll need to make some of that too (we highly suggest keeping some on hand at all times; see p. 40 for instructions on how to make it).
- Take your eggs out of the fridge to come to room temperature a half-hour before starting to bake.
- Butter 2 - 9-inch round cake pans well and flour (you can also line the bottom of each pan with parchment paper for easier removal) and set aside. Preheat the oven to 350°F.
- In a large mixing bowl, whisk together the flour, baking powder, baking soda, cinnamon, ginger, nutmeg, cloves, and salt until well combined. Set aside.
- In a separate large mixing bowl, whisk together the oil, eggs, brown sugar, granulated sugar, sour cream, crushed pineapple, clementine juice and zest, carrot-infused gin (including the gin-soaked carrots), and cinnamon-infused gin until fully combined.
- Add the grated carrots into the wet ingredients and mix until well combined. If you are using nuts or raisins, stir those in too.
- Pour the wet ingredients into the dry ingredients and mix with a wooden spoon or rubber spatula until just combined, making sure not to overmix the batter.
- Pour the cake batter evenly between both prepared cake pans.
- Bake at 350°F for 30 - 35 minutes or until the tops of the cakes are set and a toothpick inserted into the centre of each one comes out clean.
- Remove from the oven and allow the cakes to cool in the pans for about 20 - 25 minutes.
- Once the cakes have cooled, gently run a knife around the edges of the pans to loosen and then remove the cakes from the pans and place on a wire rack to finish cooling.

Ginny Syrup

- In a small microwave-safe bowl, combine the sugar and water. Microwave on high for 1 minute; it should be boiling. Give it a stir and then boil for 1 more minute. Remove from the microwave, let cool for 5 minutes and then stir in 2 tablespoons of cinnamon-infused gin. Set aside.

Frosting

- Melt the white chocolate in the microwave, or in a bowl over hot water. Let cool slightly.
- Meanwhile, in the bowl of a stand mixer fitted with the paddle attachment, or in a large mixing bowl using a hand-held mixer, beat the cream cheese until smooth. Add the butter and mix for 1 minute until well combined and smooth. Add in the gin.
- Slowly add the powdered icing sugar 1 cup at a time and continue mixing until your frosting is fully combined, scraping down the sides of the bowl as needed.
- Add the melted chocolate to the frosting and mix until fully incorporated. Your frosting should be fluffy and easily spreadable (NOT super thick like a buttercream). Add more powdered icing sugar to get the consistency you like, being careful not to add too much.
  If it gets too thick, just add a touch more gin to loosen it up.
- Pop your frosting into the fridge while waiting for the cake to cool completely.

Assemble

- Level the tops of each cake with a knife or cake leveler. Place 1 of the cakes on a cake stand. Poke holes in the cake with a wooden skewer. Drizzle or brush half the ginny syrup over the cake. Wait 1 minute to let it soak in and then spread a generous amount of frosting on top of the cake.
- Place the second cake layer on top of the first and repeat the process (i.e. poke holes, brush with the remaining ginny syrup, and then frost).
- Frost the sides and top of the cake with the remaining frosting. Decorate with crushed pecans and orange zest.

Vanilla Gin Custard

Serves: 6

Total Time: 1 hour, plus chilling time

GINSPIRATIONS

- You'll love this ginny vanilla-rich custard. It's simple and yet so elegant. You can bake your custard in either 1 big pan or individual ramekins. Just ensure you place it in the water bath during baking to keep it moist.

- To serve, you can eat it as is or with a side of fresh berries. We recommend dipping a biscotti in as well.

- You'll want to use a vanilla gin such as Sir Edmond Bourbon Vanilla Infused Gin for this recipe (or infuse your own gin with vanilla). Pair it with an **Earl Grey Mar-Tea-Ni** (p. 227) for a decadent after-dinner treat.

GINGREDIENTS

¾ cup of white granulated sugar

½ teaspoon of Kosher salt

4 large eggs, beaten

1 vanilla bean, seeds scraped and reserved

4 cups of heavy whipping cream

5 tablespoons of gin

Fresh berries for serving (*optional*)

GINSTRUCTIONS

- Preheat the oven to 300°F.

- In a large bowl, whisk together the sugar, salt, eggs, and vanilla bean seeds. Whisk in the cream and gin.

- Transfer the mixture to a 3-quart baking dish or individual custard ramekins. Set the dish/ramekins inside a roasting pan.

- Put the roasting pan on the oven rack and then carefully pour boiling water into the pan to come halfway up the sides of the baking dish filled with custard.

- Bake the custard until it is firm on the edges but still slightly loose in the centre, approximately 40 - 50 minutes.

- Remove the custard dish from the roasting pan.

- Let it cool slightly and then place the dish in the fridge to chill and completely set (approximately 3 - 4 hours).

- Serve chilled with fresh berries. For optimal temperature and texture, take it out of the refrigerator about 10 minutes before serving.

fun fact:

Up until the 1970s, British navy officers received a daily ration of gin. Ordinary sailors received a daily shot of rum.

Made this GINspired recipe? Post your photo on Instagram and tag @the.gin.shop.ca

gINspired   185

"friends and family loved it! We like that the cake is not too sweet. It contrasts nicely with the sauce and whipped cream, both of which are crucial."

Susan Sirovyak, test cook

gingerbread Cake

Serves: 9
Total Time: 1 ½ hours

GINSPIRATIONS

- Warm gingerbread cake reminds Heather of crisp autumn days, cozy sweaters, and sitting at her grandmother's table.

- This cake is rich, moist, and especially delicious when served warm with the **Caramel Gin Sauce** (p. 215). We have a feeling it will soon be your traditional autumn favourite too.

- You can use a hand mixer to mix most of the GINgredients, but we highly recommend using a wooden spoon to stir in the boiling water. Otherwise, it can fly around and you don't want boiling water flying around. It's important that the water is boiling. Trust us on this.

- We used **Whitley Neill Rhubarb and Ginger Gin** in our cake. It really adds a ginger punch. Pair it with a **Pump Up the Jam** (p. 230) to create your own autumn memories.

GINGREDIENTS

2 cups of all-purpose flour

1 teaspoon of baking powder

¾ teaspoon of baking soda

½ teaspoon of salt

1 teaspoon of ground ginger

½ teaspoon of ground cinnamon

¼ teaspoon of grated or ground nutmeg

½ cup of butter, softened

⅔ cup of brown sugar, lightly packed

½ cup of molasses

1 large egg, beaten

¼ cup of **Whitley Neill Rhubarb and Ginger Gin**

⅔ cup of boiling water

Optional garnishes: **Caramel Gin Sauce** (p. 215) and/or whipped cream

GINSTRUCTIONS

- Grease and flour an 8 x 8-inch square pan. Preheat the oven to 350°F.

- In a medium-sized mixing bowl, stir together the flour, baking powder, soda, salt, ginger, cinnamon, and nutmeg. Set aside.

- In a separate large mixing bowl, add the butter and use a hand or electric mixer to beat it until it's light and fluffy. Gradually add the brown sugar and beat thoroughly until creamy and well combined. Stir in the molasses.

- Add the beaten egg into the creamed mixture and blend it well. Stir in the **Whitley Neill Rhubarb and Ginger Gin**.

- Add the flour mixture (dry ingredients) to the creamed mixture a third at a time, mixing well after each addition.

- Gradually and gently add the boiling water, stirring with a wooden spoon until well incorporated.

- Spoon the batter into the prepared pan. Bake for about 50 minutes, or until a skewer or toothpick inserted into the centre comes out clean. Let cool for 10 minutes.

- Serve warm with **Caramel Gin Sauce** (p. 215) and freshly whipped cream.

Gin, Lemon, & Coconut Cake

Serves: 10 to 12

Total Time: 1 ½ hours, plus cooling time

GINSPIRATIONS

🍸 This gin-soaked cake is summer in a slice. It needs a little more attention, but is so worth the effort, especially if you're celebrating a special occasion.

🍸 The gin syrup keeps it super moist and hydrated (of course!) and adds to the yum factor. You can make the cakes the day before and assemble it all closer to when you wish to serve it.

🍸 We used Tinkerman's Citrus Supreme Gin because of its citrus notes and hints of vanilla. Grab a slice of this spectacularly moist and luscious cake and pair it with a **Rangpur Citrus Spritz** (p. 224).

GINGREDIENTS

Cake

½ cup of butter, softened

½ cup of heavy whipping cream

½ cup of coconut milk

2 cups of all-purpose flour

2 ½ teaspoons of baking powder

¼ teaspoon of salt

4 large eggs, room temperature

1 ¼ cups of white granulated sugar

1 tablespoon of gin

Zest of 1 lemon

¾ cup of desiccated coconut

Gin Syrup

½ cup of white granulated sugar

4 tablespoons of fresh-squeezed lemon juice

¼ cup of gin

Topping

1 cup of heavy whipping cream

2 tablespoons of powdered icing sugar

1 teaspoon of gin

1 cup of lemon curd

Lemon zest

Toasted coconut

GINSTRUCTIONS

- Preheat the oven to 350ºF. Grease and line 2 - 9-inch round baking pans with parchment paper. Grease the parchment paper too.

- In a small saucepan, heat the butter, cream, and coconut milk. Once the butter is melted, set the pot aside to cool slightly.

- In a small bowl, stir together the flour, baking powder, and salt.

- In a large mixing bowl, place the eggs, sugar, gin, and lemon zest. Using an electric mixer, beat until the eggs are frothy and pale. Gradually stir in the flour mixture. Stir in the desiccated coconut.

- Slowly pour the warm milk and butter mixture into the batter and beat slowly until just combined.

- Divide the batter between the baking pans and bake for 22 - 24 minutes or until a skewer or toothpick inserted into the centre comes out clean. Cool the cake in the pans on a wire rack.

Gin Syrup

- In a small saucepan, bring the sugar and lemon juice to a boil. Boil it hard for 5 minutes. Remove the pan from the heat and stir in the gin.

Topping

- In a separate bowl, use an electric mixer to beat the heavy whipping cream until soft peaks form. Add the powdered icing sugar and 1 teaspoon of gin. Continue to beat until the cream is stiff (when the peak is held vertically and the cream holds its shape). Be careful not to overbeat it and turn it into butter.

Assemble

- Remove each cooled cake layer from the pan. Place 1 cake layer on a serving plate.

- Poke holes into the cake using a wooden skewer. Brush the cake layer generously with gin syrup. Spread ½ cup of lemon curd on top.

- Gently place the second cake on top. Poke holes into the cake using a wooden skewer. Brush the cake layer generously with the remaining gin syrup.

- Decorate the sides and top of the cake with whipped cream, drizzle with the remaining lemon curd, and garnish with the lemon zest and toasted coconut. Keep in the fridge until ready to serve.

fun fact:

Besides enjoying a good gimlet, the British navy is said to have used gunpowder to ensure the gin they were receiving was high quality. The gin would be poured onto gunpowder, and the strength confirmed by seeing how well it lit, hence the term 'navy strength.'

Lemon Raspberry Gin Trifle

Serves: 12 to 14

Total Time: 2 hours, plus chilling time

GINGREDIENTS

Raspberry Compote

(or use 1 jar of **Raspberry Gin Jam** (p. 68)

1 ½ cups of fresh raspberries

2 tablespoons of powdered icing sugar

2 tablespoons of gin

Custard

1 small box of instant vanilla pudding mix (3.9 oz)

1 cup of 2% milk

1 ½ cups of heavy whipping cream, cold

2 tablespoons of gin

Trifle

⅔ cup of good quality lemon curd

¼ cup + 2 tablespoons of gin

1 package of lemon swiss rolls

1 package of raspberry swiss rolls

Topping

1 cup of heavy whipping cream

2 tablespoons of powdered icing sugar

1 tablespoon of lemon zest (plus extra for garnish)

2 tablespoons of gin

Optional garnishes: ¼ cup of crushed pistachios, fresh raspberries

GINSPIRATIONS

🍸 Trifle has to be one of the yummiest desserts out there and easy to boot! You basically layer a bunch of things in a big bowl and somehow it turns into this amazing dessert.

🍸 Preparation is key to making this dessert super fast to throw together. Make your compote and custard first. If you happen to have some **Raspberry Gin Jam** (p. 68) on hand, that works wonderfully too.

🍸 The biggest challenge will be finding the lemon and raspberry swiss rolls. We know many grocery store bakery departments sell them as well as specialty bakeries. If you live in Canada and want to splurge a bit, go to M&M Market and get yourself a Too Tall Lemon Cream Cake and a Too Tall Raspberry White Chocolate cake. You'll need half of each cake but woohoo do they taste amazing in this recipe. These are decadent layered sponge cakes that slice up beautifully and are easy to arrange in the trifle.

🍸 You can also change up the swiss roll flavour. Try a chocolate swiss roll with the raspberry...divine! There is gin in every delicious layer of this dessert. We used Glendalough Wild Botanical Gin because of its combination of elderflower, bilberry, rose, lemon, and Heather. Pair this light and fruity summery dessert with a **White Lady** (p. 236).

GINSTRUCTIONS

- Make the raspberry compote (or use 1 jar of **Raspberry Gin Jam (p. 68)** and skip this step).
- Put half the raspberries into a small saucepan with the powdered icing sugar. Mash the raspberries to release the juice. Turn on the heat to medium-high and bring the raspberries to a boil. Turn the heat down to a simmer and cook until the fruit is breaking down and the juices thicken slightly, about 4 - 5 minutes. Remove from the heat and set aside to cool for 10 minutes. Once slightly cool, gently stir in the remaining raspberries and the gin. Put in the fridge to chill completely.

Custard

- In a small bowl, whisk together the instant vanilla pudding mix and 1 cup of milk until smooth. In a large bowl of a stand mixer, add the 1 ½ cups of whipping cream. Whip on high until firm peaks form.
- Remove the bowl from the mixer. Fold in the pudding mix and 2 tablespoons of gin until well incorporated. Set aside.
- In a small bowl, mix the lemon curd with 2 tablespoons of gin.

Trifle

- Slice the swiss rolls into ⅔-inch slices and arrange around the sides of a large glass trifle bowl, alternating lemon and raspberry rolls. Break up remaining slices and roughly fill the bottom of the bowl. You should have the cake covering the sides and bottom of your dish completely. Drizzle ¼ cup of gin over the cake and leave to soak for a few minutes.
- Spoon half the curd mixture in random blobs over the cake layer. Spoon half the cooled raspberry compote (or gin jam) over the top. Add another layer of swiss rolls. Dot the rest of the curd over it randomly along with the remaining raspberry compote.
- Pour the custard over everything, then chill, uncovered, for at least 30 minutes to firm up.

Topping

- In the large bowl of a stand mixer, add 1 cup of cold heavy whipping cream. Whip on high until firm peaks form. Add the powdered icing sugar, lemon zest, and gin. Whip on high until stiff peaks form.
- Spread the whipped cream on top of the custard layer. Decorate the trifle with fresh raspberries, lemon zest, and crushed pistachios and drizzle with a touch of lemon curd if you have any remaining. Chill well in the fridge. Keep leftovers in the fridge.

fun fact:

If you're watching your waistline but don't want to give up the cock- tails, try a gin and tonic or soda. Amongst the lowest cocktail in calories, a gin and soda comes in only at around 100 calories, which means you can eat more cake.

Apple Pie à la Gin

Serves: 6

Total Time:
1 ¼ hours

GINSPIRATIONS

- How do you like them apples? As a mom, Heather can confirm this is Mom's apple pie (for moms that like their gin and apples!)

- What we love about this pie is that you can make it as-is for a yummy apple pie OR change it up to truly take it up a notch and make it your own.

- Add a cup of blueberries into the filling if you want apple blueberry pie. Use our **Gin Pie Pastry Dough** (p. 196). Use a streusel topping instead of a top pastry crust (our personal favourite). Or, forget the pastry and turn it into an apple crisp.

- If you are using the streusel topping, drizzle some of our **Caramel Gin Sauce** (p. 215) over the top to create a to-die-for caramel apple pie or crisp.

- Change the gin for a totally different flavour. We like to use a spiced gin such as Darnley's Spiced Gin. Serve your pie with GINfused vanilla ice cream or whipped cream and extra **Caramel Gin Sauce** (p. 215). Pair it with **Earl Grey Mar-Tea-Ni** (p. 227) and you will win the award for best apple pie ever.

GINGREDIENTS

Crust

Pastry for 2-crust pie OR 1 bottom crust and streusel topping

Filling

6 cups of apples, peeled, cored, and thinly sliced
½ cup of brown sugar, firmly packed
2 tablespoons of cornstarch
1 teaspoon of ground cinnamon
¼ teaspoon of salt
⅛ teaspoon of ground nutmeg
1 tablespoon of lemon juice
¼ cup of gin

Streusel Topping *(optional)*

½ cup of all-purpose flour
½ cup of oats
½ cup of brown sugar, firmly packed
½ teaspoon of cinnamon
⅛ teaspoon of nutmeg
⅓ cup of butter, softened

Optional Garnish: Caramel Gin Sauce (p. 215)

GINSTRUCTIONS

- Prepare the bottom crust in a 9-inch pie pan. Preheat the oven to 425°F.

- In a large bowl, combine all filling ingredients. Gently toss together until the apples are well coated. Spoon the filling into the pastry-lined pie pan. Top with remaining pastry or streusel topping.

- If using pastry, fold the edge of the top pastry under the bottom pastry. Press together to seal and flute the edge. Cut slits into the top of the pie.

- **Alternatively, use a streusel topping instead of a top pastry crust.** Simply combine ½ cup of flour, ½ cup of oats, ½ cup of firmly packed brown sugar, ½ teaspoon of cinnamon, a dash of nutmeg, and ⅓ cup of softened butter until crumbly. Sprinkle over the filling and then bake.

- Bake at 425°F for 40 - 45 minutes or until the apples are tender and the crust is golden brown.

- Cool slightly and then drizzle **Caramel Gin Sauce** (p. 215) over the top if desired and serve with ice cream or whipped cream.

Gin. Because everyone needs a hobby.

Key Lime Pie with a Twist

Serves: 6
Total Time: 1 ½ hours, plus chilling time

GINSPIRATIONS

🍸 Ahhhhh Key Lime Pie, a citrusy, sweet-tart, creamy pie with the perfect sweet-to-pucker ratio. It's light and bright with a crisp, not-too-sweet graham cracker crust. Add a twist of gin and you have a pie made in heaven.

🍸 Key limes differ from the more commonly available Persian limes (aka regular large limes found in the grocery store) in that they are smaller, have more seeds, have a thinner rind, produce more juice, and have a tart, acidic flavour. If you can't find them, you can easily substitute juice from Persian limes in this recipe. Just be sure to avoid bottled lime juice - it just isn't the same as fresh-squeezed, so only use it in a pinch.

🍸 If you want a stronger lime flavour, add more juice and another tablespoon of zest.

🍸 The sour cream in the recipe really adds a creamy texture you'll love. You can substitute full-fat Greek yogurt if you wish. DO NOT use low-fat or fat-free sour cream or condensed milk. It won't work. Trust us on this. You need the full fat to thicken your filling.

🍸 Allow your pie to set and rest at least 3 hours in the fridge before garnishing. It will taste much better if you do.

🍸 We used a lime gin for the recipe **Tanqueray Rangpur**. Pair your pie with a **Rangpur Citrus Spritz** (p. 224) for a delightful dessert treat.

GINGREDIENTS

Graham Cracker Crust

6 tablespoons of butter, melted
1 ½ cups of graham cracker crumbs
¼ cup of white granulated sugar

Key Lime Filling

1 tablespoon of lime zest (about 2 - 3 key limes or
    1 large regular lime)
¾ cup of fresh-squeezed key lime juice
    (about 24 - 25 key limes, or 3 - 6 regular limes)
1 - 14 oz can of sweetened condensed milk
½ cup of sour cream
¼ cup of gin
3 egg yolks

Whipped Cream Topping

1 cup of heavy whipping cream, very cold
1 tablespoon of gin
3 to 4 tablespoons of powdered icing sugar

Optional Garnishes

Lime slices
Lime zest

fun fact:

Juniper is a tough shrub that grows in many different parts of the world from North America and throughout most of Northern Europe and Asia. It can grow at varying elevations and is evergreen, so it's possible to obtain juniper berries throughout the year.

GINSTRUCTIONS

Graham Cracker Crust

- Preheat the oven to 350°F.

- Melt the butter in a small dish in the microwave and set aside. Add the graham cracker crumbs and sugar to a small mixing bowl and stir to combine. Pour in the melted butter and stir with a fork until mixed.

- Pour crust mixture into a 9-inch deep-dish pie plate. Use your fingers to press the crumbs evenly across the bottom and up the sides of the pie plate.

- Bake for 6 - 8 minutes, just until golden, but not browned. Remove from the oven and cool completely on a wire rack.

Key Lime Filling

- Preheat the oven to 350°F.

- Wash, dry, and zest the limes. Set zest aside until ready to use. Squeeze ¾ of a cup of lime juice (about 24 key limes or 6 Persian limes).

- Add the lime juice, sweetened condensed milk, sour cream, gin, egg yolks, and lime zest into the bowl of a stand mixer. Mix on low until combined, then increase the speed to medium-high for 2 - 3 minutes. Scrape down sides once or twice.

- Continue whipping until the batter is thickened. It should be a pale yellowish-green and creamy. It could take 5 minutes or slightly more. *DO NOT SKIP THIS LONGER WHIPPING STAGE*.

- Pour the filling into the cooled graham cracker crust. Make sure your crust is totally cooled before adding the filling. Place it in the fridge or freezer for a few minutes if needed to get it totally cool.

- Bake for 20 - 25 minutes or just until the centre is set but still jiggles slightly when shaken. *Do not allow the edges to brown!*

- Remove the pie from the oven to a cooling rack and cool for 30 minutes. Place the pie in the fridge for at least 3 hours before garnishing. If you remove it sooner, it will not be quite as set as if you had let it sit longer in the fridge, however, it will still taste good.

Whipped Cream and Garnish

- Once your pie has rested in the fridge for at least 3 hours, make the whipped cream.

- Pour the cold heavy whipping cream into a cold mixing bowl and whip at high speed until stiff peaks form.

- Add the gin and powdered icing sugar, mixing on low speed until combined, and then increase the speed to medium-high and whip it until very thick, almost to a light butter stage.

- Either pipe the ginny whipped cream in rosettes onto your pie or just spread evenly across the entire pie. Garnish with lime slices and zest.

gin Pie Pastry Dough

Makes:
one 9-inch pie crust

Total Time: 2 hours,
plus extra chilling time

GINGREDIENTS

6 tablespoons of unsalted butter

¼ cup of lard or vegetable shortening

2 tablespoons of ice-cold gin

1 ¼ cups of all-purpose flour, divided (¾ cup and ½ cup)

1 tablespoon of white granulated sugar

½ teaspoon of salt

2 tablespoons of ice water

GINSPIRATIONS

- Heather totally admits that she's never been very good at making pie pastry. She'd either get her mother to make it or just buy a crust already made. Until she discovered she could put gin in her pastry!!! And what a game-changer that was.

- The gin is THE secret to a no-fail, flaky pie crust every time. Every pie crust needs moisture. Not enough moisture and the dry ingredients can't come together. Too much moisture and you have a pie crust that doesn't flake.

- The gin works to pull the ingredients together, but then because the alcohol content evaporates in the oven, it leaves you with the flakiest pie crust ever!

- The combination of butter and lard is important too. The butter adds flavour and the lard adds stability. If you use all butter, your crust will not set correctly.

- Be sure to chill your dough at least an hour before you roll it out, overnight is great too (no more than 2 days). If you want to freeze your dough, triple wrap it with plastic wrap and store it in the freezer for up to 1 month. When ready to use, let it defrost in the fridge for 24 hours.

- Double the recipe if you need 2 crusts. We used Blue Sapphire Gin. Try changing the gin up for a different pastry flavour every time.

GINSTRUCTIONS

- Cut the 6 tablespoons of butter into ½-inch pieces. Place the cut-up butter, as well as the lard or shortening, in a dish and then into the freezer.

- Add the gin to a small cup and place it in the freezer as well.

- Fill a measuring cup about a ½ cup full of cold water along with a few ice cubes, and put it in your refrigerator. Leave the butter, shortening, gin, and water in the freezer/refrigerator for 30 minutes.

- To the bowl of your food processor, add ¾ cup of all-purpose flour, ½ teaspoon of salt, and 1 tablespoon of white granulated sugar. Pulse until just combined.

- Add the chilled butter and lard/shortening. Pulse until it is combined and there are no streaks of flour left. Add the last ½ cup of flour.

- Pulse until it is combined, broken up, and evenly distributed around the bowl.

- Pour the mixture into a large bowl and add 2 tablespoons of ice-cold gin and 2 tablespoons of ice water. With a wooden spoon or stiff spatula work the dough into a ball. Turn the dough out, shape into a disk, wrap with plastic, and refrigerate for an hour.

- Once the dough is chilled and you're ready to roll, remove it from the refrigerator and take the plastic wrap off. On a well-floured surface, roll the dough out.

- Once the dough is rolled out, use the rolling pin to loosely roll it up and transfer it into the pie plate. Press into the pie plate, trim off the extra dough, and pinch the edges.

- Line the crust with aluminum foil and pie weights or coins and bake at 375°F for 25 minutes to prebake the crust. Alternatively, fill and bake following the instructions of the pie recipe you are using.

Made this GINspired recipe? Post your photo on Instagram and tag @the.gin.shop.ca

Scrumptious Pumpkin Pecan Cake

Serves: 6
Total Time: 1 ½ hours

GINSPIRATIONS

- This cake could just be your new autumn go-to cake. It's SUPER easy to make and oh-so-yummy. It's kind of like a cross between a pumpkin lava cake and a cobbler. With cake on the top and a ginny hot caramel sauce on the bottom, how can you go wrong?

- Make sure your baking powder is fresh and that you use it. Your cake won't work without it.

- Once you add the hot water and gin for the topping, do not stir. Just leave it. **WE REPEAT DO NOT STIR.** You'll ruin your cake if you do.

- You can add a dash of extra gin into the hot water topping if you want a stronger gin taste. The alcohol will cook off so how ginny it tastes will depend on the gin you use.

- We used a fall gin for this recipe Darnley's Spiced Gin. Pair your dessert with a **Canadian Tuxedo** (p. 226) and serve it with some vanilla ice cream for the pinnacle of pumpkin perfection.

i work so i can buy gin so i can tolerate work.

GINGREDIENTS

Cake

1 cup + 3 tablespoons of all-purpose flour

2 teaspoons of baking powder

½ teaspoon of salt

¾ cup of white granulated sugar

1 teaspoon of ground cinnamon

½ teaspoon of ground nutmeg

½ teaspoon of ground cloves

½ cup of pumpkin puree

¼ cup of milk

¼ cup of melted butter or vegetable oil

1 tablespoon of gin

Topping

½ cup of white granulated sugar

½ cup of light brown sugar

¼ cup of chopped pecans

1 ½ cups of VERY hot water

1 tablespoon of gin

GINSTRUCTIONS

- Preheat the oven to 350°F.

- In a medium bowl, stir together the flour, baking powder, salt, sugar, and spices. Set aside.

- In a smaller bowl, stir together the pumpkin, milk, melted butter, and gin until combined. Pour the wet ingredients into the dry ingredients and mix to create a thick batter.

- Pour into a small 8-inch casserole dish with high sides.

- In a separate bowl, stir the white granulated sugar, brown sugar, and pecans together to create the topping. Sprinkle evenly over the top of the batter (yes, it will seem like a lot of sugar).

- Pour the hot water over the entire thing. **DO NOT STIR - RESIST THE URGE!** Sprinkle the gin over it all. Add an additional table-spoon or more of gin if you like it more ginny.

- Place the baking dish on a baking sheet in case it bubbles over during baking. Place both in the oven and bake for 40 - 50 minutes or until the middle is set.

- Cool 5 - 10 minutes before serving. Serve warm with vanilla ice cream and a sprinkle of pecans.

Ginspired

IF ¾ OF YOUR DRINK IS THE M
MIX WITH THE BEST

FEVER-Tr

ELDERFLOWER
TONIC
WATER

MADE WITH NATURAL FLAVOURS
INCLUDING HANDPICKED ELDERFLOW

x200 ml   No artificial sweeteners

gin & Tonic Loaf

Serves: 8 to 10

Total Time: 1 ½ hours, plus cooling time

GINSPIRATIONS

🍸 You can't go wrong with a nice loaf and this one already has the gin and tonic in it. While you don't need to add the glaze, it really does make it extra yummy. You can use either lime or lemon zest, depending on what you prefer.

🍸 For gin, we used Whitley Neill Brazilian Lime Gin. You'll definitely want to use something with a little more lime or lemon or even elderflower aromatics for this recipe. Pair a slice with a **Breakfast Martini** (p. 225) and you have a wonderful mid-morning (or anytime) snack.

fun fact:

Did you know, there's a World gin Day? It's celebrated each year on the second Saturday in June!

GINGREDIENTS

Loaf

1 cup of all-purpose flour

2 teaspoons of baking powder

½ teaspoon of salt

1 cup of unsalted butter softened, plus extra to grease

1 cup of white granulated sugar

3 large eggs, beaten

Zest of 1 lime

⅓ cup of gin

Syrup

¼ cup of white granulated sugar

¼ cup of **Fever-Tree Elderflower Tonic Water**

2 tablespoons of gin

Glaze

½ cup of powdered icing sugar

2 tablespoons of gin

Lime zest

GINSTRUCTIONS

• Preheat the oven to 350°F. Grease and line a 2-lb loaf pan with parchment paper.

• In a small bowl, combine flour, baking powder, and salt. Set aside.

• In a large bowl, beat butter and sugar until light and fluffy, about 5 minutes. Gradually add eggs, beating well after each addition. Add lime zest, followed by the gin.

• Fold in dry ingredients and mix just until combined. Do not over mix. Spoon batter into the prepared loaf pan and bake for 55 - 60 minutes or until a skewer inserted into the centre comes out clean.

• Meanwhile, make your sugar syrup. Gently heat the granulated sugar and tonic water in a small pot, stirring often, until the sugar dissolves. Turn up the heat and boil for 1 minute. Remove from the heat and add 2 tablespoons of gin.

• As soon as the loaf comes out of the oven, poke holes into the top with a skewer and drizzle the gin syrup over the top. Cool the loaf in the pan on a wire rack.

• Make a glaze by mixing together powdered icing sugar with 2 tablespoons of gin.

• Remove cooled loaf from pan, transfer to a board and peel off parchment. Pour the glaze over the top. Sprinkle it with lime zest. Leave the loaf to set before serving.

Toffee Gin Banana Bread

Serves: 8 to 10

**Total Time:
1 ½ hours**

GINSPIRATIONS

This recipe was based on a super easy banana bread recipe that Heather's aunt and uncle gave her many years ago. We've updated it here to include the toffee, toffee gin, and glaze.

If you've never made toffee gin, now is the time. It can be used in so many lovely recipes, plus it makes a super yummy cocktail.

It's a great idea to keep extra powdered toffee and toffee gin on hand, so you can whip up this banana bread any time your freezer is filling up with ripe bananas.

Serve your loaf either slightly warmed or at room temperature and give it a slather of butter if you are so inclined. It stores well in the freezer, just be sure it is tightly wrapped or in an airtight container.

We used Sipsmith London Dry Gin to make our toffee gin. Pair your toffee gin banana bread with a **Rose & Gin Negroni** (p. 236).

GINGREDIENTS

Toffee Gin

1 package of hard toffee candies such as Werther's Original

1 cup of gin

Banana Bread

2 very ripe bananas, mashed

1½ teaspoons of baking soda

½ cup of white granulated sugar

¼ cup of toffee powder + extra for garnish

2 tablespoons of toffee-infused gin

1 large egg, at room temperature and lightly beaten

¼ cup of canola oil

1½ cups of all-purpose flour

Optional add-ins: ½ cup of chocolate chips or chopped nuts

Toffee Gin Glaze

2 tablespoons of toffee gin

1 tablespoon of milk

½ cup of powdered icing sugar

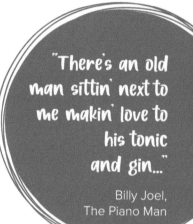

"There's an old man sittin' next to me makin' love to his tonic and gin..."

Billy Joel,
The Piano Man

GINSTRUCTIONS

- **Toffee GINfusion:** If you don't already have some on hand, make your toffee-infused gin at least 5 days beforehand. In a blender or food processor, grind the hard toffee candies into a fine powder.

- In a mason jar, add ½ cup of the toffee powder (keep the rest for the banana bread and other recipes). Pour 1 cup of gin into the jar. Seal tightly and shake vigorously to combine the gin and powder well. Store in a cool dry place for 5 days, giving it a good shake at least once a day.

- Preheat the oven to 300°F. Grease a 9 x 5-inch loaf pan.

- To make the banana bread, add the bananas to a large mixing bowl. Mash the bananas with a potato masher or fork. Sprinkle the baking soda over the mashed bananas and wait a minute or 2 for it to dissolve into the bananas.

- Add the sugar, toffee powder, toffee gin, beaten egg, and oil. Stir with a wooden spoon until well blended. Stir in the flour until just combined. Stir in any optional add-ins.

- Spoon the batter into the prepared loaf pan and bake for 45 - 55 minutes or until a skewer or toothpick inserted into the centre comes out clean. Remove the pan from the oven and let it cool on a wire rack.

- Make the glaze by placing the powdered icing sugar into a small bowl. Add the toffee gin and milk. Mix until fully combined. You may find it quite thick to start. It should be just runny enough to drip off a spoon slowly. Keep adding in a drop of gin at a time or a tablespoon of powdered icing sugar until you reach your desired consistency.

- Remove the cooled loaf from the pan and transfer it to a serving plate. Pour the glaze over the top. Sprinkle with powdered toffee or larger toffee bits, if desired. Leave the loaf to set before serving. Slice it as thick as you want and enjoy!

Made this GINspired recipe? Post your photo on Instagram and tag @the.gin.shop.ca

Dreamy Sevilla Orange Gin Cake

Serves: 10 to 12

Total Time: 2 hours, plus chilling time

GINSPIRATIONS

🍸 Remember orange dreamsicles? Well this dreamy cake tastes just like that, but with a bit of an upgrade. It's a light, flavourful, orangy cake that couldn't be more perfect for a birthday or gathering.

🍸 You can totally make the cake in a 9 x 13-inch pan if you prefer or even turn it into cupcakes.

🍸 The frosting requires that you keep this cake in the fridge so be sure to wrap any leftovers up and keep them chilled.

🍸 We used **Tanqueray Sevilla Orange Gin** in this recipe. It has a vibrant orange scent and colour and an intense citrus flavour that goes perfectly in this cake. Serve your cake with some vanilla ice cream and pair it with a **GINger Sevilla Mimosa** (p. 224).

GINGREDIENTS

Cake

2 ¾ cups of all-purpose flour

¼ cup of cornstarch

1 tablespoon of baking powder

½ teaspoon of salt

1 cup of unsalted butter, room temperature

1 ¾ cups of white granulated sugar

4 large eggs, at room temperature

1 cup of buttermilk

¼ cup of freshly squeezed orange juice

¼ cup of **Tanqueray Sevilla Orange Gin**

2 tablespoons of fresh orange zest

3 - 5 drops of orange gel food colouring (*optional*)

Orange Gin Syrup

¼ cup of white granulated sugar

¼ cup of water

2 tablespoons of **Tanqueray Sevilla Orange Gin**

Frosting

1 ½ cups of heavy whipping cream

¼ cup of **Tanqueray Sevilla Orange Gin**

¼ cup of powdered icing sugar

1 small box of instant vanilla pudding (3.9 oz)

1 cup of 2% milk

3 - 5 drops of orange gel food colouring (*optional*)

Optional Garnishes

Orange zest

Orange slices

GINSTRUCTIONS

- Preheat the oven to 350°F. Grease 2 - 9-inch round cake pans (or a 9 x 13-inch pan). Measure and cut a round of parchment paper to fit the bottom of each pan. Place the parchment paper round in the bottom of each pan and grease well.
- In a medium-sized bowl, whisk together the flour, cornstarch, baking powder, and salt and set aside.
- Add the butter to a large bowl of a stand mixer. Cream the butter. Add the sugar and mix on medium speed for 3 minutes or until light and fluffy, scraping down the sides of the machine as necessary.
- Beat in the eggs, 1 at a time, scraping down the sides of the bowl in between each addition.
- Turn the mixer to low and add the flour mixture. Just before it's completely mixed in, add the buttermilk, orange juice, **Tanqueray Sevilla Orange Gin**, and orange zest. Blend until combined, but don't overmix! Pay special attention to the bottom of the bowl.
- Divide the batter equally between the 2 prepared pans and spread out evenly.
- Bake in the centre of the oven for about 35 minutes, or until the cake springs back when touched lightly and is just beginning to pull away from the edges of the pan.
- Let the cakes cool for 10 minutes before turning out of the pans and onto a wire cooling rack. Let the layers cool completely.

Gin Syrup

- While your cakes are baking and cooling, prepare your orange gin syrup. In a small microwave-safe bowl, combine the sugar and water. Microwave on high for 1 minute; it should be boiling. Give it a stir and then boil for 1 more minute. Remove from the microwave, let cool for 5 minutes and then stir in 2 tablespoons of **Tanqueray Sevilla Orange Gin**. Set aside.

Frosting

- In a large stand mixer bowl (cold), add 1 ½ cups of heavy whipping cream. Beat on high until firm peaks form. Add in the **Tanqueray Sevilla Orange Gin** and powdered icing sugar. Whip until combined. Remove the bowl from the stand mixer.
- In a small bowl, whisk together the vanilla pudding mix and 1 cup of milk. Stir well, making sure there are no lumps.
- Gently fold the pudding mix into the whipped cream, folding until the pudding mixture is well blended with the whipped cream. Add a few drops of orange gel colouring if using. Chill your frosting in the fridge until you are ready to use it.

Assemble

- Level the tops of each cake with a knife or cake leveler. Place 1 cake on a cake stand. Poke holes in the cake with a wooden skewer. Drizzle or brush half the **Tanqueray Sevilla Orange Gin** syrup over the cake.
- Wait 1 minute to let it soak in and then spread a generous amount of frosting on top of the cake.
- Place the second cake layer on top of the first and repeat the process (i.e. poke holes, brush with the remaining ginny syrup, and then frost).
- Frost the sides and top of the cake with the remaining frosting, if desired. Decorate with orange zest and orange slices. Store the cake in the fridge.

Made this GINspired recipe? Post your photo on Instagram and tag @the.gin.shop.ca

White Chocolate Gin Fudge

Serves: 8

**Total Time:
2 ¼ hours**

GINSPIRATIONS

🍸 Fudge is great any time of year, but especially around the holidays. If you are looking for a yummy treat to eat or give, gin fudge is it.

🍸 You can totally change up the flavour by changing your add-ins and garnishes, so try different variations such as nuts, dried fruit, or citrus zest. Your add-ins shouldn't be too sweet as the fudge is very sweet to start with.

🍸 We especially love pistachios with dried raspberries and a hint of lime zest. Delish!! But make your fudge your own. Try changing up your gin as well. We used Bombay Sapphire Gin with this recipe.

GINGREDIENTS

12 oz package of Baker's White Chocolate

¾ cup (1 can) of sweetened condensed milk

1 cup of gin

Optional add-ins: zest, dried cranberries or raspberries, nuts, etc.

Optional garnishes: zest of lime, lemon, or orange, crushed nuts, dried cranberries

GINSTRUCTIONS

- Line an 8 x 8-inch pan with parchment paper or tinfoil, with ends extending over sides.

- In a large microwave-safe bowl, microwave 12 oz of white chocolate and ¾ cup of sweetened condensed milk on medium for 2 - 3 minutes or until the chocolate is almost melted. Remove from the microwave and stir until the chocolate is completely melted.

- Stir in the gin. Stir in any add-ins such as nuts, dried fruit, or zest.

- Spoon the fudge into the prepared pan. Spread it out evenly.

- Garnish as desired, pressing any zest, nuts, or dried fruit into the top of the fudge slightly.

- Place the pan in the fridge and chill for at least 2 hours or until firm.

- Remove the pan from the fridge and gently lift fudge from the pan using the parchment paper or foil 'handles'. Cut and serve. Store your fudge in the fridge.

fun fact:

Gin is truly for the refined palate. Similar to the way that truffles are collected, juniper berries must be foraged in the woods and hand-picked.

Empress Cupcakes

Serves: 24

Total Time: 1 hour, plus cooling time

GINSPIRATIONS

- Looking for a Valentine treat? Something pink or purple for your wedding shower or event? Look no further because these pretty, little delights are sure to please.
- The cupcakes themselves are fairly quick to mix up. If you aren't a fan of lemon, feel free to replace the lemon with lime or 1 ½ teaspoons of pure vanilla extra.
- We also highly recommend using raspberry liqueur in your frosting. It adds a yummy hint of raspberry.
- Be sure to use coloured gin such as **Empress 1908 Gin**. It makes all the difference. If, for some reason, you'd rather not have pink or purple cupcakes, use a clear gin instead. Serve your cupcakes with a **Club Quarantine** (p. 228) cocktail for a lovely dessert your guests will adore.

GINGREDIENTS

Cupcakes

2 cups of cake flour

2 teaspoons of baking powder

¾ teaspoon of Kosher salt

1 ½ cups of white granulated sugar

¾ cup of unsalted butter, room temperature

3 large egg whites, room temperature

1 large egg, room temperature

Juice and zest of 1 small lemon (about 2 tablespoons of juice and 2 teaspoons of zest)

1 cup of **Empress 1908 Gin**

2 tablespoons of sour cream

Few drops of pink or purple food colouring

Frosting

1 cup of butter, softened and at room temperature

4 - 5 cups of powdered icing sugar

¼ cup of **Empress 1908 Gin**

Few drops of raspberry liqueur or pink or purple food colouring

Optional garnishes: fresh raspberries

fun fact:

After Sir Francis Chichester became the first man to successfully circumnavigate the world solo in a sailboat, he credited his success to a daily glass of pink gin, and said the saddest day was when the gin ran out.

GINSTRUCTIONS

- Preheat the oven to 350°F. Line 2 - 12 cupcake baking pans with cupcake liners.

- In a large bowl, whisk together the flour, baking powder, and salt. Set aside.

- In another large bowl, add the sugar and butter and beat with an electric mixer until light and fluffy.

- Add the egg whites, 1 at a time, fully incorporating after each addition. Add the egg and lemon juice and zest, mix to combine.

- Alternate adding the flour mixture and gin, starting and ending with the flour. Stir in the sour cream until well combined. Add 1 - 2 drops of pink or purple food colouring if you want a pink or purple cupcake.

- Fill each cupcake liner halfway with batter. Smooth the tops with a spatula. Bake for 20 - 25 minutes, or until a toothpick inserted into the centre comes out clean. Transfer to a wire rack to cool for 10 minutes, then remove the cupcakes from the pans and transfer onto the rack to cool completely.

- While your cupcakes are cooling, make your frosting. Ensure your butter is at room temperature. Place the butter in a large mixing bowl and beat it for a few minutes to loosen it and make it supple. Add in 4 cups of powdered icing sugar and beat again until your frosting is smooth.

- Carefully add in the **Empress 1908 Gin** 1 spoonful at a time, beating each time, until combined. Add in a few drops of raspberry liqueur or pink food colouring for an added pink boost. Taste your frosting and add additional powdered icing sugar or gin until it reaches the desired consistency.

- Pipe or spread the frosting on each cooled cupcake and top with a fresh raspberry. Store cupcakes in a sealed container at room temperature for 2 - 3 days. Or freeze unfrosted cupcakes 1 month.

gin Caramel Peanut Butter Cups

> **Serves: 12**
>
> **Total Time: 30 minutes, plus chilling time**

GINSPIRATIONS

Peanut butter cups are a fav in Heather's house. Every holiday it seems to be the candy of choice for her boys. Once everyone was old enough, she decided to give the candy a bit of a twist, so of course, she added gin. But not just any gin... **Caramel Gin Sauce** (p. 215). So now you have ALL the best in the candy world - chocolate, peanut butter, caramel, AND gin. What's not to love??!

You will adore these perfect DIY candies. They are quick to make and keep in the freezer. Make them for your family or give them as gifts.

The trickiest part is getting the melted chocolate on the bottom and sides well covered. Once you have that, you are in the home stretch. We use a small pastry brush to help ensure good coverage. You can also swap out the peanut butter for almond butter if you prefer.

For gin, we used Monkey 47. Pair your candy with a Chocolate Martini for a sweet, rich, chocolatey, ooey-gooey treat.

> i rescued some gin. it was trapped in a bottle. i saved the day.

GINGREDIENTS

1 ½ cups of semisweet or dark chocolate chips

⅓ cup of smooth or crunchy peanut butter (almond butter works too)

1 tablespoon of gin

4 tablespoons of powdered icing sugar

½ cup of **Caramel Gin Sauce** (p. 215)

Optional garnish: flaky sea salt

GINSTRUCTIONS

- Line a mini muffin tin with 12 mini paper liners. If you don't have mini paper liners, use regular size ones in a regular- sized muffin tin instead; it should make half as many.

- Place the chocolate in a microwave-safe dish. Melt the chocolate in the microwave in 30-second increments. Alternatively, melt over a double boiler.

- Once your chocolate is melted, spoon about 1 heaping teaspoon of chocolate into each liner and use a small brush or back of a spoon to swirl the chocolate around and coat the bottoms and almost all the way up the sides. You want to make sure your fillings are fully contained, so be sure it's well coated.

- Next, mix together the peanut butter, gin, and powdered icing sugar, adding enough sugar and stirring until you have a dough that's almost workable with your hands.

- Spoon out 2 teaspoons of the peanut butter mixture and add it into each of the liners, nestling it in the chocolate-lined paper liner. Tap it down with your finger to smooth out any lumps.

- Top the peanut butter with about 1 teaspoon of the **Caramel Gin Sauce** (p. 215) - enough to seep into the cracks and just barely cover the peanut butter. Don't overfill unless you want messy cups.

- Lastly, top the caramel with the remaining melted chocolate and use a brush or spoon to smooth and seal the edges. Sprinkle with a touch of sea salt flakes (optional) and set in the fridge or freezer to set.

- You can store these chocolates in the fridge or in the freezer, though we prefer the freezer because it keeps the caramel set and they're a little easier to eat that way.

Ginny Snack'n Cake

Serves: 9

Total Time: 1 hour

GINSPIRATIONS

🍸 Heather's not sure if a snack'n cake is a Canadian thing or not, but she's had them her entire life. When she was a child, a snack'n cake meant whipping up a boxed cake mix, pouring it in a baking pan, baking it, and then topping it with a can of frosting. Then she'd SNACK on it after school or for a weeknight dessert.

🍸 There are 3 must-haves (and have-nots!) to call a cake a snack'n cake: 1. You don't need an electric beater to mix it up; 2. It is generally made in an 8 x 8-inch pan (so small); and 3. It is FAST to put together.

🍸 This recipe is SO versatile you can make it ANY flavour you want - no need for a box mix. It stirs together in moments, and you can customize it however you like. You can double the recipe if you want to make it 9 x 13-inch. Or, it also makes 10 - 12 cupcakes.

🍸 For gin, use a gin that complements the flavour of the cake you are making. For example, we used **Whitley Neill Pink Grapefruit Gin** for our citrus version of the cake or you could use **Whitley Neill Rhubarb and Ginger Gin** if you are making a chocolate cake. You can also change up your tonic water; we especially love **Fever-Tree Elderflower Tonic Water**. Pair your cake with a **Gin Hard Seltzer** (p. 229) and you have a perfectly delicious sweet snack or anytime treat.

GINGREDIENTS

Cake

1 ½ cups of all-purpose flour

1 cup of white granulated sugar

2 teaspoons of baking powder

⅛ teaspoon of salt

2 large eggs, room temperature

½ cup of 2% milk

¼ cup of **Whitley Neill Pink Grapefruit Gin**

¼ cup of sour cream

3 tablespoons of vegetable oil

Other flavouring as desired *(see below)*

Optional Cake Flavour Add-Ins

Vanilla: Add a teaspoon of pure vanilla or the inside of 1 vanilla bean into the wet ingredients. Try using a vanilla gin too.

Lemon, Lime, or Orange: Add 2 teaspoons of zest and 1 tablespoon of fresh juice (lemon, lime, or orange) to the wet ingredients. Try using a matching citrus gin too.

Chocolate: Add ¼ cup of cocoa powder to the dry ingredients. Then, once your batter is all mixed together, stir in ½ cup of chocolate chips before pouring it into your pan.

Berry: Once your batter is in the pan, spoon jam of any flavour in a few big dollops on top. Then, gently run a knife through the jam and batter to swirl it together. You can also sprinkle a few berries on top of the batter if you like (blueberries and raspberries work best).

Optional Toppings

Gin Glaze

    ½ cup of powdered icing sugar

    2 tablespoons of **Whitley Neill Pink Grapefruit Gin**

    1 tablespoon of 2% milk

Gin Buttercream Frosting

    1 cup of butter, softened, at room temperature

    4 - 5 cups of powdered icing sugar

    ¼ cup of **Whitley Neill Pink Grapefruit Gin**

Powdered icing sugar

Lemon or lime curd and whipped cream

Fresh berries

Chocolate chips

Sprinkles

Syrup

¼ cup of white granulated sugar

¼ cup of any flavour of **Fever-Tree Tonic Water**

2 tablespoons of **Whitley Neill Pink Grapefruit Gin**

Made this GINspired recipe? Post your photo on Instagram and tag @the.gin.shop.ca

fun fact:

Juniper berries are loaded with antioxidants. The bitter seed is effective in fighting infection, aiding digestion, and relieving bloating. A glass of gin might be just what the doctor ordered!

WHITLEY NEILL

HANDCRAFTED GIN

PINK GRAPEFRUIT FLAVOURED GIN
GIN AUX ARÔMES NATURELS DE PAMPLEMOUSSE ROSES

INSPIRED by the CITRUS GROVES of SPAIN, this gin is infused with zesty PINK GRAPEFRUIT. On the palate, sweet citrusy notes give way to a balanced grapefruit burst.

JOHNNY NEILL

43% alc./vol.   IMPORTED·IMPORTÉ   750 mℓ

GINSTRUCTIONS

- Preheat the oven to 350°F. Grease an 8 x 8-inch baking pan.

- In a large mixing bowl, whisk together the flour, sugar, baking powder, and salt.

- In a separate small bowl, whisk together the eggs, milk, **Whitley Neill Pink Grapefruit Gin**, sour cream, oil, and any liquid flavour add-ins (such as vanilla or citrus juice).

- Pour the wet GINgredients into the dry and stir until just combined, ensuring that all the flour is incorporated and no dry spots remain. Be careful not to overmix.

- Pour the cake batter into the greased baking pan. Bake the cake until the centre is firm and the cake is golden on top, about 30 - 35 minutes. Remove from the oven and let it cool in the baking pan on a wire rack.

- Meanwhile, make your gin syrup and the topping of your choice.

- To make your gin syrup, gently heat the granulated sugar and **Fever-Tree Tonic Water** in a small pot, stirring often, until the sugar dissolves. Turn up the heat and boil for 1 minute. Remove from the heat and add 2 tablespoons of **Whitley Neill Pink Grapefruit Gin**.

- Once the cake is cool, poke holes into the top with a skewer and drizzle the gin syrup over the top. Let it soak in a minute before serving as it is, or adding frosting or a glaze.

Glaze

- Place the powdered icing sugar into a small bowl. Add the **Whitley Neill Pink Grapefruit Gin** and milk. Mix until fully combined. You may find it quite thick to start. It should be just runny enough to drip off a spoon slowly. Keep adding in a drop of gin at a time or a tablespoon of powdered icing sugar until you reach your desired consistency. Pour the glaze over the top of the cooled cake. Let it set for a few minutes before serving.

Gin Buttercream

- Make sure your butter is at room temperature. Place the butter in a large mixing bowl and beat it for a few minutes to really loosen it and make it supple. Add in 4 cups of powdered icing sugar and beat again until your frosting is smooth.

- Carefully add in the **Whitley Neill Pink Grapefruit Gin** 1 spoonful at a time, beating each time, until combined. Taste your frosting and add more powdered icing sugar or gin until it reaches the desired consistency. Note: to make it chocolate, add ¼ cup of cocoa powder along with the powdered icing sugar. This recipe makes more than you'll need for this cake so save the remaining for something else (you can easily freeze it).

- Frost the cooled cake and decorate it with chocolate chips, sprinkles, or berries.

Boozy Chocolate Sauce

Makes: 4 cups of sauce

**Total Time:
45 minutes**

GINSPIRATIONS

🍸 If you want to relive those days of an epic hot fudge sundae, then this is the sauce for you. Yes, there are faster chocolate sauce recipes out there. And yes, you could go out and just buy chocolate syrup, but if you're looking for good, old-fashioned hot fudge sauce, look no further. It gets thick when cold, so you'll have to heat it up to pour it.

🍸 Caramelizing the sugar and dairy is important to the flavour and texture of the sauce, so don't skip this step. Cook it until it is a deep tan colour.

🍸 You can also totally make this sauce your own. Add some orange zest, cinnamon, or a few drops of mint extract. Or, add some cinnamon plus a pinch of cayenne or ground chipotle to make an amazing Mexican-style fudge sauce.

🍸 The recipe does make a lot, so half the recipe if you like or give some to a friend.

🍸 We used Black Fox Oaked Gin for our sauce. You want one with some depth of flavour (aged gin works really well). Make your best banana split sundae and pair it with a **Gin Old Fashioned** (p. 233) for a new and improved old-fashioned soda fountain experience.

GINGREDIENTS

½ cup of unsalted butter

1 cup of white granulated sugar

1 cup of light corn syrup

2 cups of heavy whipping cream

¾ teaspoon of Kosher salt

⅔ cup of 10% cream (light cream or whole milk)

¼ cup of cocoa powder

2 tablespoons + 1 teaspoon of water

¼ cup of gin

1 teaspoon of vanilla extract

8 oz of excellent quality semi-sweet chocolate, chopped

GINSTRUCTIONS

- Place the butter, sugar, corn syrup, heavy whipping cream, salt, and light cream in a large, heavy-bottomed saucepan. Heat the pan over medium heat until it comes to a boil, stirring frequently.

- While the cream mixture is cooking, in a large bowl, whisk together the cocoa powder, water, gin, and vanilla into a thin paste.

- Chop the chocolate into small pieces and add to the chocolate paste.

- When the cream mixture comes to a boil, lower the heat so that it maintains a slow simmer but doesn't boil up in the pan. Stir frequently and boil it until it reaches a light caramel colour, about 20 - 30 minutes (less time if you half the recipe).

- Once the cream mixture is a lovely shade of deep tan, pour it into the bowl with the chopped chocolate and cocoa paste. Allow it to sit for a minute or 2 and then whisk until smooth. If you see any lumps, strain it just to make sure it is completely smooth.

- Let cool slightly and then pour into jars. Store your sauce in the fridge for up to 2 weeks if you used very fresh dairy (less if you didn't).

- Once cooled, the sauce will be very thick. Scoop some sauce into a microwave-safe dish and warm it up slightly to be able to pour it.

- Use on ice cream, brownies, hot or cold chocolate, cheesecake topping, or any dessert that calls for chocolate sauce.

Caramel Gin Sauce

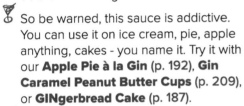

Makes: 3 cups of sauce

**Total Time: 15 minutes,
plus cooling time**

GINSPIRATIONS

Heather is a big caramel sauce fan. She could literally drink this sauce - it's so good. It always reminds her of a Happy Days episode (yes, she's that old) where Mrs. Cunningham is making a bourbon caramel sauce and keeps taste testing it until she is very tipsy and the sauce is pretty much all gone. You could totally do that with this gin caramel sauce.

So be warned, this sauce is addictive. You can use it on ice cream, pie, apple anything, cakes - you name it. Try it with our **Apple Pie à la Gin** (p. 192), **Gin Caramel Peanut Butter Cups** (p. 209), or **GINgerbread Cake** (p. 187).

If you want a salted caramel sauce, stir in a dash of sea salt flakes at the end. We highly recommend using a toffee GINfusion. We used Beefeater Gin and made it into toffee-infused gin.

GINGREDIENTS

2 cups of brown sugar, firmly packed

1 cup of salted butter

¾ cup of heavy whipping cream

¾ cup of gin (preferably an infused gin such as toffee gin)

1 teaspoon of vanilla extract

Dash of sea salt (*optional* if you want more of a salted caramel flavour)

GINSTRUCTIONS

- In a medium saucepan, combine the brown sugar and butter. Bring to a boil over medium heat.

- Reduce the heat, stir in the cream and gin, and simmer for 4 minutes.

- Remove from heat and stir in the vanilla. Stir in a dash of sea salt if you want a salted caramel sauce, and an extra dash of gin if you want a more boozy sauce.

- Let cool. Pour into a sealable jar (such as a mason jar).

- Store, covered, in the fridge for up to 2 weeks or freeze for up to 3 months.

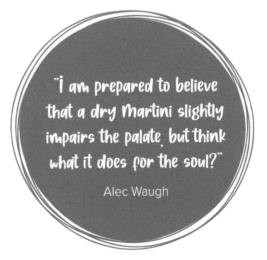

"I am prepared to believe that a dry Martini slightly impairs the palate, but think what it does for the soul?"

Alec Waugh

G&T Ice Cream

Serves: 4 to 6

Total Time: 15 minutes, plus freezing time

GINGREDIENTS

1 cup of white granulated sugar

2 tablespoons of freshly squeezed lemon juice

3 tablespoons of gin

½ cup of **Fever-Tree Tonic Water** (any flavour)

2 ½ cups of heavy whipping cream

GINSPIRATIONS

Heather had her first gin and tonic ice cream in Ireland. Before that, she had no idea it even existed. When she got home, she dusted off her ice cream maker, determined to recreate this creamy treat.

Here you have a light and citrusy ice cream with a very definite hit of gin. It's very simple to make. The hardest part is waiting for it to freeze.

We highly suggest using a high quality tonic brand such as **Fever-Tree**.

We used Warner Edwards Elderflower Gin because it is like summer in a glass, but remember - change the gin, change the flavour. Scoop this boozy ice cream onto your cone for a cool and tasty summer delight.

GINSTRUCTIONS

- In a large mixing bowl, add the sugar, lemon juice, gin, and tonic water and whisk together until the sugar is dissolved.

- Pour in the cream.

- Whisk the cream until it maintains the texture of a thick milkshake – be careful not to overwhip it!

- Transfer the ingredients to a freezer-proof container, (or use an actual ice cream container if you have one) and allow to freeze. Or, transfer to your ice cream maker and process according to the manufacturer's instructions.

- Wait until frozen (times may vary depending on your freezer, but wait at least a few hours) before serving.

I have fantastic gintuition.

FEVER-TREE
MEDITERRANEAN
TONIC WATER
EAU TONIQUE
MÉDITERRANÉENNE
200 ml

Boozy Chocolate Ice Cream

Serves: 4 to 6

Total Time: 45 minutes, plus overnight chilling, plus freezing time

GINSPIRATIONS

🍸 This is hands down the best gin chocolate ice cream EVER! It's versatile enough that you can add in whatever you like for additional flavour and yet just the base is amazing on its own.

🍸 We highly recommend using an ice cream machine for this recipe, but it does work without one too.

🍸 The cinnamon is optional, but it adds a nice Mexican hot chocolate vibe which is really tasty. You can add a tiny bit more gin during churning/freezing if you want a stronger gin flavour.

🍸 Try different add-ins. Personally, we love chocolate chunks, mini peanut butter cups, or toffee bits. But our absolute favourite is adding in a swirl of **Raspberry Gin Jam** (p. 68). Soooo gooood.

🍸 For gin, we use Martin Miller's Winterful Gin, but you can definitely switch it up to try different botanical flavour profiles.

GINGREDIENTS

5 large egg yolks

¾ cup of white granulated sugar, divided into 2 x 6 tablespoons

¼ cup of Dutch-processed or natural cocoa powder

1 teaspoon of ground cinnamon *(optional)*

1 cup of 2% or whole milk, room temperature

1 ¾ cups of heavy whipping cream

¼ teaspoon of Kosher salt

1 tablespoon of gin

Optional add-ins: ½ cup of chocolate chips or chunks, nuts, mini peanut butter cups, cookie bits, toffee bits, **Raspberry Gin Jam** (p. 68), etc.

GINSTRUCTIONS

• Create your ice cream base. In a large metal bowl, prepare an ice bath by putting a little cold water with a lot of ice. Place another metal bowl in the ice bath without getting any of the cold water or ice into it. Set aside.

• In a glass or metal medium-sized bowl, whisk together the egg yolks and 6 tablespoons of sugar until just combined and set aside.

- In a heavy-bottomed pot (over no heat yet), whisk together the cocoa powder, cinnamon (if using), and the remaining 6 tablespoons of sugar.

- Slowly stream in ¼ cup of milk. You need to add the milk slowly to the cocoa powder or else the cocoa powder will clump up. Continue adding the remaining ¾ cup of milk in a slow steady stream until you get a smooth, bubbly chocolate milk mixture.

- Whisk the cream and salt into the chocolate milk mixture and heat over medium heat. Heat until the mixture just barely reaches a simmer; it should quiver and have tiny bubbles on top but not be boiling.

- Remove the pot completely off the heat.

- Scoop ¼ cup of this hot chocolate milk mixture and slowly stream it into your egg yolk mixture. This tempers the eggs, meaning it brings the eggs to the same temperature as the hot chocolate milk without cooking the eggs. It's VERY important that you stream this hot chocolate mixture in really slowly so that you don't scramble the eggs.

- Repeat this process 3 more times or until you've added 1 cup of the hot chocolate mixture to the yolks.

- Dump your new egg yolk and hot chocolate milk mixture back into the pot and return it to a low heat.

- With a heat-resistant spatula, stir continuously until the mixture significantly thickens, about 2 - 5 minutes. You'll know the mixture is thick enough because it will coat the back of the spatula and leave a line if you run your finger across it. Note that the mixture won't be incredibly thick at this point but just thick enough. It will thicken much more as it cools in the fridge.

- Once the mixture is thick, stir in the gin.

- Next, pour the mixture into the bowl sitting inside your prepared ice bath. Stir for a few minutes to cool down the custard.

- Once the ice cream base (aka custard) is cooled down, remove it from the ice bath, dry the bottom of the bowl, cover the bowl with plastic wrap, and place in the fridge overnight. The longer it sits, the better it tastes (up to 24 hours).

Make the Ice Cream with an Ice Cream Maker

- Be sure to add the section of the machine that needs freezing into the freezer the night before (if you have that with your machine). Place the ice cream base in your ice cream maker and turn it on. After 3 - 5 minutes add your optional add-ins (e.g. chocolate chips, nuts, etc) as the maker churns. You need to add your add-ins at the beginning of the churn or they won't fully incorporate. Churn until thick and ice cream-like. You can eat it out of the ice cream maker as is or put it into a container and freeze for 4 hours or until firm.

Make the Ice Cream without an Ice Cream Maker

- Add the ice cream base and any optional add-ins into a large freezer-safe container. Stir well to combine. Place in the freezer and freeze for 1 hour. Give it a good stir. Place back in the freezer and allow to freeze until firm, 6 - 8 hours. Note that your add-ins may sink to the bottom, so giving it a good stir after an hour really helps that. You can stir more often if you like.

gin is just like time. There is never enough.

GINfused Wild Blueberry Pie filling

Makes: 2 ½ cups

Total Time: 15 minutes

GINGREDIENTS

5 cups of fresh or frozen wild blueberries

½ cup of gin

½ cup of white granulated sugar

2 tablespoons of freshly squeezed lemon juice (about ½ a lemon)

5 tablespoons of cornstarch

⅛ teaspoon of salt

¼ teaspoon of cinnamon *(optional)*

1 teaspoon of lemon zest

1 teaspoon of gin *(optional)*

GINSPIRATIONS

🍸 Never buy pie filling again! Seriously, this homemade GINfused wild blueberry pie filling is super easy and beyond delicious. It can be used on ice cream, for a cheesecake topping, on pancakes or waffles and, of course, PIE! We use it in our **Blueberry & Gin Cobbler** (p. 177) and our **Drunken Blueberry Cheesecake** (p. 169) for an extra yummy kick.

🍸 We do recommend you add the cinnamon as it brings out the flavour of the blueberries nicely. We also add a teaspoon of gin at the end for an extra flavour boost, but that is totally optional.

🍸 You can freeze the filling, but make sure you thaw it in the fridge overnight and give it a good stir to get any lumps out before you use it. We don't recommend using a microwave to thaw it.

🍸 You can use any type of gin, but we suggest a gin with a lemon or more fruity flavour profile. Or try a combination! For this recipe, we used Dixon's Wicked Blueberry Gin.

GINSTRUCTIONS

- Wash the blueberries carefully. If using frozen, partially thaw before using.

- In a medium saucepan, combine ½ cup of gin, sugar, lemon juice, cornstarch, salt, and cinnamo (if using). Stir together until ingredients are combined and the cornstarch and sugar are mostly dissolved.

- Add the blueberries and stir to coat with the liquid.

- Cook over medium heat until the mixture comes to a gentle boil, about 5 minutes, only stirring occasionally. Mixing too much will crush your berries as they cook.

- Once the filling has come to a boil and thickened, remove the pan from heat and gently stir in the lemon zest and an additional 1 teaspoon of gin (if using).

- Allow your pie filling to cool 15 - 20 minutes before using as a topping or cool completely if using as pie filling.

"maybe you could swing by my room around ten. Baby, bring the lemon and a bottle of gin."

Ed Sheeran, Don't

gin O'Clock

it's always
gin O'Clock somewhere!

NO. TEN MARTINI

GINGER SEVILLA MIMOSA

RANGPUR CITRUS SPRITZ

COLSON

BREAKFAST MARTINI

BERRY TASTY GIN SMASH

CANADIAN TUXEDO

CLASSIC GIN CAESAR

CHEF'S LITTLE HELPER

CUCUMBER GIMLET

EARL GREY MAR-TEA-NI

HIKER'S MARTINI

CLUB QUARANTINE

FUNDY PEACH GIN & TONIC

GIN HARD SELTZER

PUMP UP THE JAM

IT'S ABOUT THYME GIN & TONIC

KAZUKI NEGRONI

JASMINE

SERRANO CILANTRO G&T

PURPLE LADY PUNCH

GIN OLD FASHIONED

SEASIDE MARTINI

SPA WATER CAESAR

MAD MARTINI

GIMLET

GIN BASIL SMASH

LARRY'S WHITE LONDON

MARTINEZ

ROSE & GIN NEGRONI

WHITE LADY

WATERMELON GIN PUNCH

Martini Primer

About the Martini

The Martini seems to transcend the test of time and trend. Martinis appear on cocktail menus of all calibers the world over. They are household verbiage in even alcohol-abstaining households. But as ubiquitous as a Martini is, ordering one can be somewhat confusing. Shaken? Stirred? Dry? Dirty? Vesper? For a three-ingredient cocktail, ordering a Martini requires a hell of a vocabulary.

The oriGINs of the Martini have been up for debate for ages. There are three main schools of thought: those who believe the Martini is simply named after vermouth brand, Martini & Rosso; those who point fingers at bartender Martini di Arma di Taggia of the Knickerbocker Hotel in New York for the drink's creation; and those who believe the folk tale of a Mr. Martinez.

Rumour has it that during the gold rush, in the small mining town of Martinez, California, a fella struck it rich. When he went to his local watering hole to celebrate his riches, they were out of Champagne. The barkeep whipped up a concoction of gin, vermouth, bitters, and maraschino liqueur, thus dubbed the "Martinez Special". The first-ever publication of the drink was in Jerry Thomas' 1862 manual *The Bartender's Guide*. As the story goes, the miner stopped by Thomas' bar and introduced him to his "Martinez Special". While the Martini was called the "Martinez Special" in the book, no one has been able to prove this origin story.

Today, no one puts maraschino in a Martini, but the base spirit of a Martini is still polarizing. While it may be commonplace to order a gin or vodka Martini, as history has it, a Martini is traditionally gin, not vodka. The vodka cocktail is actually known as a 'Kangaroo", however, bartenders know what you mean if you order a vodka Martini. But you're reading this book, which means you're a gin person!

Shaken or Stirred?

If you've ever heard Sean Connery fielding the question, 'shaken or stirred,' you may think shaking is the way to go. But this question is the cause for many debates amongst serious imbibers. Though Bond would disagree, many people believe shaking 'bruises' the alcohol and reduces the clarity of the drink.

To properly stir a Martini at home, fill a pint glass with ice cubes (the larger the better) and build your Martini over it. Spin a bar spoon around the edge of the glass for a minimum of thirty seconds, or until the outside of the glass is thoroughly chilled and cloudy.

Dry, Wet, or Dirty?

This isn't an x-rated question! Adding this to your Martini order will determine just how you want it made. Ordering a dry Martini actually means you want less vermouth or none at all. Vice-versa, a wet Martini means you'd like more vermouth. The phrase 'perfect Martini' points to a Martini with a perfect ratio of sweet and dry vermouth, while 'dirty' means the bartender will pour olive brine with a heavy hand. *Did you know? The original recipe for a Martini called for equal parts gin and vermouth! Nowadays, a standard Martini calls for just a splash of vermouth.*

Glassware

Up or on the rocks? While your standard Martini is served up - meaning in a stemmed glass - there are folks who prefer their Martinis on the rocks.

Garnishing

While olives are standard fare for most Martinis, lemon peel is a perfectly acceptable finale. Ask for your Martini with a twist if you'd like a hint of citrus.

no. TEN Martini

This is how we prefer our Martini. Did you know that **Tanqueray No. TEN Gin** is the only gin to be inducted to the San Francisco World Spirits Competition Hall of Fame?

GINGREDIENTS *(Serves 1)*
1 oz of Tanqueray No. TEN Gin
⅓ oz of dry vermouth
Optional garnish: Lemon curl or olive

GINSTRUCTIONS
Combine the **Tanqueray No. TEN Gin** and dry vermouth in a cocktail shaker with ice. Shake well (or stir if preferred). Strain into a chilled Martini glass.

Rangpur Citrus Spritz

The rare Rangpur lime is an ingenious choice to bring a distinct and bold flavour to **Tanqueray Rangpur**. With the zestiness of lime and mandarin orange, this gin is the best kept secret of the British-Indian tradition.

GINGREDIENTS *(Serves 6)*

1 ½ cups of **Tanqueray Rangpur Gin**
1 cup of Champagne or sparkling white wine
½ cup of Cointreau or Triple Sec
1 bottle of **Fever-Tree Club Soda**
¾ cup of fresh lemon juice
½ cup of simple syrup
10 dashes of orange bitters
Pineapple slices and fronds, grapes, star anise, and fresh nutmeg to garnish

GINSTRUCTIONS

Add a generous amount of ice to a punch bowl. Pour in ingredients and stir to combine. Garnish with star anise, grapes, and pineapple slices. Grate fresh nutmeg over the entire mixture.

Ginger Sevilla Mimosa

Today, Mimosas are the liquid secret to the best brunch ever, fueling boozy breakfasts and daylight celebrations across the globe. We have a bartender from the Ritz Hotel to thank for this orange-y, bubbly cocktail - the cocktail dates back to 1925, though many credit Alfred Hitchcock for making the drink popular (he loved to sip a Mimosa or two during the lunch hour!).

GINGREDIENTS *(Serves 6)*

1 bottle of dry sparkling wine, chilled
3 cups of fresh orange juice, chilled
1 ½ cups of **Fever-Tree Ginger Ale**, chilled
2 cups of **Tanqueray Sevilla Orange Gin**
1 ½ quarts of orange sherbet

GINSTRUCTIONS

Combine the sparkling wine, orange juice, **Tanqueray Sevilla Orange Gin**, and **Fever-Tree Ginger Ale** in a large pitcher. Divide it into 6 highball glasses and top each with a scoop of orange sherbet.

Breakfast Martini

You can't make the perfect Martini without the perfect Martini glass. However, fun fact – the Martini glass only got its name in the 1990s, when Martini-style cocktails became all the rage. Prior to that, it was simply called a cocktail glass. If you'd like to do as Bond did, opt for a Nick and Nora glass for your Martini.

GINGREDIENTS *(Serves 1)*

1 spoonful of orange or peach marmalade
1 ½ oz of **Aviation Gin**
½ oz of fresh lemon juice
½ oz of fino sherry (or Triple Sec)

GINSTRUCTIONS

Add all the ingredients to a shaker filled with ice. Shake until the outside of the shaker is icy to the touch. Strain into a coupe or Martini glass.

Colson

The Colson is named after Larry Colbran and Heather E. Wilson. They mashed their names together for this summer-inspired cocktail. It's one of our favourites all year long.

GINGREDIENTS *(Serves 1)*

1 oz of Peach Crown Royal
   (or another peach whisky)
1 oz of gin
1 oz of orange juice
Optional garnishes: Peach slice
   and/or a sprig of mint

GINSTRUCTIONS

Add all the ingredients to a shaker filled with ice. Shake until the outside of the shaker is icy to the touch. Strain into a coupe or Martini glass. Garnish with a peach slice and sprig of mint.

Berry Tasty Gin Smash

One of the earliest examples of a Smash appears in the form of a julep recipe in Jerry Thomas' 1862 *How to Mix Drinks*. His version – which would later evolve into what we know as the Julep – lay the groundwork for a whole category. Though he prefers bourbon in his Smash, we think gin makes it lighter and livelier.

GINGREDIENTS *(Serves 1)*

½ oz of simple syrup
4 - 5 blueberries (or other red berries of choice)
1 ½ oz of gin
1 oz of fresh lemon juice
Fever-Tree Ginger Beer

GINSTRUCTIONS

Add your berries to a highball glass with simple syrup. Using a muddler or the back of a spoon, crush down the berries into the simple syrup. Add the gin, lemon juice, and ice, and stir to combine. Top with **Fever-Tree Ginger Beer**. Garnish with a berry or two, a sprig of mint, and sip away!

Canadian Tuxedo

The "Tuxedo" cocktail dates back to 1903, where Tim Daly penned it in his book, *Daly's Bartenders' Encyclopedia*. Daly called for maple gin, but since that is hard to come by, this recipe subs in Canadian maple syrup with gin for a Canadian-approved Martini riff. Throw on your best denim-on-denim to sip this number.

GINGREDIENTS *(Serves 1)*

1 oz of gin
1 oz of dry vermouth
⅓ oz of maple syrup
3 dashes of maraschino liqueur
2 dashes of orange bitters
Lemon twist
Optional garnish: cherry

GINSTRUCTIONS

Add all the ingredients to a glass shaker with ice. Stir until the glass is cold to touch and the maple syrup is thoroughly mixed, approximately 50 rotations. Strain into a chilled Martini glass and garnish with a cherry.

Classic Gin Caesar

The Caesar was invented in 1969 by restaurant manager Walter Chell of the Calgary Inn (today the Westin Hotel) in Calgary, Alberta, Canada. He mixed vodka with clam and tomato juice, Worcestershire sauce, and other spices, creating a drink with a uniquely spicy flavour. We say scrap the vodka, amp up the spices, and pile on the garnishes. Our favourite recipe is below, but feel free to tweak to your needs. Heather lives in Atlantic Canada, so seafood is always the move. Kate likes hers spicy. Sometimes too spicy, so fresh cucumber and pickled beans help cut the heat.

GINGREDIENTS *(Serves 1)*

1 fresh lime
2 oz of gin
Salt, pepper
2 dashes of oyster sauce
2 dashes of BBQ sauce
1 dash of hot sauce (or to taste)
Clamato juice
Garnish of choice

GINSTRUCTIONS

Run a cut lime around the edge of a glass. Rim the glass with salt. Fill the glass with ice and add the gin. Add salt, pepper, oyster sauce, BBQ sauce, and hot sauce to taste. Top with Clamato juice and stir thoroughly. If needed, add ice to the top of the glass and garnish. Go wild with the garnishes - everything from celery to pickled beans to bacon to grilled shrimp will do the trick.

Made this GINspired recipe? Post your photo on Instagram and tag @the.gin.shop.ca

Chef's Little Helper

A spin-off from a dirty Martini, the Chef's Little Helper cocktail makes use of a GINfusion technique called "fat-washing". It's a fun, easy-to-make alternative that provides layers of flavour and texture to your standard Martini. Make it ahead of time and keep it in your fridge!

GINGREDIENTS *(Serves 1)*

2 oz of olive oil-infused gin
   (see GINfusion recipe)
1 oz of dry vermouth
Optional garnish: olives

GINSTRUCTIONS

Add ingredients to a mixing glass with ice. Stir until the glass is cold to touch, approximately 30 rotations. Strain into a chilled Martini glass. Garnish with olives.

GINFUSION

Combine a 26 oz bottle of gin (preferably one you're fond of sipping neat, as this is for a Martini) and 4 oz of olive oil in a container with a tight lid. Stir vigorously to combine. Place the container in the freezer for 8 - 12 hours until the olive oil separates from the top of the mixture and solidifies. Remove the solid olive oil, and strain the spirit through a coffee or fine filter.

Note: you can also add fresh herbs, like rosemary or thyme to your GINfusion to add even more depth of flavour.

Cucumber Gimlet

It was said that Royal Navy surgeon Sir Thomas Gimlette would encourage men at sea to mix lime juice with their gin rations. This cocktail prevented diseases like scurvy, which raged when vitamin C wasn't present. While we're sure you eat your fruits and vegetables today, a few squeezes of a lime and a hit of simple syrup makes for a lively, bright cocktail.

GINGREDIENTS *(Serves 1)*

2 tablespoons of diced cucumber
¾ oz of simple syrup
2 oz of gin
¾ oz of lime juice
Optional garnish: 1 slice of cucumber

GINSTRUCTIONS

In a cocktail shaker (if you don't have a shaker, try a mason jar with a lid), muddle the cucumber and simple syrup. Add gin, lime juice, and plenty of ice and shake thoroughly. Strain into a chilled Martini glass and garnish with a cucumber slice.

Earl Grey Mar-Tea-Ni

Created by Audrey Saunders and her award-winning bar Pegu Club, her goal with the Mar-Tea-Ni was to get people drinking gin again. We think it worked.

GINGREDIENTS *(Serves 1)*

¾ oz of lemon juice
1 oz of simple syrup
1 ½ oz of Earl Grey tea-infused gin
1 egg white
Martini glass ½ rimmed with sugar
Optional garnish: lemon twist

GINSTRUCTIONS

Measure all the ingredients into a mixing glass. Add ice and shake hard to a ten-second count. Strain into a chilled Martini glass, ½ rimmed with sugar. Garnish with a lemon twist.

GINFUSION

1 - 26 oz bottle of dry gin
4 tablespoons of loose-leaf Earl Grey tea
   (or 4 tea bags)

Combine the gin and tea in a large glass bottle. Allow it to sit for 2 hours. Strain the tea out and use in your favourite cocktails.

Club Quarantine

This breezy riff on a classic Moscow Mule calls for **Fever-Tree**'s spicy ginger beer and **Empress 1908 Gin**'s disco-hued spirit to add a little groove to your at-home happy hour. This was a drink that got us through quarantine!

GINGREDIENTS *(Serves 1)*

1 bushel of mint
½ oz of fresh lime juice
¾ oz of simple syrup
2 oz of Empress 1908 Gin
Top with **Fever-Tree Ginger Beer**
Optional Garnish: mint crown

GINSTRUCTIONS

Add the mint to a shaker with the lime juice and simple syrup. Gently muddle - you want to bring out the flavours, not crush the herb! Add the **Empress 1908 Gin** and ice, and shake thoroughly. Strain into a rocks or lowball glass filled with fresh ice. Top with **Fever-Tree Ginger Beer** (try the **Fever-Tree Smoky Ginger Ale** if you like a little smokiness). Garnish with a mint crown.

Hiker's Martini

Whether you are out on a hike or just want to pretend, the Hiker's Martini will invigorate you like a walk in the woods. Raging Crow's utterly unique, woodland-inspired gin transports you to a serene forest scene (even if you're stuck in the city).

GINGREDIENTS *(Serves 1)*

1 oz of **Raging Crow Nazdrowka Vodka**
1 ½ oz of **Raging Crow Spruce Tip Gin**
1 oz of dry sherry
Optional garnish: lemon peel

GINSTRUCTIONS

Add ingredients to a mixing glass filled with ice. Stir for 50 turns of a spoon then strain into a chilled coupe glass. Garnish with a lemon peel.

Gin Hard Seltzer

Also known as hard soda, hard seltzer is essentially alcoholic, low-calorie, low-carb, and flavoured fizzy water. It was also THE drink of 2020 and the lockdown. This is our version.

GINGREDIENTS *(Serves 1)*

1⅓ oz of **Whitley Neill Pink Grapefruit Gin**
½ oz of grapefruit juice
½ oz of fresh lemon juice
½ oz of simple syrup
Fever-Tree Club Soda
Optional garnishes: grapefruit twist
    and sprigs of lavender or thyme

GINSTRUCTIONS

Add ice to a highball glass. Add the **Whitley Neill Pink Grapefruit Gin**, grapefruit juice, lemon juice, and simple syrup. Top with **Fever-Tree Club Soda**. Garnish with a grapefruit twist and a fragrant herb sprig of your choice.

Fundy Peach Gin & Tonic

The gin and tonic first gained popularity in the British colonies, as the quinine in the tonic water was found to be a potent deterrent to malaria-carrying mosquitoes. However, the bitterness of the quinine was unpalatable, so gin was added to make the drink taste better. This Fundy Peach G&T has the hint of sweetness from the peach and a whiff of the sea thanks to the **Fundy Gin**.

GINGREDIENTS *(Serves 1)*

1 ½ oz of **Still Fired Distillery Fundy Gin**
½ oz of Peach Schnapps OR 3 - 5 drops of peach bitters
3 oz of **Fever-Tree Aromatic Tonic Water**
Optional garnish: peach slice

GINSTRUCTIONS

In a glass of your choice, pour the **Fundy Gin** and Peach Schnapps (or peach bitters) over ice. Top with **Fever-Tree Aromatic Tonic Water** (add to your taste – we don't like our drinks watered down too much so only use 3 oz but you can add more if you like). Garnish with a fresh peach slice.

It's about Thyme Gin & Tonic

No G&T of quality can be made without a high-quality tonic (if you're picky about your gins, why aren't you picky about your tonic, after all?). Artisanal mixers like **Fever-Tree** are recommended for flavour, selection, and quality. The ingredients in this drink are relatively simple and that's on purpose: it lets the flavours of the tonic and gin shine through!

GINGREDIENTS *(Serves 1)*

1 - 2 fresh sprigs of rosemary
A few fresh basil leaves
Several fresh sprigs of thyme
½ of a lime, juiced
2 oz of **Aviation Gin**
4 - 6 oz of chilled **Fever-Tree Lemon Tonic Water**

GINSTRUCTIONS

Add the rosemary sprigs, basil leaves, thyme sprigs, and lime juice to a cocktail shaker and lightly muddle. Strain and pour the contents of the cocktail shaker into your glass of choice. Add **Aviation Gin**, **Fever-Tree Lemon Tonic Water**, and ice. Gently stir to combine.

Pump Up the Jam

The benefits of jam over simple syrup in a cocktail are more than just a time-saving step. Jam is sweet like simple syrup, but it has an extra boost of being fruity! Plus, if you use really good jam like ours, it has a thickness to it that makes the best cocktail. Pick your favourite jam, your go-to gin, and shake away.

GINGREDIENTS *(Serves 1)*

1 tablespoon of **Raspberry Gin Jam** (p. 68)
1 ½ oz of **Whitley Neill Rhubarb and Ginger Gin**
½ oz of lemon juice
A splash of sparkling white wine
1 lemon wedge

GINSTRUCTIONS

Add ice to a wine glass. Mix 1 hefty tablespoon of jam with a splash of water and pour it into a cocktail shaker. Don't worry if the jam settles at the bottom. Add 1 ½ oz of **Whitley Neill Rhubarb and Ginger Gin** and lemon juice and shake thoroughly. Pour into the glass. Top it off with sparkling white wine and a lemon wedge.

Jasmine

The Jasmine was first created by Paul Harrington in 1992 when a classmate sidled up to the bar he was working at and said, "*make me something new.*" Since Harrington had recently made a Pegu Club cocktail for another customer, he decided to riff on that classic for his friend. He kept the two main ingredients, gin and orange liqueur, but subbed out lime for lemon and Campari liqueur instead of Angostura bitters. He named the drink Jasmine after the friend that asked for it.

GINGREDIENTS *(Serves 1)*

1 ½ oz of gin
⅓ oz of Campari
1 oz of Triple Sec (or Cointreau)
¾ oz of freshly squeezed lemon juice
Optional garnish: twist of grapefruit peel

GINSTRUCTIONS

Add all the ingredients to a shaker filled with ice. Shake until the outside of the shaker is icy to the touch. Strain into a coupe or Martini glass. Garnish with a twist of grapefruit peel.

Kazuki Negroni

When Orson Wells tried his first Negroni in 1947, he reportedly said "*The bitters are excellent for your liver. The gin is bad for you. They balance each other.*"

GINGREDIENTS *(Serves 1)*

1 ½ oz of **Sheringham Distillery Kazuki Gin**
1 oz of sweet vermouth
1 oz of Campari
Optional garnish: orange slice or twist

GINSTRUCTIONS

Add all ingredients to a rocks glass with ice. Stir to mix. Garnish with a twist or slice of orange.

Purple Lady Punch

Punched-up version of the classic pink lady that tastes even better with friends! Start with this recipe and double or triple as needed, depending on your number of guests.

GINGREDIENTS *(Serves 1)*

1 ½ oz of **Empress 1908 Gin**
½ oz of Campari
1 oz of lemon juice
1 oz of Triple Sec or Cointreau
Optional garnish: orange slice

GINSTRUCTIONS

Add ice to a glass. Add the **Empress 1908 Gin**, Campari, lemon juice, and Triple Sec. Stir to combine. Garnish with orange slices.

Serrano Cilantro G&T

We love a refreshing G&T, but sometimes it's time to spice things up. Stir in a few slices of hot pepper and garnish with some cooling sprigs of cilantro for a more savoury, spicy riff on this highball.

GINGREDIENTS *(Serves 1)*

4 sprigs of cilantro
½ oz of lime juice
1 ½ oz of **Aviation Gin**
Fever-Tree Tonic Water, to taste
Optional garnish: serrano pepper

GINSTRUCTIONS

Muddle 4 sprigs of cilantro with ½ oz of lime juice in the bottom of a glass. Add 1 ½ oz of **Aviation Gin**. Top with ice, tonic, and slices of serrano pepper to taste. Sip and enjoy!

Seaside Martini

A take on the classic dry Martini with a cucumber twist and slightly salty goodness of the **Sheringham's Seaside Gin**, reminiscent of a day at the beach.

GINGREDIENTS *(Serves 1)*

2 oz of Sheringham Distillery Seaside Gin
Splash of dry vermouth (or to taste)
Optional garnish: sliced cucumber rounds

GINSTRUCTIONS

Add **Sheringham Distillery Seaside Gin** to a mixing glass filled with ice. Stir for 50 turns of a spoon. Add a splash of dry vermouth to a chilled Martini glass. Give it a good swirl and then discard excess vermouth (or keep it if that is your taste). Strain the **Sheringham Distillery Seaside Gin** into the chilled (and vermouth rinsed) glass. Garnish with cucumber rounds floating on top.

Gin Old Fashioned

How old fashioned is the Gin Old Fashioned cocktail? Pretty old - it dates all the way back to 1862, when Jerry Thomas published his namesake coctail tome, the *Jerry Thomas' Bartenders Guide: How To Mix Drinks*. He uses a richer, maltier Holland gin for his, but we prefer ours with **Raging Crow's Caw-Caw-Phany Gin**.

GINGREDIENTS *(Serves 1)*

Orange peel
Splash of simple syrup (or a sugar cube)
2 dashes of orange bitters
1 tsp of **Fever-Tree Club Soda**
2 oz of **Raging Crow Caw-Caw-Phany Gin**

GINSTRUCTIONS

Add the orange peel, simple syrup, bitters, and **Fever-Tree Club Soda** to a glass. Muddle with the back of a spoon until well combined (and sugar is dissolved if using a sugar cube). Add a large ice cube. Give it a stir, and run an orange peel around the rim of the glass for flavour. Drop in the peel, top with the **Raging Crow Caw-Caw-Phany Gin**, stir, and savour!
Pro Tip: Avoid pouring gin directly on the ice. It will make it melt quicker!

Mad Martini

The Martini has prompted a great deal of poetry and inspirational quotes. Writer E. B. White called it *"the elixir of quietude"* while journalist H. L. Mencken said it was *"the only American invention as perfect as the sonnet"*. However, given the murky origins of the Martini, whether or not it's truly American is still disputed **(see Martini Primer** – p. 222).

GINGREDIENTS *(Serves 1)*

3 fresh basil leaves
1 ½ oz of **Mad Lab Gin6**
1 ½ oz of white vermouth
3 dashes of plum bitters

GINSTRUCTIONS

Add the fresh basil leaves, **Mad Lab Gin6**, white vermouth, and plum bitters to a cocktail shaker. Muddle gently with a muddler or the back of a spoon to release the aromas of basil. Add ice to the shaker and shake until the outside of the shaker is cold. Strain into a tall glass with ice and enjoy!

Spa Water Caesar

While Caesars still reign as a morning-after recipe, this lighter riff on the classic Canadian cocktail is even more refreshing. It uses tomato water (the juice of tomatoes), which makes it perfect for a hot weekend morning. Best of all, the drink is easy to batch, making it low effort to make.

GINGREDIENTS *(Serves 1)*

1 ½ oz of romeo's gin
Tomato water (see recipe below)
Optional garnishes: spicy beans, cherry tomatoes, fresh parsley, and/ or serrano peppers

GINSTRUCTIONS

Tomato water: Cut up ½ pound of fresh tomatoes. Feel free to add freshly cut serrano peppers; add it all to a blender with salt and pepper and purée. Wrap a bowl in cheesecloth or fine strainer, and let the tomato mix strain in the fridge overnight. The next day, toss the pulp mixture. Voila – tomato water!

Add 1 ½ oz of **romeo's gin** to a highball glass or mason jar filled with ice. Top with tomato water. Garnish with ingredients of your choice. We love fresh herbs and a hot pepper, but spicy beans, tomatoes, or bacon are all yummy too.

Gimlet

The Gimlet rose to popularity after it was mentioned in the 1953 Raymond Chandler novel *The Long Goodbye*. The main character, Philip Marlowe, said, *"A real Gimlet is half gin and half Rose's Lime Juice and nothing else. It beats Martinis hollow."* This line secured the Gimlet's place in history.

GINGREDIENTS *(Serves 1)*

2 oz of dry gin
¾ oz of simple syrup
¾ oz of lime juice

GINSTRUCTIONS

Add all the ingredients to a cocktail shaker with ice. Shake until the outside of the shaker is frosted, about 30 - 45 seconds. Strain into a coupe glass. Enjoy!

Gin Basil Smash

This modern classic was invented in 2008 in Hamburg, Germany by bartender Jörg Meyer. Meyer originally called his creation the Gin Pesto, a very fitting name for a basil-forward sip. It seems that over time, the name transformed into more of a description of its preparation. Make sure your lemon juice is fresh! If it isn't, tone down the simple syrup.

GINGREDIENTS *(Serves 1)*

6 - 7 fresh basil leaves
⅔ oz of simple syrup
1 oz of fresh-squeezed lemon juice
2 oz of gin
Optional garnish: basil sprig

GINSTRUCTIONS

Add basil leaves, simple syrup, and lemon juice to a cocktail shaker. Muddle gently with a muddler or the back of a spoon to release the aromas of basil. Add ice and gin to the shaker and shake until the outside of the shaker is cold. Double-strain into a chilled cocktail glass with ice. Garnish with a basil sprig.

Larry's White London

Larry (Heather's spouse) loves gin. This cocktail is his riff on a White Russian.

GINGREDIENTS *(Serves 1)*

1 oz of gin
1 oz of Kahlua
1 oz of Irish cream
1 oz of cream or milk

GINSTRUCTIONS

Add ingredients to a rocks or lowball glass. Stir and enjoy. Easy peasy.

Martinez

Think of the Martinez as a cross between a Martini and a Manhattan. Made with Dutch genever over dry gin, this malty Martini riff called for both sweet and dry vermouth, plus a splash of orange Curacao. This is our take on a classic.

GINGREDIENTS *(Serves 1)*

2 oz of genever
2 oz of sweet vermouth
1 bar spoon of maraschino liqueur
1 dash of Angostura bitters
Optional garnish: lemon peel and 3 brandied cherries

GINSTRUCTIONS

Add all ingredients to a cocktail shaker filled with ice. Shake thoroughly until the outside of the shaker is frosty. Strain into a chilled coupe or Martini glass. Garnish with lemon peel and 3 brandied cherries.

Rose & Gin Negroni

While the usual Negroni is bracingly bitter, a bit of ginger and a splash of rose water gives the classic drink spicy, floral flavours. Try this when you've grown weary of Negronis!

GINGREDIENTS *(Serves 1)*

2 slices of fresh ginger
1 oz of rose water (or to taste)
1 oz of gin
1 oz of Campari
1 oz of red vermouth
Optional garnish: slice or twist of orange

GINSTRUCTIONS

Muddle 2 small slices of fresh ginger in a glass with rose water. Add ice to the glass. Add the gin, Campari, and red vermouth. Stir to mix. Garnish with a twist or slice of orange. Enjoy!

White Lady

When it comes to gin cocktails, this is one of the classics. Invented by Harry MacElhone of Harry's New York Bar in Paris in the 1930s, it's frothy and light with hints of bright citrus. It pairs particularly well with desserts!

GINGREDIENTS *(Serves 1)*

1 ½ oz of gin
¾ oz of Cointreau (Triple Sec)
¾ oz of lemon juice
⅓ oz of simple syrup
1 small egg white
Optional garnish: lemon peel

GINSTRUCTIONS

Add all ingredients to a cocktail shaker and shake without ice. Add ice and shake until chilled. Strain into a cocktail glass. Garnish with a lemon peel.

Watermelon Gin Punch

This breezy summer punch combines everything you want from a hot-weather drink: thirst-quenching watermelon, refreshing mint, and an ample amount of gin. Serve it in a hollowed-out watermelon for the best effect.

GINGREDIENTS *(Serves 8)*

1 watermelon
12 fresh mint leaves
1 cup of simple syrup
1 cup of lemon juice (fresh is best)
2 cups of gin

GINSTRUCTIONS

Purée the flesh of the watermelon in a food processor. Strain out the seeds. In a large punch bowl, muddle 12 mint leaves with a splash of lemon juice. Add the puréed watermelon juice, 1 cup of simple syrup, 1 cup of lemon juice, and 2 cups of gin. Stir to mix, add ice and serve.